SECRET
SAN DIEGO

SECRET
SAN DIEGO

The Unique Guidebook
to San Diego's Hidden Sites,
Sounds, & Tastes

Frank Sabatini, Jr.

WITH PHOTOGRAPHS BY
Linda Rutenberg

ECW PRESS

The publication of *Secret San Diego* has been generously supported by the Canada Council, by the Ontario Arts Council, and by the Government of Canada through the Book Publishing Industry Development Program. **Canadä**

NATIONAL LIBRARY OF CANADA CATALOGUING IN PUBLICATION DATA

Sabatini, Frank
Secret San Diego: the unique guidebook to San Diego's hidden sites, sounds & tastes / Frank Sabatini, Jr.
Includes index.
ISBN 1-55022-588-X
1. San Diego (Calif.) — Guidebooks. I. Title.
F869.S22S22 2003   917.94'9850454   C2003-902194-7

Original series design: Paul Davies, ECW Type and Art, Oakville, Ontario.
Series editor: Laura Byrne Paquet.
Typesetting: Martel *en-tête*.
Imaging and cover: Guylaine Régimbald – SOLO DESIGN.
Production: Johanna Neuschwander.
Printed by Transcontinental.

Distributed in Canada by Jaguar Book Group,
100 Armstrong Avenue, Georgetown, Ontario L7G 5S4.

Distributed in the United States by Independent Publishers Group,
814 North Franklin Street, Chicago, Illinois 60610.

Published by ECW PRESS
2120 Queen Street East, Suite 200, Toronto, Ontario M4E 1E2.

ecwpress.com

PRINTED AND BOUND IN CANADA

TABLE OF CONTENTS

Introduction   9

How to Use *Secret San Diego*   10

Other Resources   11

Acknowledgments   12

SECRET . . .

ABBEY   13

ADULT   15

AGENDA   16

ANIMAL ENCOUNTERS   17

ANIMATION   20

ARCHIVES   20

ASIAN FABLES   21

ASTROLOGY   22

AUTOS   23

AVOCADOS   24

BAKERIES   25

BALLROOM DANCING   27

BEACHES   29

BEER SCHOOL   32

BINGO   33

BOOKSTORES   34

BRAZILIAN   36

BREAKFAST   37

BREWERIES   40

BRITISH ISLES   43

BUDDHA   45

BUFFETS   47

BUGS BUNNY   48

BURIAL GROUND   49

CAESAR SALAD   49

CANDY STORES   50

CELEBRITY SCRAWLING   51

CHAPELS   52

CHICKEN PIE   56

CHILDREN'S STUFF   57

CHINESE LAUNDERER   60

COFFEEHOUSES   60

COMICS 64
CONCERT VENUE 65
COTTAGES 66
COUNTRY-WESTERN 67
CUBAN 69
CURFEWS 70
CURRENCY 70
CYCLING 71
DEEPAK 73
DIVAS 74
DOG BEACHES 75
EAST AFRICAN 75
EDIBLE STOGIE 76
EXPENSIVE SOUP 77
FARMERS' MARKETS 78
FAUX PAS 79
FENG SHUI 81
FETISH WEAR 81
FILIPINO 82
FLYING SAUCERS 84
FOOTBRIDGES 85
FREE ADMISSIONS 87
FREE RIDE 90
FRENCH 90
FUNGI 91
GAMES AND PUZZLES 91

GARDENS 92
GLASS 97
GLASS PIPES 98
GOLD MINES 99
GONDOLAS 100
GROCER 101
HAMBURGERS 101
HAUNTINGS 104
HEAVENLY BODIES 107
HERBS 108
HOME FURNISHINGS 110
JAZZ 113
JEWISH DELIS 115
JOAN CRAWFORD 118
JUNK 119
KALUA PIG 120
KITES 120
KNITTING AND
    FABRICS 121
LAWRENCE WELK 122
LGBT 123
LODGINGS 126
MARTINIS 130
MASSAGE 131
MEAT MARKETS 132
MEMORIALS 133

MINI-CABS   136
MISSIONS   136
MOVIE SCREENS   139
MUSEUMS   142
NECESSITIES   147
NEIGHBORHOOD BARS   148
NEW ORLEANS   151
NIKI DE SAINT PHALLE   153
NUDITY   155
OBSERVATORY   156
OLD RIDE   157
OLYMPICS   159
OUTLET MALLS   160
OVER THE LINE   161
PEANUT BUTTER   162
PERSIAN   163
PET TREATS   163
PIANO BARS   164
PICNICS   166
PIMP   169
PIZZA   169
POLISH   171
PROPHYLACTICS   172
PUPPETS   173
RANCHES   173
RETRO NOVELTIES   175

ROTATING HOME   176
SANDCASTLES   177
SCALPERS   177
SCHNITZEL   178
SCULPTORS   179
SECOND HELPINGS   180
SHAKESPEARE   181
SHAWARMA   183
SHOES   183
SHORTCUTS   184
SINGLES   185
SLEEPING QUARTERS   187
SMOKE   189
SPAS   191
SQUARE DANCING   193
SURVIVORS   194
SUSHI   195
SWIMMING POOLS   197
TEA   198
TEDDY BEARS   201
THAI   201
THEATER   203
THRIFT   208
TIJUANA   210
TIME CAPSULE   212
TIMPANO   214

TORTILLAS 214

TRADER JOE'S 215

TRAILS 216

TREES 218

TUNA MELT 219

24/7 220

USED GARB 221

VAULT 222

VEGAN 223

VICTORIAN 225

VIEWS 226

WAFFLES 229

WATER TAXIS 230

WEATHER 231

WHIRLPOOL 232

WINE STORAGE 233

WINE STORES 233

WING 234

The Secret Future 236

Photo Sites 237

Subject Index 238

Location Index 248

Alphabetical Index 255

INTRODUCTION

It wasn't too long ago that San Diego seemed like a blank canvas waiting for a mad artist to splatter it with color and texture.

When I relocated here in the mid-1980s, the downtown skyline appeared pitifully dwarfed by the vast blue sky. Innumerable streets fell silent at nightfall. And newcomers generally complained about the lack of culture, gourmet restaurants, and chic shops, despite their tenacious love for the city's breathtaking landscape and flawless weather.

In what seemed like a blink of an eye, a portrait of vitality emerged. Steel rods began sprouting like California poppies, giving way to sparkling neoteric high-rises and multicolored commercial plazas. Prestigious restaurateurs rushed to the scene on the shirttails of trendy retailers. And the city's historical landmarks and natural elements that had long given San Diego its sleepy charm finally married into big-city living.

But rapid growth obscures the type of good secrets contained in this book. Those secrets are brought into focus through my own experiences as well as those of myriad sun-starved visitors I have hosted with enthusiasm over the years. San Diego, I've learned, requires many sets of eyes and legs to keep up with its mutating identities.

Travel writers and photographers love coming here to capture such obvious fodder as the world-famous San Diego Zoo, the historic Hotel Del Coronado, big Navy shipyards, and bright, endless beaches. Yet if you want to discover the city's smaller jewels, which are equally precious, then you will need to veer off the beaten track. The text you are about to read takes you there.

HOW TO USE
SECRET SAN DIEGO

This book is arranged alphabetically, by subject. But don't let one entry title, such as "Secret Breakfasts," fool you into thinking the meal is finished after you've read it. Skip ahead and you will also find noteworthy tidbits that relate to morning fare under "Secret Celebrity Scrawling" and "Secret Waffles."

Cross-referencing abounds, even when it isn't spelled out. And it should, since secrets often spawn other secrets that lurk nearby. Thus, the book provides you with a foundation for discovery as you zero in on your favorite subject matter and flip from page to page.

Because San Diego is fraught with multiple area codes, you may need to dial an area code before the main phone number to reach a place that is just on the other side of a freeway. The previously reigning area code for metropolitan San Diego, 619, has diminished in scope. It now applies only to areas from Mission Valley all the way south through downtown, and on to the city of San Ysidro at the Mexican border. It also extends east to the cities of La Mesa, El Cajon, Santee, and Alpine. The 858 area code has taken effect in neighborhoods and cities just north of Mission Valley, and gives way to 760 in the northern reaches of the county.

Restaurant hours are omitted for good reason: they change with the tides of our tourist season, and tend to vacillate according to the levels of daily consumer traffic. And food prices are included only if a particular dish is delightfully cheap or exorbitantly expensive.

Lastly, don't go home without taking advantage of the locations I recommend under "Secret Views." But don't stop there. Ask the locals you meet at these vantage points for more suggestions. They are usually the types who have invested a good deal of time exploring San Diego's stunning landscape — and cherish it as much as I do.

OTHER RESOURCES

A wealth of free publications is yours for the taking at numerous restaurants and coffeehouses throughout San Diego County. Many publications, such as *City Beat*, *The Reader*, and *Downtown News*, offer extensive listings for theater productions, outdoor festivals, underground bands, and touring museum exhibits. Additionally, the *San Diego Union-Tribune* features a calendar-rich pullout section on Thursdays, called *"Night & Day."* Local news and events pertaining to the gay, lesbian, bisexual, and transgender community are well covered in the *Gay and Lesbian Times*, *Update*, and *Buzz Magazine* — free publications found mostly throughout the neighborhoods of Hillcrest, North Park, and University Heights.

Updated information about tour boat operators, Jet Ski rentals, and other aquatic activities is available at the **San Diego Visitor Information Center** (I-5 and Clairemont Drive, Mission Bay, 619-276-8200). For walking maps and current information about downtown nightlife, call or visit the **Gaslamp Quarter Association** (614 5th Avenue, Suite E, Downtown, 619-233-5227). General information about hotels, business conventions, and city attractions can be obtained by calling the **San Diego Convention and Visitors' Bureau** (619-236-1212) or by visiting the bureau's **International Visitors' Information Center** (11 Horton Plaza, Downtown).

ACKNOWLEDGMENTS

Hidden throughout this book are a thousand acts of personal support given to me by family, friends, and colleagues. My enormous thanks to Jim Hennum, Kelly Terry, Vik Shetty, and Chris Huard, who contributed words, wit, and encouragement. And to my parents, two sisters, aunt, and George Christy for cheering me on through all of my writing endeavors; and most of all to Jerry Gentry, who stands by with unfailing belief through thick and thin.

SECRET
ABBEY

Okay, I lied. It's really a small, cozy restaurant, but with enough candles inside to brighten up the altar of a large 15th-century monastery. The kitchen is the only area that uses electricity inside **The Abbey Café** (127 University Avenue, Hillcrest, 619-692-0311). Its creaky wood-floored dining room is illuminated nightly by nearly 600 candles, placed wherever there is a flat surface: on the fireplace mantel, tabletops, and window ledges. Most of them sit on six lengthy rows of individual bracket shelves that dominate an outside wall in the narrow courtyard. The spectacle is cleverly controlled. Each row of tea lights, beginning with the top, gets lit every 15 minutes, starting at 6 PM. The rows burn out systematically throughout the evening. And by closing time, the wall is dark. A velvet collection bag and several other church artifacts complete the Gothic ambiance. The menu is eclectic — homemade soups, fancy salads, and gourmet pasta dishes, plus meat and fish. One of the more unusual dishes worth trying is from the appetizer list — a Middle Eastern specialty called zatar. It's a curious blend of nearly 80 dry herbs and spices that are presented on the perimeter of a plate with olive oil in the center. Accompanying pita bread serves as your mop.

SECRET
ADULT

Since the days when Alexander the Great conquered the known world, and even before, there have been camp followers who've made money serving the needs of sex-starved military men. San Diego, being a military town, continues that grand tradition with adult-oriented venues sprinkled all over the city. By far the greatest concentration is to be found in the Loma Portal district, along Midway Drive and Rosecrans Street. There are four strip clubs, five pornographic peepshow stores, and one sex shop with fantasy booths.

The most tucked away has to be the **Adult Depot** (3489 Kurtz Street, Loma Portal, 619-224-8466), located ironically close to the Home Depot. But in getting there, you either know the way or else you can't find it from here. Those who have given it thought travel through the parking lot of the **Sports Arena** (3500 Sports Arena Boulevard) and exit through the back onto Kurtz Street. Others take Hancock Street off Rosecrans Street, and travel a huge and meandering loop that doubles back onto Kurtz. Located in a sea of auto body shops and industrial garages, this isn't a place everyone stumbles upon in their daily rounds — and that's its major draw. Privacy to peruse and experience its offerings is practically an ironclad guarantee when scanning the store's selection of latex and leather party wear, lotions, and dildos — or when stepping into the video arcade to see what's on the small screens. Pay a separate entrance fee and walk through a door into a darkened adult theater with two small rooms. Owned by All Worlds Video, a major player in the gay video porn industry, this relative newcomer to the adult theater scene in town has already remodeled and expanded its facilities to accommodate a burgeoning audience.

Scattered between all reaches of the county is **F Street Adult Video and Gifts** (619-236-0841) with eight bright stores that resemble mainstream music shops. A few locations, however, are taking heat from the city to transplant themselves further away from residential areas. **Midnight Adult Book and Video Centers** (619-299-7186) is the other major established chain. It has three stores in San Diego and one in the southern coastal town of Imperial Beach.

S E C R E T
AGENDA

In the early 1900s, San Diego was a backwater coastal village without a plan. It lacked impressive business districts, playgrounds, and worthy sculpture. Yet it impressed visionaries with its subtropical climate and fertile soil, hospitable to every sort of tree, shrub, grain, and flower. At the **San Diego Public Library** (820 E Street, Downtown, 619-236-5820), visitors will find the city's first fully completed plan for urban rise: *San Diego — A Comprehensive Plan for Its Improvement*. The largely forgotten work was authored in 1908 by landscape architect John Nolen of Cambridge, Massachusetts. His proposals for improvement were based largely on personal criticism of lackluster city planners: "Little or nothing has been done to secure for the people the benefits of any of its great natural resources, nor to provide those concomitants without which natural resources are so often valueless."

The eight-chapter plan was never officially adopted by the city, much to the dismay of conservative environmentalists. But his recommendations for preserving 1,400 acres of city park space (now Balboa Park), and protecting the caves and coves of affluent La Jolla, panned out as immature San Diego became a confident adult during the 20th century.

SECRET
ANIMAL ENCOUNTERS

Diehard fans of sea mammals and other marine life may want to skip the Shamu show and register instead for **SeaWorld's** year-round **Trainer for a Day program** (500 Sea World Drive, Mission Bay, 877-436-5746). It's a rare opportunity to don a wetsuit for an intimate splash with the dolphins, or grab hold of a dorsal fin for a chilly tow through the pool. Participants get an up-close look at training methods that focus on an array of keen animal behaviors demonstrated in daily shows. But there's work involved. The seven-hour day begins at 8:30 AM with stuffing hundreds of pounds of smelt, herring, and squid with vitamins before loading them into refrigerators. The cost is $395, which includes a separate day's admission into the park. Participants must be at least 13 years old. Make reservations three weeks in advance. Additionally, the little-known **Dolphin Interaction Program** (DIP) begins with a brief learning session before you enter the water in wet gear for 25 minutes (age 6 or older, $135). For the regular admission price ($42.95), visitors can hand-feed the bottlenose dolphins at **Rocky Point Preserve**. Be patient if you're empty-handed, because chances are still strong that these friendly cetaceans will give you a chance to pet their rostrums.

In the third week of October, San Diego's **Jarrett Meeker Foundation** (619-670-1333) holds a one-night fundraiser that brings people and kids face to face with some of the animals at the **San Diego Zoo** (Park Boulevard, Balboa Park, 619-234-3153). The cause is a good one: it sends disadvantaged children to summer classes at the zoo. For $75, attendees are given a private tour of the park led by animal trainers plus the zoo's zany "scientist," Dr. Zoolittle. You'll get to handle snakes, lemurs, and exotic birds. **Spooky Sleepovers** ($89 for non-member campers) are offered the same month, giving children a chance to go trick-or-treating around the petting area and sing songs around the campfire at the park's rustic Camp Timbuktu. Dinner and breakfast are included; advance reservations required.

A little-known secret among tourists is the **photo caravan safari** at San Diego's **Wild Animal Park** (15500 San Pasqual Valley Road, Escondido, California, 800-934-2267). Participants hop into the back of an open pickup truck and traverse hundreds of rugged acres for a stunning behind-the-scenes brush with giraffes, wildebeest, rhinos, and ostriches. Tours are offered three times a day throughout most of the year ($100 to $150). Or prowl where few visitors are allowed to venture in a three-hour **Walk on the Wild Side** tour that leads you to the bedrooms of the park's tigers, okapis, and elephants. It's one of the best opportunities to meet animal ambassadors and see firsthand the meal preparations and feeding routines these creatures enjoy.

You've earned your whale sightings if you paddle out by kayak about four miles offshore with **Aqua Adventures** (1548 Quivira Way, Mission Bay, 619-523-9577). Laborious as it may sound, you'll get closer to gray whales than you would by motor boat as they migrate from Arctic waters to the warm lagoons of the Baja Peninsula. These graceful mammals revel in the hush of the open ocean as much as you will. Tours are conducted by certified kayak instructors (8 AM to noon, January and February, $75).

To avoid the cattle boat whale outings available through **San Diego Harbor Excursions** (1050 N Harbor Drive, Downtown, 619-234-4111), experienced boat operators can rent a 26-foot powerboat and launch their own whale tours from **Seaforth Boat Rentals** (1641 Quivira Way, Mission Bay, 619-223-1681 or 888-834-2628). For $90 per hour extra, you can rent a captain.

No signs or advertisements exist for the two chubby harbor seals residing on the grounds of the **Bahia Hotel** (998 W Mission Bay Drive, Mission Bay, 858-488-0551). Known as Natasha and Estaban, they were rescued over 12 years ago by SeaWorld San Diego officials and given to the hotel for a life on Easy Street. Their unassuming salt water, kidney-shaped pool is accessible to passersby, who obviously disobey the "no feeding" sign judging from the astonishing girth of these creatures. Enter the main parking lot and veer left toward the Bahia restaurant.

At any given time, nearly 100 exotic hookbill birds are in residence at **Freeflight** (2132 Jimmy Durante Boulevard, Del Mar, California, 858-481-3148), a small, out-of-the-way avian boarding school and breeding center with outdoor facilities that are open to the public. For a $1 admission, visitors can hold and pet a variety of species that appear as though they are waiting for some human cooing and cawing. Among the more affectionate ones: Abbey, a hyacinth macaw; Targa, a Moluccan cockatoo; and Picante, a golden conure — all of which have clawed their way up to "permanent resident" status.

SECRET

ANIMATION

From thought provoking to utterly deranged, *Spike & Mike's Festival of Animation*, and its *Sick & Twisted* spin-off series, offer some brilliant hijinks in the form of animated short films that are presented seasonally at the **Museum of Contemporary Art** (700 Prospect Street, La Jolla, 858-454-3541). Too creative to be called "cartoons," the classic, G-rated works in the general festival (April and May) appeal to the intelligentsia of conceptual art, with the creators turning life's complexities into poignant caricatures of themselves. The ebullience is fueled by more salacious subject matter in the *Sick & Twisted* series (September and October), such as rooftop sex and inbreeding, which are easier to snicker at in the company of close peers than parents, offspring, or first-time dates. The shows feature between 15 and 20 "shorts" from animators all over the world.

SECRET

ARCHIVES

A treasure chest of the region's official documents, maps, and ephemera, along with an astounding collection of 2.5 million photographs, is available for public examination at the **San Diego Historical Society Museum and Research Archives** (1649 El Prado Way, Balboa Park, 619-232-6203). The opening of the facility in 1983 united several important archival resources that had been previously unavailable to the public, primarily because the collections were stored in cramped and disconnected spaces. History buffs today will marvel at the nearly 4,000 linear feet of manuscripts. And they will get to see how San Diego looked over 100 years ago: what was being worn or driven or sailed.

Tucked behind the Diversionary Theatre (see "Secret Theater") is a mini-library of sorts that serves as a time capsule for San Diego's gay, lesbian, bisexual, and transgender community (see "Secret LGBT"). Established in 1987, the **Lesbian and Gay Historical Society of San Diego** (4545 Park Boulevard, Suite 205, University Heights, 619-260-1522) houses books, periodicals, newspapers, and personal collections of social activists that reflect the city's rich LGBT history. The space is used often by researchers, students, and curious visitors, who drop by to poke through the acid-free storage boxes that preserve local gay and lesbian publications dating back to the early 1970s. In one of the boxes are the original volumes of *One,* a former international publication that began in Los Angeles in 1953, long before the gay press blossomed. Open to the public on Sundays (11 AM to 2 PM), and on the second and fourth Wednesdays of each month (6 PM to 8 PM).

SECRET
ASIAN FABLES

Since 1989, **The Asian Story Theater** (619-587-2816, www. asianstorytheater.com) has been skillfully adapting Asian children's stories for the stage, bringing to life ancient literary characters that are as beloved throughout the Far East as Mickey Mouse is in North America. Recent productions have shed light on a mischievous monk escort known as the Monkey King — his adventures are lifted from chapters of a novel written by a Chinese government official in the early 1600s. And the story of Mulan was presented by the theater to San Diego audiences long before Disney produced it as an animated movie. The colorful performances, held in early April, feature original scores and handmade Chinese shadow puppets that interact with costumed actors. Performances are held at the **Lyceum Theatre** (79 Horton Plaza, Downtown, 619-235-8025).

SECRET
ASTROLOGY

Like most people might expect of Southern California, San Diego has its fair share of tarot readers and mystics. A stroll down **El Prado Way** in **Balboa Park** on almost any given day puts you in touch with those lucky few who bear licenses to operate beneath the ornate Spanish Colonial façades that grace the midway.

But serious astrologers will bridle at being grouped in that set. On the second Friday of every month, the **San Diego Astrological Society** (888-405-6825) presents lectures by big-name authors and researchers in the field. Horoscope columnist Michael Lutin of *Vanity Fair* has been a regular over the years. So has Rob Hand, known worldwide for translating ancient astrological text from the Middle East and Greece into English. Non-members are always welcome, but save the questions about your love life and career for a seer, because these are meetings without readings. The lectures are held at the Joyce Beers Community Center (1220 Cleveland Avenue, Hillcrest).

SECRET
AUTOS

One would never expect to find more than 120 classic American automobiles displayed on the grounds of a prestigious winery, just steps away from where award-winning varietals are poured for public tasting. But the businesses of crushing grapes and collecting cars blend naturally at **Deer Park Winery and Auto Museum** (29013 Champagne Boulevard, Escondido, California, 760-749-1666). The 50-acre vineyard, located about 45 miles north of San Diego, offers visitors an overview of the evolution of automobiles, particularly convertibles. Among the rare and restored vehicles on display: a 1928 Model A sport coupe; a 1948 Crosely convertible; a 1953 Cadillac Eldorado convertible; and two decades worth of finned classics, starting from the 1950s. The entire collection is housed in three separate buildings on the bucolic property, also known for producing fumé blush, petite syrah, and full-bodied cabernet sauvignon.

In a more predictable setting, visitors can gawk at 80 beloved vehicles representing different eras of the 20th century at the **San Diego Automotive Museum** (2080 Pan American Plaza, Balboa Park, 619-231-2886). The structure, built in 1935, served as barracks for Navy corpsmen during World War II. Today, it boasts an impressive collection of rare chassis, including one of three Bizzarinis ever built in a "spider" design, and a circa 1910 Flying Merkle motorcycle. The museum is open daily (10 AM to 5 PM). Admission is $3 for children and $7 for adults.

SECRET
AVOCADOS

The reason to buy avocados at roadside stands isn't freshness. Truth is, no matter where you buy them, it could take a few days before they ripen and become soft enough for making guacamole. But when you buy them roadside, you'll find better prices — and you can soak up the local color of the surrounding landscape. Avocados have long been a major source of income for growers in the North County area of San Diego, particularly around the quaint town of Fallbrook. About 6,000 acres in the area are devoted to avocado growing, although recent droughts have significantly reduced the number of trees and growers over the past several years.

The best roadside stands operate quietly along Mission Road in Fallbrook (about a 45-minute drive north on I-15 from downtown San Diego). Two of them offer a wide variety of other seasonal fruits and vegetables as well. **Rancho Fruit Market** (2591 E Mission Road, Fallbrook, California, 760-731-2924) is the largest curbside market in the region, selling about as many avocados per day as the leading supermarkets, but for about 25 percent less. And they're all freshly picked. The vendor also offers a large variety of fruits, nuts, and vegetables. Alongside the stand is an abundant field of spiky plants that resemble a mini pineapple plantation. The leaves of these aloe plants are cut regularly and sold for use in cosmetic and medicinal products. **Exotic Limes and Fruits** (1397 E Mission Road, Fallbrook, California, 760-728-1722) is further down the road toward Fallbrook's town center, on the left side of the street. As the name implies, it features farm-fresh limes and lemons along with the high-calorie, vitamin-rich green fruit that everyone wants to bring home and mash. But eat them on San Diego soil before traveling home to any-where outside of the United States. Otherwise, you'll be feeding the customs agents.

SECRET
BAKERIES

You'll need the nose of a hound dog to sniff out the few bakeries in town that fire up their ovens every day at the crack of dawn to make fresh-baked breads, cookies, and cakes. Most of the big supermarket chains, such as **Von's**, **Ralph's**, and **Albertson's**, have convenient bakery sections, but I generally find them below standard compared to the secret, individually owned establishments.

Depending on what time you visit, the checkout lines at **V.G. Donuts and Bakery** (106 Aberdeen Street, Cardiff, California, 760-753-2400) might be horrendously long. But they move fast. Since 1969, this family-owned landmark, situated about 100 yards from the beach, has supplied sugar-craving residents with luscious cakes, airy donuts, and mouthwatering cinnamon rolls. With the exception of an expanded catering business, nothing has changed. Longtime customers find familiar faces here and relate like kin to the founder's two sons, who now run the business. And the "V.G." in the name still stands for "very good." Tables and barstools set the stage for folksy chitchat, espe-cially on busy weekday mornings, when designated donut gofers drop by en masse on the way to their offices.

At **Flour Power Custom Bakery** (3211 Holiday Court, La Jolla, 858-558-1199), it's all about cakes — elaborately detailed cakes festooned with English buttercream frosting, chocolate mousse, or cream cheese.

Like some high-end art gallery, the bakery takes appointments if you need a private consultation or wish to browse the catalogues for decorating ideas. Walk-ins will find a modest selection of fresh cookies and a limited number of leftover cakes in the display racks. The shop is tucked away in the small Villa Norte Shopping Center.

More than 20 types of breads, hand-shaped using the European artisan technique, are baked fresh daily at **Bread and Cie** (350 University Avenue, Hillcrest, 619-683-9322). The dough is started with live yeast cultures to produce crusty loaves in flavors such as rosemary olive oil, walnut-scallion, fig-anise, and jalapeño-cheese. But the kitchen's biggest secret is its 10,000-pound stone hearth oven, imported from France. An indoor-outdoor seating area makes it a perfect lunch spot for grabbing a gourmet sandwich. And the interior walls showcase paintings and photographs from local artists, which change every two weeks. About a mile west in the community of Mission Hills is **À La Française** (4029 Goldfinch Street, Mission Hills, 619-294-4425), a little French bakery and restaurant popular for its fresh croissants, Danishes, scones, and, of course, excellent French bread. The bakery is easy to miss, so look for the outdoor flower stand where Fort Stockton Drive intersects Goldfinch.

In a remote outpost about an hour's drive northeast of San Diego is a bustling bakery known as **Dudley's** (30218 Highway 79, Santa Ysabel, California, 760-765-0488), which bakes up 3,000 loaves of specialty bread each day. The bucolic setting seems strange for a bakery of this caliber until you realize that it's a popular stop for motorists heading to the nearby historic gold-mining town of **Julian**, seven miles up the road. The bakery, which opened in 1963, features about 15 varieties of home-style breads, cookies, and an ever-present supply of date-nut bars. **Crossroads Gift Shop** is connected to it, offering Native American jewelry and crafts, plus a sparkling selection of gems and minerals. In the same tiny shopping complex is the **Julian Pie Company** (21976 Highway 79, Santa Ysabel, California, 760-765-2400), a quieter outlet compared to its wildly popular location in the heart of Julian (2225 Main Street, Julian, California, 760-765-2449). There, throngs of San Diegans line up in autumn for fresh apple and boysenberry pies, sold whole or by the slice. They have to come this far to see the leaves change colors. If you're making a day trip to the area, go east on I-8 out of San Diego, connect onto Highway 67, then continue through the city of Ramona to Highway 78 for about 12 miles. Should you want to savor the region's tranquility, turn left onto Highway 79 from Dudley's, and drive one mile to the **Santa Ysabel Indian Mission** (23013 Highway 79, Santa Ysabel, California, 760-765-0810). The structure was founded in 1818 and priests still celebrate Mass there for Native Americans and visitors.

Better than flowers to some, the edible bouquets at **Cookies by Design** (5658 Mission Center Road, Suite 301, Mission Valley, 619-295-4083) can be tailored to every occasion under the sun. It's a national franchise, but one with a low profile. The shop is small and inconspicuous, upstaged by larger neighboring retailers in a generic strip plaza. But the fresh cookie arrangements are flamboyant — a perfect rescue when you're stuck for something to give on birthdays, anniversaries, or other joyous occasions.

SECRET

BALLROOM DANCING

The swirling chiffon, plunging necklines, flawlessly tailored slacks, and mirror-like polished spats that are the trademark of ballroom dancing have a firm toehold in San Diego. Several international champions hail from our city, and many teach in dance schools around the county. In the past decade, the amount of floor space dedicated to ballroom dance classes has exploded. If you have arrived in San Diego with two left feet and all the rhythm of a water buffalo, three schools tucked away in inauspicious places will speed you on your way to displaying the dapper air of Fred Astaire and the delicate grace of Ginger Rogers.

Champion Ballroom Academy (3580 5th Avenue, Hillcrest, 619-291-7722 or 858-481-3307) is uniquely situated on the second floor of a two-story building overlooking one of San Diego's main avenues. Floor-to-ceiling windows add light to an already-airy dance floor. You can sign up for two private classes or a group class, along with a dance party on Friday or Saturday evenings ($29). Downstairs is the **Ballroom Boutique** (619-291-1601), a convenient lifesaver in case you forgot to pack your flaming-orange, sequined, form-fitting dance outfit.

The **Starlight Dance Studio** (6506 El Cajon Boulevard, Unit H, North Park, 619-287-9036) offers international ballroom, American ballroom, country-western, West Coast swing, and nightclub dance classes. If there is a John Travolta waiting to emerge from within you (and, please, warn somebody if this is the case), check out the *Saturday Night Fever* dance every second Saturday of the month, with funk, hip-hop, disco, and rhythm and blues dancing ($8). The public is also welcome to attend free "very beginner" lessons in West Coast swing dancing, held Sunday evenings.

Absolutely Dancesport (2400 Kettner Boulevard, Suite 101, Little Italy, 619-531-1700) is the largest studio in the city, with 12,500 square feet of dance space. Along with the other styles of ballroom and swing dancing, the instructors also teach salsa, Argentine tango, country-western, and ballet. This studio is in the Little Italy section of San Diego, a fast-growing area with wonderful restaurants and storefronts, many with hidden patios and gardens in the back. The studio offers private and group dance instruction and programs for children and teens. Its introductory special features two private lessons, a group lesson, and a practice session — all for $25. Lessons are 45 minutes long. You can pop in on their practice parties (8:45 PM to 10 PM) every Friday. Students and their guests get in free; visitors pay a cover ($10).

Finally, while swing dancing in recent years has become a phenomenon across the nation, we've had our own **San Diego Swing Dance Club** (619-491-1808) since 1970. This non-profit organization specializes in West Coast swing, which is the California state dance and a sophisticated descendant of jitterbugging. The club holds its dances every Sunday at **La Mesa Women's Club** (5220 Wilson Street, La Mesa, California, 619-466-4362) and welcomes visitors, with or without partners. The dances are preceded by a beginner class (included with admission).

SECRET
BEACHES

The **Children's Pool** (850 Coast Boulevard, La Jolla) is an odd structure jutting into the ocean off the La Jolla cove. Originally, a semi-circular concrete seawall was built in hopes of creating a protected swimming area for children. Sand quickly settled and filled in the curvature and created a sheltered beach. But less than 10 years ago, a flank of seals showed up on the sands to sunbathe. Because they are a federally protected species, we humans had to cede use of the beach to them. The area has since been renamed **Seal Rock Mammal Reserve**. On some days, there may be more than 150 of the innocent-looking creatures lazing around. You can walk all the way out to the end of the seawall for a spectacular view of both the seals and coastal La Jolla. The area is popular with scuba divers because of the reefs just offshore. Best bet: arrive early in the morning during high tide. There are fewer people around to pester the seals and the high water coaxes the seals higher up on the beach, where you can view them better.

The path to **Beacon's Beach** (Neptune Avenue and Leucadia Boulevard, Leucadia, California) is winding and treacherous. That fact, coupled with a hidden location behind homes on the street above, has kept this beach a favorite among locals. If you have a surfboard, you'll get a classic view of the California coastline that only surfers, sailors, and pilots ever see. Officially, the beach is named **Leucadia State Beach**, but area residents will look at you quizzically if you call it that. During World War II, there was a navigational beacon here, so Beacon's is the name that stuck. Leucadians have built up a plethora of legends and myths about their beloved strip of sand. One claims that early Native Americans believed the ocean currents brought healing powers and anti-aging properties to the water at Beacon's. I'm guessing the legends have more to do with tequila-inspired bonfire stories than with historical accuracy. But if there's a grain of truth in it, a dip in the surf can't hurt.

Moonlight Beach is located at the very end of Encinitas Boulevard in the coastal town of Encinitas. This is a broad white-sand beach with picnic tables, volleyball courts, fire rings, and public parking. The view as you come over the hill on Encinitas Boulevard and descend

down to the level of the beach is postcard Southern California. Yet every time I've visited a friend who lives just a block away, the beach has been wide open with plenty of room to stroll or plant a blanket for the day. If you're looking for quiet sands, this is a good bet. Back at the top of the hill, and a block north on Highway 101, is the quaint business district of Encinitas, with numerous mom-and-pop restaurants, bookstores, and clothing shops.

S E C R E T
BEER SCHOOL

Shamu the killer whale. Dolly Dolphin. O.P. Otter. Visitors to **SeaWorld San Diego** (500 SeaWorld Drive, Mission Bay, 619-226-3901) count on seeing this cast of characters at the adventure park, but what they don't expect is to learn how beer is brewed or — better yet — to taste free samples. During **Budweiser Beer School** at SeaWorld's Anheuser-Busch Hospitality Center, a certified beer master covers the 22-step brewing process from the mill to the bottle, with all the fermenting, aerating, and chill-proofing that goes on in between. Along the way, guests learn about the history of Anheuser-Busch, which owns and operates SeaWorld, Busch Gardens, and several other theme parks in the country. In addition to tasting several products during class (Budweiser, Bud Light, Michelob, Killarney's Red Lager, and Doc's Hard Lemon), adult consumers 21 years or older can get two free samples of beer at the Hospitality Center. Here, you'll also find a restaurant, gift shop, and the Clydesdale Hamlet, occupied by 12 feather-legged Budweiser Clydesdales and a traditional Dalmatian guard dog.

S E C R E T
BINGO

The number of charitable bingo halls in San Diego has diminished by over 50 percent in the last five years due to the construction of Native American gaming casinos in East County. California's ban on smoking in bars, restaurants, and indoor charity functions certainly hasn't helped, either. But after peeking into **Bingo and More** (3511 5th Avenue, Hillcrest, 619-296-1900), it's easy to believe that the game still ranks as the largest recreational activity in the United States. The store is easier to pass by than it is to forget. Bingo paraphernalia abounds, with more than 500 different items designed expressly for hardcore gamers. There are "square waiters," used to mark numbers you wish would be called; seat cushions for the long duration in waiting for them; lucky charms to add hope; and "bingo control pills," which speak for themselves. Products can be shipped to anywhere in the US, Canada, Mexico, or Europe.

Bingo is presented with a tasty little secret at **St. Mary Magdalene's** church (1945 Illion Street, Bay Park, 619-276-4538). On the last Tuesday of the month, players eat for free: sloppy Joes, spaghetti, or chicken. One of San Diego's oldest bingo halls is **Blessed Sacrament** (4540 El Cerrito Drive, College Area, 619-582-5722). Games are held under the church every Friday night.

Native Indian casinos pay out three times more in their jackpots, and they're exempt from the state's smoking ban. For instance, **Sycuan Casino** (5469 Casino Way, El Cajon, California, 619-445-6002) holds bingo three times a day and once in the evening, with pots reaching upwards of $15,000. Look for the big white tent at **Viejas**

Casino (5000 Willows Road, Alpine, California, 619-445-5400). Payouts on regular games average a whopping $1,000.

Bingo with a campy gay twist is held on Wednesdays (9 PM) and Saturdays (7 PM) at **Bourbon Street** (4612 Park Boulevard, University Heights, 619-291-4043). The games are emceed by drag queens, who dole out kitchen appliances, rubber chickens, and padded toilet seats as prizes.

SECRET
BOOKSTORES

One of the few places where young nihilists in black garb (I swear they are required by law to wear it) co-exist peacefully with doe-eyed New Agers is within the narrow aisles of a beloved San Diego landmark, the **Controversial Bookstore** (3021 University Avenue, North Park, 619-296-1560). Located on a busy thoroughfare in the city's North Park community, and sandwiched between a discount shoe store and a mom-and-pop pizza joint, the store has stocked astrological tomes and Marxist manifestoes for well over 25 years. Walk in off the street and you are immediately enveloped in the perfume of packaged incense and aura-cleansing sage wands. Various crystals sparkle for sale beneath the front counter, along with Tarot decks and self-help videos. The shelves along the walls in the back will bring you from Edgar Cayce's psychic dreams to Sartre's existentialist play *No Exit,* and just about any counterculture point in between. There is even a used section in the far back of the store where you'll find books with cryptic margin notes written by caffeine-soaked college grad students. Be an anti-establishment beatnik, or just carry books that make you seem like one! This is also a great place to pick up information about offbeat events in San Diego.

The Prince and the Pauper Collectible Children's Books (3201 Adams Avenue, 619-283-4380 or 800-454-3726) squeezes roughly 85,000 titles of scarce, out-of-print juvenile books into a 4,000-square-foot shop in the community of Normal Heights. Faded memories spring back to life when you happen upon Nancy Drew, Tom Swift, the Hardy Boys, and Oz books — most of them neatly contained in their original series. There are about 180 subject categories in all. The massive pickings yield nearly 4,000 new titles as well.

An eclectic selection of new and used books, many by obscure local authors, make **Blue Stocking Books** (3817 5th Avenue, Hillcrest, 619-296-1424) a cherished community den for readers and poets alike. A little antique desk in the back of the store serves as the lectern for open readings and poetry orations every Monday (7 PM). You'll find 30 years worth of collected tomes on everything from architecture and metaphysics to horror and ancient history.

A jaunt across the street brings you to much rarer books by authors such as Ray Bradbury and J.R.R. Tolkien. If it's out of print, you stand a chance of finding it at **5th Avenue Books** (3838 5th Avenue, Hillcrest, 619-291-4660). A couple storefronts away is **Bountiful Books** (3834 5th Avenue, Hillcrest, 619-491-0664), where I've found a good many nature essays by Henry David Thoreau and past editions of the *Journal of San Diego History,* published over the last several decades by the **San Diego Historical Society** (1649 El Prado Way, Balboa Park, 619-232-6203).

S E C R E T

BRAZILIAN

South American cuisine has slowly inched its way into San Diego's dining scene with the recent arrival of **Rei do Gado** (939 4th Avenue, Downtown, 619-702-8464). At the center of it all is the traditional Brazilian grill, called a *churrascaria*. Diners are served a steady stream of fabulous skewered meats until they turn over their table markers to red (for stop). When green, it's an all-you-can-eat repast of filet mignon, top sirloin, pork loin, chicken, and Brazilian sausages. A salad buffet provides balance to the meal with offerings such as fried bananas, yuca root, eggplant, and sliced oranges. You'll need a strong appetite and a few ounces of self-control to reach a comfortable finish. Sunday through Thursday ($23.95); Fridays and Saturdays ($27.95).

There are no grills or red meats at **Melodia Brazilian Seafood and Vegetarian Kitchen** (101 N Coast Highway, Encinitas, California, 760-942-8380). But there are plenty of traditional vegetarian and seafood specialties to keep carnivorous appetites at bay. Grilled salmon, mahi mahi, and shrimp stroganoff are among the seafood specialties crafted with verve by the restaurant's Brazilian owners. Some of the vegan entrées are downright exotic: mineiro (okra, squash, and farofa served with rice, beans, and sautéed bananas) and carioca (rice, beans, mock sausage, collard greens, and bananas). Brazilian hospitality is evident; the owners are talkative and they don't rush you out after the check is paid.

You can walk out of **Terra Brazil** (1002 N Coast Highway, Encinitas, California, 760-635-7549) with imported chocolates in one hand

and a new piece of swimwear in the other. Nearly everything in the store originates from Brazilian manufacturers — swimwear, lingerie, hammocks, and music CDs. Traditional edibles are big draws as well, particularly the farofa and robust coffees. Bilingual editions of the *Brazilian Pacific Times* are available for keeping up with the community's regional cultural events.

S E C R E T

BREAKFAST

I'm always mystified by the hordes of people I see clamoring to get into **Denny's** and **Coco's** on weekend mornings while less expensive, more unusual places go unnoticed. When it comes to our most important meal of the day, I'm sticking to where the non-conformists eat (see also "Secret Waffles").

The owner of **Jimmy Carter's** (3172 5th Avenue, Hillcrest, 619-295-2070) says people ask him all the time if the restaurant is affiliated with the toothy, ex–peanut farmer, ex-president. Sorry, same name, but no relation. The non-partisan menu includes mostly American breakfast fare, except for several incongruous Indian-style choices, such as dhosa (made with rice, lentils, and chicken curry) and pesarattu (a satisfying "pancake" of beans, onions, peppers, ginger, and cilantro). And while soup isn't normally on my mind in the morning, I start thinking about it as soon as I arrive here. Rarely can I pass up a cup of Indian dahl, infused with more than 16 exotic spices. It's a wonderful complement to everything on my plate. Big storefront windows and a corner-lot location provide tangential views of Balboa Park's giant eucalyptus trees. The neighborhood begins crowding in by 9 AM on weekends.

The huevos rancheros breakfast at **Cecil's Cafe** (5083 Santa Monica Avenue, Ocean Beach, 619-222-0501) is superior to the version at hundreds of other places that serve it. A generous pile of scrambled eggs, topped with chunky salsa, covers two fresh tortillas. And the accompanying rice and beans reveal a nice hint of cumin. Pancakes are light and airy; omelettes come in many varieties. The dining room looks out to the ocean, and the view is all yours if you can seize one of the few tables along the front windows. Conveniently, the **Ocean Beach Pier** is in very close range. A roundtrip walk on it takes about 15 minutes, should you want to burn off a pat of butter.

It's dull, dingy, and frozen in time. But that's what makes **Hob Nob Hill** (2271 1st Avenue, Bankers Hill, 619-239-8176) so popular among the locals who eventually find it. The heavy wooden chandeliers, fluorescent-lit pie cases, and dusty bric-a-brac confirm the restaurant's half-century age. Located in a mellow residential area about three miles north of Downtown, it attracts a medley of business and theater folk, along with devoted seniors who have a keen sense for sniffing out the best blue-plate specials in town.

The breakfast menu at **The Mission** (2801 University Avenue, North Park, 619-220-8992; and 3795 Mission Boulevard, Mission Beach, 858-488-9060) is a tasty scramble of American and Mexican fare that doesn't weigh you down with fatty goo. Forget those cheese-loaded omelettes, gristly sausage links, and oily hash browns. The plates flying around this beatnik-looking restaurant are loaded with seasonal fruits, fresh veggies, and homespun granola — perfect fuel for an afternoon of swimming or bike riding. My recommendations: the Pappas Loco — a hearty mélange of potatoes, grilled jalapeños, black beans, avocado, and a smattering of cheese. The strawberry-granola hotcakes are unbelievably large and fluffy. And health nuts will love the Zen breakfast, composed of scrambled egg whites, braised tofu, and brown rice. Tables and booths are tightly arranged. A wide-open deconstructed interior, with its exposed rafters and ventilation tubing, does little to mute the din when the place is busy. But the food is well worth the extra decibels.

Whenever I go to **Johnny's Family Restaurant** (2611 El Cajon Boulevard, North Park, 619-291-8239) for breakfast, I usually end up eating lunch because the menu is chock-full of tempting, homey dishes that seem straight out of a Fannie Farmer cookbook. Old-fashioned *real* turkey dinners, Swiss steak, and Monte Cristo sandwiches are among the hard-to-find kitchen specialties served any time of the day. And nowhere else in San Diego will you find cold buttermilk offered on a beverage list. The owner says he keeps it on the menu because of a small but serious demand. I did once forgo lunch for the popular feta cheese and black olive omelette that I remember fondly. Corned-beef hash and pancakes are also hot sellers. The restaurant is big and clean — and staffed by chatty, warm-hearted waitresses who you might guess are imported from the Midwest. I especially like it here because there is rarely a line to get in.

A drive up the coast to downtown Carlsbad brings you to one of the prettiest breakfast patios in San Diego County. The **Daily News Café** (3001 Carlsbad Boulevard, Carlsbad, California, 760-729-1023) is no less famous for its omnipotent omelettes than for its beautiful, landscaped surroundings. The restaurant is part of the Tudor-style **Carlsbad Inn Beach Resort** (760-434-7020), but draws plenty of sandal-clad locals with their morning newspapers in tow. Come here if you like to people watch, because the patio is positioned within perfect eyeshot of the boulevard. And the beach is just a few steps away. Regular customers rave about the cinnamon French toast and breakfast parfaits, a summery blend of fresh fruit, non-fat vanilla yogurt, and granola.

SECRET
BREWERIES

Say it with gusto: *Dunkelweisen!* Doesn't matter what it means when you're drinking it — but when you finish that last *prost*, you might be interested to know that it's a word on the menu to describe a rich microbrewed winter variety of Hefeweizen beer. It's just one of the brews that you'll find at **Karl Strauss Brewery** (9675 Scranton Road, Sorrento Valley, 858-587-2739). The building, surrounded by a lavish Japanese garden, is so tucked away that it's a wonder visitors get here without guidance. Of course, with a selection of 10 homemade brews on tap, the return trip could be difficult, too. Entering from the parking lot through a narrow gate, you cross over a wooden bridge and wind along a woodland path through bamboo and evergreen trees. The scene that spills out as you emerge is like a picture from an Asian silk print. A long, low-roofed teahouse delicately hovers over a large, quiet koi pond stocked with ghostly white and orange fish. The restaurant is almost entirely glass windowed and features generous outdoor seating on multilevel terraces. At night, with lanterns glimmering in the distance, it's easy to forget this place is smack in the middle of one of the county's largest light industrial and high-tech manufacturing areas. Also worth tasting is the Karl Strauss oatmeal stout, a rich Irish concoction made with oatmeal flakes, and the La Jolla

Hefeweizen, a Bavarian-style wheat beer with hints of banana, cloves, and vanilla. The brewery has three other locations around town, all of which are more visible and less landscaped.

San Diego Brewing Co. (10450 Friars Road, Mission Gorge, 619-284-2739) is a sports bar first and brewery second. There are two satellite dishes, 15 televisions, and two wide screens that deliver an encyclopedia of sports games to nearly every table and booth. But only four homemade brews are offered: gold, amber, nut brown, and a mild-tasting smoked stout. Other taps dispense "guest" microbrews that are made elsewhere by other companies. A sign on the door stating "We're open, get in here" might be more effective if the brewery were closer to the street. Like so many destination spots in San Diego, it resides in an architecturally prosaic strip plaza. But it's worth a visit if you're on the hunt for *any* type of sports game. Brewing equipment is visible behind a glass wall near the long oak bar — and the homemade sausage and barbecue pizzas are all perfect come-ons for guzzling down more beer.

Beer connoisseurs come to the **Coronado Brewing Co.** (170 Orange Avenue, Coronado, California, 619-437-4452) for the Silver Strand Steam, a fairly obscure ale that is brewed and fermented with lager yeast. About four other beers are made on the premises, including the light and refreshing Coronado Golden. The place fills up quickly in the late afternoon on Fridays and Saturdays, but is otherwise quiet.

Smoking isn't allowed on the patio, which means there is less competition for landing a table outside here than at other places. A well-rounded food menu includes moderately priced sandwiches and salads, although the garlic fries and beer match up as perfectly as cookies and milk.

S E C R E T

BRITISH ISLES

One would never think of heading to the **Little Italy** district for slow-tapped ale and cottage pie. But if you want to sample the cheery ambiance of San Diego's oldest British pub, you'll have to fend off the alluring smells of pizza and spaghetti sauce when making your approach. **Princess Pub and Grille** (1665 India Street, 619-702-3021) is flanked by a bevy of Italian restaurants — some long established, others that have popped up since the street was redesigned with more sidewalk space. An imposing painting of Princess Diana looming over the dining area serves as an odd cue to indulge, rather than pause in thought. Wet your whistle at the commodious bar, equipped with 18 beer taps. Play darts. Order fish and chips. Everything you want from a British pub is right here.

Further north up the street, a mile outside of Little Italy, **Shakespeare's Pub & Grill** (3701 India Street, Middletown, 619-299-0230) is where the other half of the city's Brits and Anglophiles gather. The authentic grub is particularly sought-after during Friday happy hours and when European Premier Soccer League matches emanate from the large-screen satellite tellies. A spacious outdoor deck with ample seating provides scads more sunshine than do pubs in England. **Shakespeare's Corner Shop** (3719 India Street, Middletown, 619-683-2748) is a few doors down, in the back of a small courtyard raised above street level. It carries a tremendous selection of imported British delicacies such as pickled walnuts, jarred minced meat, and the English version of Heinz baked beans — paler, with a thinner sauce.

When a friend told me about **All Things Bright and British** (8401 La Mesa Boulevard, La Mesa, California, 619-464-2298), he coyly admitted to spending almost $100 in a single visit, though he intended to pick up only a few things. The store touts itself as a British "supermarket," although it isn't nearly quite that big. It does, however, carry one of the largest and most tempting selections of British teas and imported food items in the region. And it's in a fitting location, nestled among antique stores, quaint eateries, and coffee shops that bring Old World charm to **La Mesa Village.**

Whether you're hankering for a Cornish pastie or traditional pork pie, **Bit O' Britain** (2860 State Street, Carlsbad, California, 760-434-9130) bangs them out fresh, along with a variety of other baked goods made daily. You'll also find a large variety of canned, packaged, and frozen products that are purchased directly from vendors throughout the UK.

If a battle of the pubs ever broke out, the Irish would prove a formidable challenge to the British, with their free-flowing Guinness and unconquerable corned beef — just like what you'll find at **The Field** (544 5th Avenue, Downtown, 619-232-9840). Piece by piece, the homey bric-a-brac and interior wood was shipped over from an Irish farmhouse. Much of the wait staff comes from the Motherland too — young adults on temporary work permits gathering a taste of American culture while giving patrons a sample of theirs with those charming brogues. The corned beef is consistently lean. And if you've never tried boxty, then do so here. It's a potato pancake wrapped around a variety of meat or veggie fillings, and topped with a roux-like sauce. Ask for a table upstairs. It's cozier and more rustic.

The Ould Sod (3373 Adams Avenue, 619-284-6594) is Irish through and through, with worn-down green wooden fittings, Irish memorabilia plastering the walls, and live Celtic music on Tuesday evenings.

Bartenders and waiters, mostly from Ireland, are the friendliest in town. The pub is sandwiched on a quaint commercial block in the newly hip community of Normal Heights. Equally popular, but somewhat more Americanized, is **Rosie O'Grady's Irish Pub and Grille** (3402 Adams Avenue, 619-284-7666), just one block down the street.

SECRET
BUDDHA

While Southern California has a reputation as a place where we all sit around in the lotus position contemplating our navels, to me there is always an incongruity in coming across a Buddhist temple in our commercial landscape. But the ancient religion thrives here, partly because of vegetarian, puka-shelled, macramé-wearing seekers of the '70s, and partly because of a significant Asian population that has called California home from its earliest days. As long as you are respectful, most temples are welcoming to visitors. Here are two of the most gorgeous ones in San Diego, which are little known outside the community of congregants who attend them.

Looking like something straight out of the '70s action television series "Kung Fu," **Chua Van Hanh Vietnamese Buddhist Temple** (8627 Fanita Drive, Santee, California, 619-448-6611) is serenely beautiful. This unexpected complex of temple, monastery, and garden, along with a large statue of Kuan-yin (the bodhisattva of compassion), is located in a part of San Diego better known for redneck cowboys and Bible Belt Christians. Bilingual dharma teachings in Vietnamese and English are held every Sunday (9:30 AM), followed by a vegetarian lunch. An English-speaking group meets on Saturdays for meditation practice. And visitors are warned ahead of time that there is a dress code as well as specific etiquette requested of visitors. Quoting directly, the rules state: "Please dress conservatively and respectfully. Especially, do not wear shorts or short skirts. Be prepared to sit cross-legged on the floor, but please do not sit stretching your legs out in front of you." And, of course, singing a chorus of "Louie, Louie" during meditation will cost you major karma demerits.

A tiny four-block district at the end of Park Boulevard in the University Heights area has turned itself from what was a nondescript backwater neighborhood 20 years ago into a burgeoning mini-bohemia. Nestled amid quaint bookstores and coffeehouses, a legitimate theater, a New Orleans–style gay bar, a Persian restaurant, and a Persian rug store, sits the **Hsi Fang Buddhist Temple** (4536 Park Boulevard, 619-298-2800). If you do nothing else, take the time to see the exquisite Buddha Hall, located on the second floor of a building that looks almost like a warehouse from the outside. An easy way to find it is to first locate the **Buddha's Light Bookstore** (4536 Park Boulevard, 619-298-2800) next door, which is very visible and considered by some to be the best Buddhist bookstore in the region. The temple is the building just south of that. For those with a deeper interest, the temple organizes summer camps, does family visitations, and holds Cantonese language and zither classes. How often have you come back from a vacation able to say, "I took a zither class?" The temple also officiates at funerals, weddings, and house blessings.

S E C R E T
BUFFETS

You'll be hard pressed to find a buffet in San Diego that features all-you-can-eat lobster tails — unless you go a few blocks outside Downtown's Gaslamp District for a visit to **Momo** (555 Market Street, 619-231-9000). To call this a restaurant is misleading because it's more like a culinary exhibition in progress, one that you'd expect to see at a Japanese food convention. The buffet bar is over 160 feet long. It's filled with Asian delights that include spicy salmon, tempura vegetables, pan-fried pork dumplings, and mounds of peeled shrimp. The baked lobster tails appear unexpectedly halfway down the bar, near an active teppanyaki grill, but still many feet before an exquisite display of sushi reveals itself. Located in a 100-year-old building, the airy, stylish space replaces the colorless character of the former **G.I. Joe Army Surplus Store**, now located two storefronts away.

Patrons under five feet tall receive a 50-percent discount at the giant Japanese buffet called **Todai** (2828 Camino Del Rio South, Mission Valley, 619-299-8996). In other words, bring the kids. The restaurant resembles a hotel banquet hall and is perfect for industrial-sized crowds. You'll find nearly 20 hot entrées, including hardcore seafood dishes such as greenlip mussels, sashimi, crab legs, and more. The Japanese noodle soup and shrimp tempura are particularly memorable. Located under the I-805 freeway, the restaurant is open seven days a week for lunch ($12.95 to $14.95) and dinner ($22.95 to $23.95).

There are two secrets to keep in mind before putting your name on the list for Sunday brunch at the **94th Aero Squadron** (8885 Balboa

Avenue, Kearny Mesa, 858-560-6771). Ask for seating along the back windows or on the patio — or request a table that comes with headphones. The restaurant, a replica of a World War I French farmhouse, has a small airport in its backyard called **Montgomery Field**. Diners can gaze out at light aircraft and helicopters that arrive and depart from three different runways, or tune in to the flight control tower with headphones wired from about a dozen tables. The lavish buffet (11 AM to 2:30 PM) combines usual breakfast fare with a fajita station, cold crab legs, and beef, ham, and lamb roasts. An old model airplane, army jeep, and duck pond are a stone's throw from the back patio.

SECRET
BUGS BUNNY

What's up, Doc? Well, the price of animation cels is up. Those cartoon characters we grew up watching on TV fetch a mighty price in the art market. Chuck Jones worked for Warner Bros. Studio and was one of the most celebrated animators. During a career spanning 60 years, he made more than 300 animated films and won three Oscars. His artwork for such characters as the Grinch, Horton (who heard a Who), Bugs Bunny, Daffy Duck, Yosemite Sam, Sylvester, and Tweety Bird brought him worldwide renown. Today, a single cel of his work easily fetches $3,000. You can feast your eyes on — and buy if you wish — these classic gems of modern media art at the **Chuck Jones Studio Gallery** (2501 San Diego Avenue, Old Town, 619-294-9880).

SECRET
BURIAL GROUND

It's an idyllic setting for an afternoon picnic, provided you don't mind lunching above 1,800 people buried beneath the manicured lawns of **Pioneer Park** (Washington Place at Randolph Street, Mission Hills). The site was once a crowded little cemetery filled with tombstones memorializing San Diego's earliest citizens, many of whom were interred before 1925. As years went by, the graveyard became unkempt, and the city took over by removing most of the headstones and planting California pepper trees in their place. About three dozen stones were spared and placed in a loose arrangement along the eastern extremity of the park. It appears as though a groundskeeper swept them off to one side before cutting the grass, and they are waiting to be put back in their proper locations. One engraving reads: "Here rests a woodsman of the world." But his exact location of burial, like all the others listed at the dedication platform, remains a guessing game.

SECRET
CAESAR SALAD

The bygone tradition of Caesar salad, made tableside, is still upheld at **Molly's** (333 W Harbor Drive, Downtown, 619-230-8909), a plush, upscale restaurant one floor below the lobby of the San Diego

Marriott Hotel and Marina. The venerable Caesar originated a stone's throw away from San Diego in 1924, inside a small Tijuana restaurant owned by Italian chef Caesar Cardini. The antics he employed when concocting the dressing and tossing the greens were later adopted by dozens of restaurateurs locally. But concerns over salmonella poisoning in the late '70s put the kibosh on making the salads from scratch. Raw egg yolks, used to bind the dressing, induced more fear than appetites. Nary a salad cart could be found afterwards. Molly's upholds the custom with pasteurized eggs. The yolks are pummeled in a bowl with eight other ingredients, such as crushed garlic, anchovy filets, olive oil, and mustard. The under-your-nose presentation is dazzling. Cardini would be proud.

SECRET
CANDY STORES

Talk about strategic placement. If you're taking in a movie at the **Hillcrest Cinemas** (see "Secret Movie Screens") and prefer to skip the concession line, **The Candy Depot** (3955 5th Avenue, Hillcrest, 619-683-2334) offers a bigger variety of bulk confections at slightly lower prices. It's conveniently located one floor below the theaters in the **Village Hillcrest** complex. The secret is that customers can load their goodies into non-crinkling bags, which are expressly designed for smuggling past the ticket takers without making a sound. Call it unethical, deceitful, or savvy business sense. The proprietors make no apologies for their advantageous location. You can easily miss the store if you ascend to the theaters by elevator from the underground parking structure. You'll need to get off at ground level and walk toward 5th Avenue from the inner courtyard to find it.

Buttery caramels, chocolate turtles, and dense truffles are lovingly displayed in a 90-year-old apothecary unit at **Creations and Confections** (Bazaar Del Mundo, 2754 Calhoun Street, Old Town, 619-296-4080). The wood cabinetry was salvaged from a San Francisco pharmacy, along with the original drug labels printed on the drawer handles. Look closely and you'll see that one of them was designated for cannabis. The pharmacy's old cash register is also part of the scheme and still works perfectly for ringing up sales.

SECRET
CELEBRITY SCRAWLING

She started out a dishwasher and ended up a star. Whoopi Goldberg's testimony to scraping plates and rinsing silverware remains scribbled over an industrial sink at the funky **Big Kitchen** (3003 Grape Street, Golden Hill, 619-234-5789), where she worked for a short stint in the early '80s while breaking into local comedy clubs. Ask for a patio seat to enjoy your whole-wheat pancake breakfast and you'll pass through the kitchen on the way. There, you will see her writing on the wall: "Don't paint over this, goddamnit — Whoopi."

SECRET

CHAPELS

This is the story of two chapels — the bright, beautiful, lovely younger sister chapel, and the tucked-away-behind-the-main-house, almost forgotten, older sister chapel.

The former is a new addition that recently opened just inside the sliding glass front doors of **Scripps Mercy Hospital** (4077 5th Avenue, Hillcrest, 619-294-8111). The Bob Baker family donated the funds for construction. You enter this little marvel through a small anteroom with water tripping down a ridged light-stone wall. Next, you curve around and pause by a niche with a modern brass screen and carved-glass prayer bowl. Another sharp turn and you enter the main chapel, where you are greeted by a stunning, wall-length, stained-glass mural designed by Mario Uribe, flowing with blue and green organic lines reminiscent of Matisse. It fills the softly hued contemplation room with a soothing light. When I visit, I feel like I am looking up at the sun from just under the canopy of a cool, tropical rainforest. The modern design is open and airy, and welcoming to all denominations.

The forgotten older sister chapel is **Our Lady's Chapel**. Her story begins in 1890, when two Sisters of Mercy opened San Diego's first hospital at the corner of 6th and Market streets. The five-bed facility was known as St. Joseph's Dispensary. In 1924, the hospital moved to its present site on 5th Avenue in Hillcrest and was renamed Mercy Hospital. A convent was built on the site to house the sisters who ran the hospital, and the chapel was constructed for prayer and meditation. This is the original church. Weddings and funerals still take place here because those who know about it recognize its time-tested

beauty. But its location, to the north of and behind the jutting
entrance of the modern hospital, makes it an easily missed piece of
San Diego's history that is still alive and well.

The **Saint Francis Chapel** (1350 El Prado Way, Balboa Park, 619-
239-2001) is located inside the **Museum of Man** (also 619-239-2001),
a building that looks like the back of a stucco-walled stable. When
you cross the Cabrillo Bridge from 6th Avenue and enter Balboa
Park's central area, the stately Spanish Colonial façade of the California Tower overshadows the museum with its little-known chantry.
Bertram Grosvenor Goodhue designed the chapel for the Panama-
California Exposition that took place in the park in 1915. Its stark
Mission-era style — with bench seating, tiled floors, and heavy
beamed ceiling — is strikingly offset by an elaborately decorated
gold-leaf altar. Appropriately, one of the figures carved into the altar
is that of the saint San Diego de Alcalá. Another little-known fact is
that the non-denominational chapel is available for wedding ceremonies. Visitors to the museum pass the chapel's shuttered doors every
day without knowing what's inside. It is not open to the public, but
those in the know can see it by making an appointment a few days in
advance.

Overlooking the west end of Mission Valley and Mission Bay Park is
a cheerful, blue-tiled dome called the **Immaculata** (5998 Alcalá
Park, Linda Vista, 619-574-5700). The structure rises from a small
city of gleaming white buildings that is the University of San Diego.
This beautiful Roman Catholic church, run by the San Diego Diocese,
holds daily Masses and is open to the public. But lesser known is
Founders Chapel, located near the church inside Founders Hall.
While the Immaculata is bigger, Founders is architecturally richer,
with a jaw-dropping ornate altar completely covered in gold leaf. It
stretches from floor to ceiling. This chapel is where most Catholic

students opt to attend Mass. Some serve as liturgical ministers during the school year. Classical concerts are also held inside. Yet few people know about the annual Red Masses celebrated on the first Monday of October. No, they aren't satanic fraternity rituals, but rather a tradition in the Christian Church dating back to 14th-century France and England. Each Mass marks the opening of a new judicial year. Catholic lawyers and judges, as well as government officials, attend them. Lawyers belonging to the Thomas More Society sponsor the ceremonies in churches around the nation. Regular daily Masses at the chapel are held Monday through Friday (12:10 PM) and Sunday evenings (7 PM and 9 PM) when school is in session.

There are two churches to see in Old Town. One is the big, looming, melancholy **Immaculate Conception Church** (2540 San Diego Avenue, 619-295-4148) on the neighborhood's main tourist artery. Beautiful dark-wood beamed ceilings and whitewashed walls enclose this incredibly somber space, insulated in silence from the crazy, flashy tourist trade taking place outside. But what many people pass by is the tiny **Chapel of the Immaculate Conception** (3950 Conde Street) a few blocks away. It is the oldest church in San Diego after the **Mission San Diego de Alcalá** (see "Secret Missions"). The structure was originally the first home in San Diego with wooden floors. It was converted into a chapel in 1858 with the backing of a wealthy rancher named Don Jose Antonio Aguirre. Local lore claims that California's most famous lovers, Ramona and Alessandro, were married here. Given that they are fictional characters from an early 19th-century novel by Helen Hunt Jackson, a lot is left to the imagination. Nonetheless, it's a romantic notion to consider.

Rose Creek Cottage (2525 Garnet Avenue, Pacific Beach, 858-490-0468) is an 80-year-old English Tudor-style cottage that looks like it was lifted straight out of a Grimm Brothers fairy tale. Weddings, receptions, and parties have been held here since the early 1960s. Being placed catty-corner on its lot spares it from appearing in stiff contrast with its odd location on a major thoroughfare in a "totally" surfer-dude beach neighborhood. The **Pacific Beach Town Council** (1706 Garnet Avenue, Pacific Beach, 858-483-6666) owns and rents out the tiny cottage, which features an outdoor patio, a Victorian garden with gazebo, and the intimate quasi-chapel space used for special affairs.

SECRET
CHICKEN PIE

Concealed beneath golden brown, flaky piecrusts are big, tender chunks of chicken and turkey that keep longtime customers pouring into **The Chicken Pie Shop** (2633 El Cajon Boulevard, North Park, 619-295-0156). Established in 1938 by a Missouri businessman, the kitchen bakes up nearly 1,800 pies a day, each topped with country gravy to augment their homey flavor. The expansive dining room is anything but chic — a nesting ground for ceramic chickens that look down to an outdated lunch counter and cart-pushing waitresses. But a rainbow of patrons adds vivid color to an otherwise dull atmosphere. Nuns, seniors, gays, military types, and families of all ethnic backgrounds turn out. The pies are a steal. They come with fake mashed potatoes, vegetable, coleslaw, roll, and dessert for $4.75.

SECRET
CHILDREN'S STUFF

Lucky are the kids who visit or grow up in San Diego. The city was practically made for them, when you consider there are four well-known theme parks at their disposal. Two of them are in San Diego proper: **SeaWorld** (500 SeaWorld Drive, Mission Bay, 619-226-3901); and the **San Diego Zoo** (2920 Zoo Drive, off Park Boulevard, Balboa Park, 619-234-3153). And the others are only a short distance north: LEGOLAND **California** (1 Legoland Drive, Carlsbad, California, 760-918-5346); and the **Wild Animal Park** (15500 San Pasqual Valley Road, Escondido, California, 800-934-2267). But hidden in between are playful diversions that hold equal appeal for active souls at a little less cost.

I could have only dreamed of such a place when I was a kid — a 5,000-square-foot arena with a two-level, full-structure maze, completely black-lit, where friends chase friends with laser tag guns. A visit to **Ultrazone** (3146 Sports Arena Boulevard, Loma Portal, 619-221-0100) is like walking through the looking glass of the popular video game "Capture the Flag." Players are equipped with flashing-light vests that are color coded to distinguish their teams. With non-blinding laser guns in hand, they fire at the blinking lights on their opponents as the arena fills with music and theatrical fog. Computerized scorecards tally up the number of hits at the end of each game, which lasts about 30 minutes under the guidance of staff instructors. The secret is to wear dark clothing for better camouflage. It's a high-tech playground located behind **Chuck E. Cheese's** (3146 Sports Arena Boulevard, Loma Portal, 619-523-4385), a sprawling arcade loaded with jungle gyms, a pizza kitchen, and a theatrical stage that features live children's entertainment, including appearances by Chuck E. Cheese himself.

On the same day we set back the clocks for daylight-saving time, a few of the streets in Downtown's Gaslamp District come alive with children and their parents in celebration of the annual **Fall Back Festival** (Island Avenue, between 4th and 5th Streets, 619-233-4692). The event (11 AM to 4 PM) is designed to show kids what San Diego was like in the mid- and late 1800s, when cowboys, Indians, and gold miners jostled for land, and horse-drawn wagons began clogging the dirt streets soon after. History reveals that those classic shoot-'em-up images we know of the Old West did indeed extend all the way to San Diego. Thus, demonstrations in gold panning, soap making, and hat design are held amid live Western music and educational displays provided by the **San Diego Historical Society** (1649 El Prado Way, Balboa Park, 619-232-6203).

Also Downtown is a curious, one-block space called **Children's Park** (Front and Island streets) that doesn't have a stick of playground equipment or any picnic tables in it. But it's freckled with a grid of grassy moguls that kids can't resist. Across the street near the trolley station is the **San Diego Children's Museum** (200 w Island Avenue, 619-233-8792), which is in transition to becoming a much bigger children's facility. It currently operates "without walls," offering only special events and field outings. The city block on which it sits is being completely demolished to make way for a more modern edifice slated to open in early 2005. It will feature a café, museum towers, and underground parking.

Up the coast in the **Village Fair Shopping Center** is the **Children's Discovery Museum of North County** (300 Carlsbad Village Drive,

Suite 103, Carlsbad, California, 760-720-0737). The facility offers kids a medieval play area, a "marketplace" with real cash registers, bubble tubes, an indoor fishing boat, and more. Closed on Mondays.

From a remote acre of land several miles off I-5, south of San Diego, a terrific water park rises from the landscape. It's known as **Knott's Soak City USA** (2052 Entertainment Circle, Chula Vista, California, 619-661-7373). The park's overall theme bows to the long boards and surf woodies of the 1950s, featuring a wave pool tower, a three-story water sports playhouse, and 16 tall and mighty water slides. Three of them are 80-foot-high vertical shoots that send riders plummeting into pools at sensational, almost unnatural, speeds. There's also a 500,000-gallon pool for wave riding, and volleyball pits and picnic areas for drying off. The park is open daily between late April and late September.

I can never leave **Belmont Amusement Park** (3146 Mission Boulevard, Mission Beach, 858-488-0668) without putting my body through a round of whacking on the **Giant Dipper Roller Coaster**, built out of wood in 1925. Don't be fooled by its modest height. The ride packs an unexpected punch, with neck-breaking curves and stomach-churning drops. If your kids are even semi-leery about getting on, best to wait until they're older, because I've seen many disembark with jittery hands and tears in their eyes. At the base of the coaster are dozens of other rides and amusements for children of all ages. The **Liberty Carousel** is an antique reproduction with hand-painted scenes of early San Diego, and the **Thunder Boats** are always a favorite with younger kids.

SECRET

CHINESE LAUNDERER

Soon Lee Chinese Laundry (1305 c Street, East Village, 619-239-5384) is perhaps the last place left in San Diego where garments are still hand-washed in old barrels and pressed to a crisp finish in heavy metal contraptions that you'd expect to see in an exhibit of early Industrial Age machinery. The small shop, directly across the street from City College and next door to the city's last remaining clapboard houses, has been in operation since 1948. It lacks as much sunlight as it does modern technology — a clue to its industrious and insular past. The owner doesn't advertise or list the business in the telephone book. That in itself makes it a good secret.

SECRET

COFFEEHOUSES

San Diego isn't Seattle. The concept of coffeehouses doesn't seem to jibe with our sun-baked, outdoor lifestyle — at least on the surface. Nevertheless, **David's Coffee House** (3766 5th Avenue, Hillcrest, 619-296-4173) is the most comfortable example I've found of what this compound word should be — a *house* where you drink coffee. The welcoming yellow walls and their monthly rotating artwork give this spot the aura of a well-loved den in someone's upscale house. Comfortable couches and a baby grand piano add to the atmosphere. It began as a place where people fighting a personal struggle with

AIDS could enjoy casual conversation in a public setting without feeling they were being stared at because of the cruel disfigurements the disease often produces. The original owner named it after his partner, David, who unfortunately succumbed to the disease. As newer drugs have changed the course of AIDS, diminishing somewhat the physical debilities it effects, the coffeehouse has broadened its mission. David's now serves clients as diverse as the city itself, many of whom may not even be aware of its origins. Yet it still maintains non-profit status, with proceeds benefiting the HIV-positive community.

It seems there is a favorite place in town for people who have chatted on the Internet in order to meet face to face. Being an eavesdropper, I noticed this trend the few times I have stopped by **Dietrich Coffee** (1080 University Avenue, Hillcrest, 619-718-9522). My suspicions were further confirmed when two friends told me that, indeed, they met Internet dates there. Whether or not you're "hooking up" with someone for the first time, the warm, polished, light-wood interior and sizable outdoor patio make it a comfortable place to stop for a while. It sits in the heart of the **Uptown District**, a planned "neighborhood within a neighborhood" in Hillcrest that was considered a model of cutting-edge urban infill when it was built in the late '80s.

Little Italy has undergone a big renaissance in just the past two years. Massive construction projects have brought in bucks, and mom-and-pop restaurants have spruced up their acts as a result. The city came in and widened sidewalks along **India Street** to allow for outdoor tables overlooking pedestrian traffic, and the whole area has a grander feel of cultural celebration to it. **Caffè Italia** (1704 India Street, 619-234-6767) taps into that spirit with mock frescoed walls, rustic accents, classical music playing in the background, and a back patio. Along with your caffeine fix, you can nosh on salads, pastries, and gourmet sandwiches. The Sunday Belgian waffle bar is a big hit.

A newspaper and magazine rack full of foreign and domestic journals adds to an atmosphere that is distinctly European. People rave about the Vietnamese coffee and banana gelato.

When **Twiggs Coffeehouse** (4590 Park Boulevard, University Heights, 619-296-0616) opened in 1992, the owners obviously had tremendous foresight — or just plain luck. The location is now a very trendy area, but back then they frequently had to call police because of drug deals going down in broad daylight outside. This roomy corner establishment has a space with green walls called the Green Room, where poetry readings as well as occasional folk guitar performances take place. On Wednesday evenings, customers can take to the open microphone; the following night is the "new talent" showcase; and on Sunday afternoons at 3 PM, people mosey in to hear the Celtic Ensemble. It's an afternoon of music, stories, and myths, backed by traditional Celtic instruments.

The **Kensington Coffee Company** (4141 Adams Avenue, Kensington, 619-280-9114) is more than just a java joint. It is a jealously defended icon of the Kensington neighborhood. With its funky basement/bebop/hippie décor and outdoor seating, it feels like a counterrevolutionary café on campus at a small ultra-liberal college. When corporate giant Starbucks opened up across the street, the neighborhood went to war, trying with all its might to stop the intrusion. Naturally, Starbucks prevailed. But in tribute to grassroots chutzpah, the Kensington Coffee Company still thrives with loyal customers devoted to the unique atmosphere that big chains can only palely imitate.

SECRET
COMICS

The future is looking bright for comic book merchants, who say the industry is thriving because of an ever-growing crop of young independent authors and numerous series popularized by blockbuster movies.

San Diego has long had its finger on the pulse. Every mid-July, it plays host to **Comic-Con International** (619-491-2475), a four-day convention that attracts more than 63,000 exhibitors and spectators from around the world. The extravaganza is held at the **San Diego Convention Center** (111 w Harbor Drive, Marina District, 619-525-5000), where visitors are treated to more than 600 hours of programming that includes films, anime, gaming, and special events. Local cartoonists will attest just how much this event has blossomed. In the mid-1970s, it was held in a single meeting room of the old **El Cortez Hotel** (702 Ash Street, Downtown, 619-338-8338), which has since been converted to private apartments.

With several locations around town, the main headquarters for **Comics-N-Stuff** (3148 Midway Drive, Loma Portal, 619-222-8908) is set back from the street and visually obstructed by a doughnut shop. But it's a treasure chest of more than 7,000 comic books, many dating back to the industry's golden age, when titles such as *Fantastic Four*, *Spider-Man*, and *The Avengers* were hot off the presses. The store is divided into neat sections that feature Japanese-language comics, new works by young European writers, and a backroom adult area revealing covers of sex-starved characters such as Aphrodisia, and Liz & Beth.

A decent selection of independent authors fills the cramped shelves at **On Comic Ground** (1629 University Avenue, Hillcrest, 619-683-7879). The small store manages to pack in a very diverse selection that includes mainstream, alternative, and underground comics from the US and Europe. Almost anything that the *Comics Journal* has recently reviewed can likely be found here. The friendly staff can point you to some of the more offbeat items.

Compared to the local competition, **Galactic Comics** (4981 Newport Avenue, Ocean Beach, 619-226-6543) carries a more limited selection of comic books. But it's one of the few places where you'll find porcelain and metal-cast statues of well-known characters that include The Girls of R. Crumb, Marvel Blade, and the Black Widow. Or how about fitting a set of Death & Purgatory bookends into your luggage?

Since the mid-1970s, the proprietors of **Southern California Comics** (8280 Clairemont Mesa Boulevard, #124, Kearny Mesa, 858-715-8669) have been buying and selling comic books, mostly from the silver and golden ages. Having amassed a huge collection, they recently moved their store into a warehouse that also offers comic book supplies, trade paperbacks, and magazines such as the *Castle of Frankenstein*, *Cinefantastique*, and the *House That Hammer Built*.

SECRET
CONCERT VENUE

Interesting thing about the electronic information age — it seems to have made bank buildings obsolete. In the last 20 years, we've watched these old bastions of stability get turned into everything from offbeat clothing stores and restaurants to hotels and dentists' offices. One such renovation that sees a lot of foot traffic is **4th and B** (345 B Street, 619-231-4343, www.4thandb.com), a vast performance space in Downtown San Diego. I'm hoping they didn't stay up all night thinking of the name for this place, but that aside, it has been a hugely successful transformation. The venue includes eight bars, one located in the old bank vault, named plainly "The Vault." Are you sensing a theme here? Perhaps when you mix booze and high-voltage music, it's best not to expect too much originality with names. The main floor can seat 850 bodies, with 242 more in the balcony, and another 309 in the mezzanine. Despite its huge size and self-locating name, it is extremely easy to drive right past and never notice the place. The outside is a windowless, utilitarian, block-long blank wall. And the sign is small and unobtrusive. But the acts that get booked here make it worth finding. The stage has welcomed the likes of B.B. King, X, Emmylou Harris, Erasure, Patti Smith, and popular club divas. It is also used for private events and converts into an amazing dance floor. Certain comedy events are sometimes free, but the offers are only listed on the club's Web site, and you have to mention that you saw them there in order to get the free tickets.

SECRET COTTAGES

Every Sunday from March through October, the **House of Pacific Relations International Cottages** (Balboa Park, 619-234-0739) hosts a party on the lawn. It's a cluster of nearly 30 small houses, representing nations such as Italy, Japan, and Iran. Each takes its turn hosting an afternoon program on the common lawn, featuring music and dance from its culture. The other cottages keep their doors open to the public on Sundays (noon to 5 PM), with historical and cultural displays depicting their nations. In the House of Ireland, you might find Irish soda bread and a fiddler, while the smell of Kielbasa sausage wafts from the nearby House of Poland amid accordion music. Admission is free, but donations are accepted. Once a year (usually in early July), all the nations join forces for an ethnic food feast not to be missed.

S E C R E T
COUNTRY-WESTERN

Just a few miles separate two worlds that have a great deal in common and a whole heck of a lot not.

On one end of the country-western spectrum lies **In Cahoots** (5373 Mission Center Road, Mission Valley, 619-291-8635). Located in the middle of Mission Valley, this sprawling nightclub is always bustling with Midwestern servicemen wearing cowboy hats and boots and getting a touch of home. It is a meat market for the hayseed set. The bar offers free country dance lessons every day (6:30 PM) except Sundays and Wednesdays. Three full-service bars ensure that everybody feels confident enough to hit the dance floor. Something called "cowboy hip-hop two-step" is occasionally featured, and although I don't know what it is, I'm willing to bet that you won't find it in Tulsa. On the first Saturday of the month is the "birthday bash." If it happens

to be the month in which your birthday falls, you pay no cover and get a goodie bag.

In the heart of Hillcrest, just up the hill from Mission Valley, is a very different land where cowboys and cowgirls can comfortably slow dance in same-sex arrangement. **Kickers** (308 University Avenue, Hillcrest, 619-491-0400) is a popular LGBT nightspot for line-dancing and two-stepping (Thursdays). Dance lessons are held on weeknights (7 PM to 8:30 PM). On Wednesdays (8:30 PM to 2 AM), the bar hosts a "karaoke café" that has become wildly popular. Regulars get dressed up in all kinds of costumes to belt out their favorite tunes on microphones, accompanied by the ubiquitous karaoke prompter.

SECRET
CUBAN

The last place you'd expect to find a Cuban restaurant — or any restaurant, for that matter — is along an eight-block stretch of Morena Boulevard that is one of San Diego's home furnishing districts (see "Secret Home Furnishings"). Set among a continuous string of kitchen and tile stores, **Andres' Patio Restaurant** (1235 Morena Boulevard, Bay Park, 619-275-4114) affirms that Cuban food *isn't* the same as Mexican or South American fare; nor is it spicy hot. The traditional pan con lechon shows off the kitchen's ability for pulling pork and making it into memorable sandwiches served on hoagie rolls. Another favorite is yuca con mojo — yuca root cooked in garlic oil and served with a side of savory black beans.

SECRET
CURFEWS

As sunbathers clear the sands on late afternoons, the vastness of city beaches comes into focus, with an intoxicating appeal for people who like sunset picnics and evening bonfires. But don't let the quiet solitude fool you into thinking that certain municipal restrictions have gone to bed with the sun. They're just beginning to rise. Cement fire rings at **La Jolla Shores**, **South Mission Beach**, **Ocean Beach**, and certain locations throughout **Mission Bay** are open from 6 AM to 2 AM. The fire curfew at **Fiesta Island** in Mission Bay Park goes into effect at 10 PM. Flames at any of the beaches cannot exceed 12 feet above the upper edge of the rings. And only "clean" wood is allowed, meaning no nails or paints in the mix. Alcohol is permitted until 8 PM on most oceanfront and bay beaches, although it's prohibited altogether at **La Jolla Shores**, **Marine Street Beach**, **Santa Clara Point**, and the beaches of **Coronado Island**. Violators who get caught will be slapped with fines of $55 or more.

SECRET
CURRENCY

Despite San Diego's steady influx of foreign visitors, there are only a few outlets in town to exchange money — and most of them are hard to find. The major banks cater only to customers with savings or checking accounts. Worse yet, they can take a couple of days to process the request. **Thomas Cook Currency Service Inc.** (800-287-7362) has four money exchange outlets stocked with global notes and coins. Two are at the airport. The bigger office is located on the upper level of Terminal 2, behind security and adjacent to the Admiral's Club. A smaller counter can be found in Terminal 1, on the lower level across from the United Airlines check-in counter. The downtown branch requires some navigation inside the abstract layout of **Horton Plaza** (177 Horton Plaza, 619-238-1596). It's on the first level, toward the structure's front entrance. Another outlet can be found at the **University Towne Center Mall** (4417 La Jolla Village Drive, Suite N17, University City, 858-453-2930), next to Nordstrom. The agency charges $6.50 on exchanges of $250 or less, and a 1.5-percent fee on transactions over that.

SECRET
CYCLING

I always expect the bike paths on Coronado Island to be crammed with other cyclists every time I go there. But even on weekends, the scenic, three-mile route beginning at **Bikes & Beyond** (1202 1st Street, #1, Coronado, California, 619-435-7180) is never congested. The path leads bicycle renters through Tidelands Park and under the lofty Coronado Bay Bridge. It eventually joins up with Glorietta Boulevard, flanked on one side by the island's majestically manicured golf course, and expensive, storybook homes on the other. Pedal further, and you end up at the western shoreline, where you'll find the historic **Hotel Del Coronado** (1500 Orange Avenue, Coronado, California,

619-435-6611), and the crème de la crème of homes along Ocean Boulevard to the north. Or turn south onto Strand Way for a brisk seven-mile cruise down the island's shadeless isthmus known as the **Silver Strand**. A wide bike path runs the length of the land, allowing you to increase your clip with little interruption. But keep in mind that the return trip can take twice as long because of headwinds.

If you are staying near Balboa Park and don't mind biking on city streets to get there, the **San Diego Velodrome** (2221 Morley Field Drive, North Park, 619-692-4919) is worth a visit. This banked outdoor track is used periodically for regulation bike competitions sponsored by the **San Diego Velodrome Association** (www.sdva.org). Few people know that it is usually open to the public when no professional racing events are taking place. On the opposite west end of the park, a hidden dirt trail hugs the canyon along Highway 163, offering bikers a hilly, tree-lined ride that runs about 1.4 miles. Notice the cluster of tall redwood trees shortly before the path ends at Laurel Street and Balboa Drive. To start the trek, go north on 6th Avenue, turn right at Upas Street, and then follow the sidewalk to the canyon's edge.

Bike riding along the Mission Beach boardwalk on weekend afternoons is a wild and crazy experience if you are not accustomed to weaving through thick waves of pedestrians, skateboarders, and inline skaters. Yet it's one of the best places for observing San Diego's bronze-bodied beach culture. The **Mission Beach Club** (704 Ventura Place, Mission Beach, 858-488-5050) rents all sorts of bikes and boards to keep you in the loop. If you're willing to lower your standards with a slightly worn-down bicycle or medium-quality surfboard, you can save a few dollars down the street at **Cheap Rentals** (3221 Mission Boulevard, Mission Beach, 858-488-5533).

Uptown, downtown, and all around the bay, San Diegans start riding their bicycles in nightgowns for just one night when the clock strikes midnight (early August). **Midnight Madness** (619-645-8068) is an annual fundraiser that began in 1973 to help finance the youth programs supported by Hostelling International-AYH and the Uptown Optimist Club of San Diego. What started as a fun idea attended by 300 has grown into a tradition that now attracts more than 2,300 riders. The 20-mile scenic bike tour begins Downtown at midnight. Cyclists dress not only in pajamas, but also lingerie and costumes ranging from King Tut to Carmen Miranda. Participants gather at the **County Administration Building** (1600 Pacific Highway, Harbor District) to embark on a route that travels past Harbor Island, Shelter Island, and Old Town. Bagels and refreshments are served at the end of the ride.

SECRET
DEEPAK

He's got thick black hair, along with *The Seven Spiritual Laws of Success* that he'll readily sell you — not to mention a business headquartered in one of the most upscale seaside spa resorts in the world. Deepak Chopra appears to be doing something right, as he is known worldwide for his books on transcendent spiritual practices and nationwide for an occasional pledge drive on PBS. The center that bears his name is a magnet for those with bucks seeking training in yoga, massage, astrological counseling services, and Ayurvedic health treatments. What many are not aware of are the free events held there, including daily meditations and frequent discussion groups. For some of them, you won't even have to sit in the lotus position. The **Chopra Center** (2100 Costa Del Mar Road, Carlsbad, California, 760-931-7566) is located in the exclusive **La Costa Resort and Spa** (760-438-9111), about 35 minutes up the coast from downtown San Diego. For those seeking alternative healing resources, Chopra's center boasts the services of Dr. David Simon, whose approach to holistic medicine brings in modern Western and ancient Vedic traditions from India. Among the more unusual and personally amusing offerings is "wellness golfing." Feel the ball, get in touch with the ball's inner child, become one with the ball, and then hit the crap out of the ball.

SECRET
DIVAS
❖

Few would guess that so much glitter and glamour explodes behind the plain, lifeless exterior of **Lips** (2770 5th Avenue, Hillcrest, 619-295-7900). How these jaunty drag queens can haul oversized plates of food through the dining room one minute, then launch into syncopated musical stage acts the next is beyond me. Not a hair or eyelash drops out of place. Lips is part dinner theater, part cabaret — a Xanadu brimming with crystal chandeliers, colored lights, and luminous décor. Since opening in 1999, it has continued to attract mainly camera-happy heterosexuals who seem to revel in the company of these anatomically mysterious *demoiselles*. When a convincing Cher announces from the small runway stage that her "girls" are taking a five-minute break to change their "lips, hips, and tits," the well-rounded supper menu becomes a mere footnote to the evening. A $15-per-person minimum is required in the dining room. Lips is open for dinner Tuesday through Sunday (6 PM to 11 PM). The atmosphere shifts to gospel drag for Sunday brunch (11 AM to 2 PM).

SECRET
DOG BEACHES

There are two beaches in San Diego where you and your dog can abandon the leash and sprint across the sands together. **Dog Beach** (west end of Ocean Beach Flood Control Channel, Ocean Beach) is the most popular. It's located a few blocks north of **Ocean Beach Park** (west end of Newport Avenue, Ocean Beach), where surfers and the homeless peacefully co-exist. Dogs are also allowed anywhere outside of the fenced areas at **Fiesta Island** (Fiesta Island Road, off E Mission Bay Drive, Mission Bay), which is a popular playground for cyclists and joggers as well.

SECRET
EAST AFRICAN

The cuisine of East Africa was always a mystery to me until I visited **Aswan African Restaurant** (7404 University Avenue, La Mesa, California, 619-464-7100). Intent on sampling the works, I opted for the dazzling weekend buffet, served on Saturdays and Sundays (9 AM to 3 PM) from a long line of silver chafing dishes that sit undisturbed until the noon crowd arrives. The spread includes genuine East African dishes such as savory fava beans (fuul-iya ceech), wilted mustard greens (goman), and delicious pastry pillows filled with curried potatoes or chicken (sambussa). Conventional brunch fare such as roast turkey and omelettes seems unexpected but keeps less adventurous eaters happy. Dinner gives way to more exotic specialties, such as the top-selling fadarayshan, a medley of lamb, beef, rice, and sautéed vegetables covered with flatbread. What you won't find here are filets, chops, or steaks. Time-honored recipes call for breaking meat apart and flavoring it with spicy curries. The restaurant is bright and attractive, adorned with fresh flowers and crafty wood giraffes. Don't pass up the Somali iced tea, made with a heavenly blend of cinnamon, ginger, and fresh lemon juice.

Smaller but equally hospitable is **Haar Ethiopian Restaurant** (2432 El Cajon Boulevard, North Park, 619-295-3735), which uses spicy red peppers in many of its dishes and brews a memorable Ethiopian coffee for groups of three or more. An oil service station next door mars its exterior charisma, but you'll feel far removed from it upon entering the rattan-filled dining room or charming wood-plank patio.

S E C R E T
EDIBLE STOGIE

Forget those chocolate cigars that get passed around when someone's first baby is born. The ones at **Terra** (1270 Cleveland Avenue, Hillcrest, 619-293-7088) are a work of art. If you can pass the finish line to dessert at this upscale American bistro, ask for the "chocolate cigar" and have your camera ready. What you'll get is triple-chocolate ganache molded into the shape of a fat cigar and wrapped in flaky phyllo pastry. It's presented in a heavy glass ashtray lined with whipped cream. And the tip is dusted in cocoa powder to create the illusion of burned-down tobacco. I've never seen anything like it.

SECRET

EXPENSIVE SOUP

You'll need a thick wallet and an adventurous appetite for the prized bill of fare at **Emerald Chinese Seafood** (3709 Convoy Street, 1st floor, Kearny Mesa, 858-565-6888). Among the many Cantonese delicacies listed on its tome-like menu is shark fin soup, made with chicken stock and presented with a whole fin floating in the middle. The cost for this broth: $450. But it's enough for eight people, so you can divide the expense to lessen the blow. The restaurant occupies the first floor of a spacious office building and caters respectfully to patrons who favor authentic Hong Kong cuisine over Americanized standards such as kung pao shrimp and Mandarin rice. Dim sum carts, fish tanks, and multigenerational Chinese families supping together prove that you'll be getting down to some authentic Asian eating.

A plethora of other traditional Asian restaurants and small noodle houses are clustered in strip plazas along **Convoy Street**, between Clairemont Mesa Boulevard and Balboa Avenue. The area doesn't fit the picture of touristy Chinatowns found elsewhere, but Chinese pictograms on most signs confirm that you've come to the right place. Don't drive away without surveying the fresh sushi bar and lunch buffet inside **Nijiya Market** (3860 Convoy Street, Kearny Mesa, 858-268-3821). The busy store offers prepared box lunches, or bento, for bargain prices, as well as very affordable soups and hard-to-find kickshaw desserts such as bread rolls filled with sweet bean paste.

SECRET
FARMERS' MARKETS

They can be found on any given day throughout San Diego County. And some are held conveniently in the late afternoon — a kind gesture to those who don't relish the thought of fondling produce at the crack of dawn. Fertile farmlands throughout Southern California and parts of Mexico supply a never-ending bounty of fruits and vegetables to about 20 different outdoor markets each week. Ambiance and offerings vary, depending on what geographic location you choose. For a complete schedule of farmers' markets in the area, call the **San Diego County Farm Bureau** (760-745-3023).

My three favorites include one in the seafront community of **Ocean Beach** (4900 block of Newport Avenue, 760-439-1612), held late in the day on Wednesdays (4 PM to 8 PM) in the middle of a street lined with antiques shops and tall palm trees. Vendors tote in everything from stuffed crêpes and affordable exotic flowers to organic vegetables and some very good, fresh Gouda cheese. There are also llama rides for the kids and live rock bands for their older siblings. The **Hillcrest** farmers' market (Department of Motor Vehicles parking lot, Normal and Cleveland streets, 619-237-1632) is where the urban set congregates on Sunday mornings (9 AM to 1 PM) over punchy salsas, scented soaps, Moroccan knickknacks, and the usual profusion of fresh produce. The best-kept secret here is found at the market's northeast corner. The fresh bread and cookie vendor slashes his prices by 50 percent during the last hour of operation. A smaller market, but one with a prettier setting, is held on Tuesdays (2:30 PM to 6 PM) in **Coronado** (Old Ferry Landing, 1st and B streets, Coronado, California, 760-741-3763). Shoppers are less folksy in comparison, but the downtown skyline glistening over the bay adds warmth and character. The experience is particularly memorable if you take the **Coronado Ferry** (San Diego Broadway Pier, 619-234-4111), which departs every hour between 9 AM and 9 PM.

SECRET
FAUX PAS

Not everyone arrives in San Diego with a command of the Spanish language. Nor does anyone need to speak it fluently. But you can spare yourself the tourist raillery by pronouncing the Big Three correctly. The affluent seaside community just north of here is **La Jolla** (La Hoya), not "La Jah-la." If for any reason you find yourself in the not-so-chic East County city of **El Cajon** (El Ka-hone), the locals will laugh you out of town if you say "El Kay-jun." And if you're headed south of the border to haggle for cheap leather goods and Mexican wool blankets, you're going to **Tijuana** (Tee-wanna), not "Tee-uh-wanna."

SECRET
FENG SHUI

Feng shui, an ancient Asian discipline, is the latest craze to sweep the West Coast during the past decade. It basically involves planning and arranging objects and colors in the environment in order to make good things happen in our lives. Whether you're looking to sweeten the marriage bed or ward off frenzied bosses, the **Feng Shui Warehouse** (1130 Scott Street, Point Loma, 619-523-2158) is known as the source to go to in San Diego. In fact, it bills itself as the world's oldest and largest supplier of *feng shui* books and products. Tucked away on a side street a few blocks from the marina area of Shelter Island, it looks more like the paymaster's office for a fishing crew than a New Age emporium. But inside, crystals, red wooden flutes, and bronze bells attached to red silk cords tell the real story. Here you'll find everything from over-the-counter quick fixes to trained experts who will consult with you to *feng shui* your entire home.

SECRET
FETISH WEAR

Try to imagine shoppers clad in sandals and т-shirts by day sporting metal-boned corsets or leather chaps by night. For over 15 years, the **Crypt on Park** (3847 Park Boulevard, Hillcrest, 619-692-9499) has quietly supplied the leather/fetish community in San Diego with a pipeline of clothing and accessories that befit those passive-aggressive fantasies we all supposedly harbor. From whips and nipple clamps to shoes, leather pants, and Goth wear, you'll find designer fetish labels such as Shrine, Tripp, and Lip Service. Or browse deeper into the inventory for raiment made by the merchant, and you've got yourself a genuine San Diego souvenir that conforms to your body better than it sticks to your refrigerator.

The proprietors of **Ringold Alley** (3408 30th Street, North Park, 619-295-7464) are the newest masters on the block with their formidable line of dildos and s&m goods from around the world. Bumble around this 800-square-foot, product-packed shop and you'll find latex from Berlin, floggers from Australia, and lascivious leather wear created by British and Canadian craftsmen.

Shopping for leather restraints on open retail floors could be risky business for discreet consumers. It would be just your luck if you stumbled upon an acquaintance from home while rifling through harnesses and blindfolds. EAT **Leather** (619-284-4713, www.eatleather. com) caters to musicians, professionals, and those who prefer something a little more customized without having to rub elbows with anyone. Sex toys, gags, chains, riding belts, and leather uniforms are ordered by phone or online. Goods are deliverable by mail or can be picked up from the purveyor's garage. Privacy is assured.

SECRET
FILIPINO

San Diego's rich cultural mosaic includes a thriving Filipino community that has established itself throughout most sections of the county, particularly within the incorporated cities of National City and Chula Vista, and the community of Mira Mesa. Yet finding a good Filipino supermarket or cultural fair can be difficult if you remain rooted on the beaten tourist track.

I love lumpia, the Filipino equivalent of egg rolls. And I've come to love them 100 times more after eating them stuffed with fresh shrimp and cream cheese. My Filipino friends insist that this wonderful variation can be found only at **Conching's Café and Ice Cream Parlor** (3400 E 8th Street, National City, California, 619-470-6598). The food here is fast and inexpensive, with all-you-can-eat deals for under $5.

Seafood City Supermarket (8955 Mira Mesa Boulevard, Mira Mesa, 858-549-0200; and 1420 E Plaza Boulevard, National City, California, 619-477-6080) carries assorted top-brand lumpia in its freezer section from manufacturers around the country. But the hot, precooked lumpia served from the store's pinoy barbecue are superior because they're made on the premises daily. Fillings include chicken, pork, mixed seafood, and beef. The steam tables further entice customers with their array of other traditional dishes, including pinakbet (mixed vegetables in sauce), dinuguan (meat cooked in pork blood), and exceptional boneless milkfish. Shoppers at the National City store are greeted near the entrance by a bronze bust of Jose Rizal, the novelist who became a national hero of the Philippines in the 1800s after writing against the Spanish oppression. His prose helped spark the country's revolution, but he was fatally shot in the process.

The annual **Filipino Family Day** takes place every mid-July among the towering water slides of **Knott's Soak City USA** (2052 Entertainment Circle, Chula Vista, California, 619-661-7373). The celebration, presented by the *Filipino Press* (525 D Avenue, National City,

California, 619-477-0940), is spread out over an open lawn to the right of the main entrance. A tented parquet floor is the scene of lively performances by the **Samahan Dance Company** (619-422-3695), giving way to games and contests in between. The dance company makes a popular encore several weeks later when it presents the annual **Philippine Cultural Arts Festival** (President's Way, Balboa Park), held on the first weekend in August. Attendance is usually higher at this event, due to the central location and tasty food offerings.

SECRET
FLYING SAUCERS

In one location, it appears as though a spaceship has landed in the trees. At another, a millennialist spiritual group earnestly awaits such an event. San Diego isn't in the same league as Roswell, New Mexico, when it comes to UFO mania, but it does offer a bit of extraterrestrial fodder for the imagination.

Behold the life-size steel flying saucer hidden behind the **San Diego Design Center** (3625 5th Avenue, Hillcrest, 619-557-8484). Finnish architect and futurist Matti Suuronen erected the structure in 1965 with hopes of mass producing it as a form of alternative housing. He called it *The Futuro*, but only 20 were made. With its oval windows and dull-green paint job, it blends inconspicuously into the treetops from a sturdy 15-foot-high pedestal. The entry hatch has remained bolted for the past several years. The structure looks like an aging mothership that has veered off-course from its inventive mission. You'll have to walk down the canyon stairway from the front of the building to see it.

In the city of Jamul, about 25 miles east of San Diego, a landing site has been determined for spaceships from 32 different worlds believed to exist by members of the **Unarius Academy of Science** (145 s Magnolia Avenue, El Cajon, California, 800-475-7062). The organization, founded in 1954 by Ruth and Ernest Norman, professes that future contact with otherworldly beings is inevitable and will spark a new spiritual renaissance on planet Earth. Its main headquarters, adorned with a flamboyant space mural, offers books, pamphlets, and lectures on the subject. In October, members hold their annual three-day Conclave Event, which includes a banner procession in a nearby park and the release of doves as a symbol of peace and awakening.

S E C R E T
FOOTBRIDGES

It's one of my favorite places to bring out-of-town guests for a wobbly stroll, provided they don't suffer a fear of heights. The **Spruce Street Suspension Bridge** (Front or Brant streets at Spruce Street, Bankers Hill) was erected in 1912 and stretches over a deep, lush canyon that seemingly divides this quiet, residential street into two different neighborhoods. But whatever side you end up on, it's still Bankers Hill, a hidden enclave of expensive two-story homes, built mostly between 1900 and 1940. The walkway is long and narrow, and tilts from side to side when more than four people cross it — an unexpected thrill considering how thick and taut these cables remain. Mature palm and eucalyptus trees, scattered cacti, and wild shrubs blanket the forbidden grounds below.

A sturdier footbridge, made of wood in 1905, spans an equally steep canyon about a half-mile south of the suspension bridge. It connects Quince Street to 3rd and 4th avenues in Bankers Hill. A walk across the **Quince Street Bridge** offers a peek at San Diego Bay and a surprising look at how some earthquake-ignorant San Diegans live — in houses and condominiums poised on the edge of these precipitous banks. Look straight down through an occasional rotted knothole in the wooden planks, and your knees start touching the ground.

You'll have a lot to ponder when traipsing across the steel **Vermont Street Pedestrian Bridge**, which extends over busy Washington Street to connect the neighborhoods of University Heights and Hillcrest. Built in 1994, the blue-painted bridge is lined with metal panels containing stamped-out quotes from the likes of Eleanor Roosevelt, Lao Tsu, Martin Luther King Jr., and Theodor Geisel (a.k.a. Dr. Seuss), who lived in nearby La Jolla. But the worn-down words embedded in the cement along the sides of the walkway are much quirkier: a listing straight from the dictionary of all the definitions of the word "bridge."

SECRET
FREE ADMISSIONS

This isn't just a free meal — it's free dinner theater! A gleaming marble-floored temple filled with the exotic perfumes of incense and curry in the evening's supper simmering in a kitchen behind the altar to Krishna sets the backdrop for the experience. The players are the congregants all around you, dressed mostly in flowing *punjabis* or traditional colorful saris. There is a sermon delivered straight from the ancient *Bhagavad-Gita* (the *Song of God*), with tales of war and plunder, courage and cowardice, pleasure and pain — all with spiritual metaphoric significance. The head of the temple, dressed in robes of saffron hue, the color of celibacy, leads the group in some chanting. And then you eat! The tradition of feeding worshipers and respectful visitors is a long and honored one in Hindu temples, stretching beyond recorded time. The **International Society for Krishna Consciousness Temple** (1030 Grand Avenue, Pacific Beach, 858-483-2500), which has stood on the same spot for 25 years, upholds the little-known custom by serving up free vegetarian fare at an open house almost every Sunday, beginning at 6 PM.

If you can survive watching movies sans the popcorn and red licorice, the **San Diego Public Library** (820 E Street, Downtown, 619-236-5820) shows old Hollywood classics, foreign films, and historical documentaries for free on Mondays (6:30 PM) in its third-floor auditorium. The 100-seat venue also features free classical and pop music concerts two Sundays a month. Eat before you come, because food is forbidden.

Visitors can save a chunk of change by taking advantage of "free Tuesdays" at several Balboa Park museums located along El Prado Way. Between two and five museums offer free admission in any given week, depending on the rotation schedule. They include the **San Diego Natural History Museum**, the **Museum of Photographic Arts**, the **Model Railroad Museum**, and the **Reuben H. Fleet Science Center**. Charges will apply to special exhibitions. Call or visit the Balboa Park administrative office Web site (619-239-0512, www.balboapark.org) to find out which museums are free.

The grandeur of Balboa Park's ornate **Spreckels Organ Pavilion** (1549 El Prado Way, Balboa Park, 619-702-8138) comes alive on

Sundays (2 PM), when guest organists evince their musical wizardry on a 4,518-pipe melodeon. The historic instrument, donated in 1914 by philanthropist John D. Spreckels, was a focal point of San Diego's Panama-California Exposition several months later.

Admission is always free at the **Timken Museum of Art** (1500 El Prado Way, Balboa Park, 619-239-5548), which houses old European works of art and classic American paintings. Among its many treasures is the famous 1634 oil, *Portrait of a Man,* by Dutch artist Frans Hals. There is also an impressive array of Russian icons kept tidy in the Putnam Foundation Collection. Closed Mondays and the month of September.

Salsa, classical, and pop music concerts enhance the Saturday shopping experience at **Seaport Village** (foot of Kettner Street, Marina District, 619-235-4014), a Disney-like plaza on the banks of San Diego Bay that caters to tourists with too many craft shops to mention. Follow your ears to the East Plaza Gazebo.

It's a free ticket to Oceania. Coconut husking, Samoan-style woodcarving, and grass hut displays are part of the ever-growing annual **Pacific Islander Festival** (Ski Beach at Mission Bay Park, Ingraham Street, at West Vacation Road, 619-699-8797). The late-September event recently moved to cooler and more spacious grounds from Downtown's Embarcadero to accommodate more food booths and colorful re-creations of villages that reflect the people of Melanesia, Micronesia, and Polynesia.

Celebrate your wins and forget your losses at free concerts held after the last race each Friday at the **Del Mar Thoroughbred Club** (2260 Jimmy Durante Boulevard, Del Mar, California, 858-755-1141). Pop and rock bands are presented weekly by a local radio station at the venue's outdoor Plaza de Mexico courtyard. The race season runs for seven weeks, between late July and early September.

SECRET

FREE RIDE

Sobriety checkpoints abound in San Diego. Yet most of the city's bar crawlers still aren't aware of the **Designated Drivers Association** program (866-373-7233). On Fridays and Saturdays (10 PM to 2 AM), more than two dozen volunteers are available to fetch the inebriated and drive them back to their homes or hotels. What's unique is that your own vehicle, rented or owned, becomes the taxi. Two volunteers arrive. One drives your car while the other follows. Gratuities are accepted to help pay for gas. Local bars and corporations fund the expanding program, which began in 2001. The service applies to all locations in bar-happy Pacific Beach, club-crazy Downtown, and the quieter North County coastal cities of Encinitas, Cardiff, Solana Beach, Del Mar, Leucadia, and Oceanside.

SECRET

FRENCH

If it weren't for the petite Eiffel Tower gracing the sign out front, I think **Liaison** (2202 4th Avenue, Bankers Hill, 619-234-5540) would remain forever undiscovered. Most San Diegans would notice it only if they were driving down this remote part of 4th Avenue as an alternate route between Downtown and Hillcrest. There are never any lines to get inside, even though people who know about it arrive with a reservation. I've yet to find a European atmosphere this authentic in San Diego. Lighting is kept low. Table linens are starched to a crisp.

And copper pots on stone walls confirm that country French sauces are on a slow boil in the kitchen. Steak and seafood dishes are of high quality, and dessert crêpes are made tableside. A word of advice regarding attire: dress lightly, because it is always unusually warm inside.

SECRET
FUNGI

It doesn't matter that San Diego's dry climate is disastrous for mushroom growth. Members and guests of the **San Diego Mycological Society** (858-566-3958) will vigilantly ferret out species that magically spring up after a rare rain. Some they eat. Others they scrutinize with hopes of adding new ones to the list of 200 fungi already documented in the region, including dead man's foot fungi, candy caps, stalked puffballs, and destroying angels, the deadliest of them all. The mushroom forays are conducted each year in the city's outskirts from October to May, depending on precipitation. An annual mushroom festival is held on the third weekend in February at the **Casa Del Prado** (Balboa Park).

SECRET
GAMES AND PUZZLES

It's literally the land of a thousand games, where visitors can connect to their inner child and rub elbows with locals while competing in chess, cards, or fantasy and historical diversions such as Dungeons & Dragons and King Arthur. The back room at **Game Empire** (7051 Clairemont Mesa Boulevard, Clairemont Mesa, 858-576-1525) offers free playing grounds on several commodious game tables. Initiate your own tournaments or jump into those led by the proprietor. The retail section brims with favorites such as Axis and Allies, Stratego, Taboo, and Feudal, plus brain-boggling 3-D puzzles that contain up to 8,000 pieces.

SECRET
GARDENS

San Diego has a semi-arid climate (see "Secret Weather"), which loosely translated means, "a little more rain than Death Valley, but don't open an umbrella store." The result: scrubby gray-brown plants no taller than your navel. It's perhaps not what early pioneers would have pictured as a gardener's dreamland. But when the population started to swell in Southern California in the 1900s, engineers and deep-moneyed pockets brought in a steady supply of water from the Colorado River and northern California. Lush landscaping soon found its way into lawns and parks around the city. And the region's potential as an ideal location for some of the most diverse botanical specimens from around the world became a reality.

Take an hour to walk around **Balboa Park** and you can admire myriad forms of cacti, wander through a maze of roses, gaze upon lily pads in a calm reflecting pool, contemplate Japanese maples in quiet Zen meditation, and rest under regal shade provided by redwood trees. The mastermind behind the transformation of what was

originally a bunch of undeveloped dry, brown mesas was **Kate Sessions**, known locally as the Mother of Balboa Park. A gardener's gardener, she gathered plants from around the world, and in 1892 struck a bargain with the city to plant 100 trees a year in the 1,400-acre park in exchange for 30 acres of land. A bronze statue of this savvy planter resides in the western end of the park, near Laurel and 6th streets.

The **Japanese Friendship Garden** in Balboa Park celebrates the sister-city status that San Diego shares with Yokohama, Japan. Inside the gate are gifts of life from that city, including Japanese black pine, azaleas, sunburst locust, and bamboo. The plants are sparsely distributed, following the Zen practice of minimalism. You won't find tons of blossoms, but you will experience serenity — especially when viewing the requisite Zen garden of raked pebbles surrounding larger boulders. The teahouse in the center of the garden features a meditation room and has a soul-soothing feel to it.

If you thirst for a touch of the American Southwest, the nearby **Cactus Garden** along Park Boulevard (next to the rose garden) offers an up-close look at one of the oldest gardens in the park, charted by Kate Sessions herself. The variety of plant life that survives desert conditions will surprise anyone whose idea of cacti is limited to the archetypal two-armed Sonoran Desert saguaros. Late winter and early spring rains trigger strange and colorful blossoms that seem oddly out of place in a desert.

On the opposite side of Balboa Park, tucked behind a shadowy arched walkway near the highly visible spire of the California Tower, lies the **Alcazar Garden**. Colorful blue and yellow Spanish tiles line the low fountains that are centrally grouped in this formal, geometrically balanced space. Large rectangular and low-walled flowerbeds are planted seasonally with profuse arrangements of annuals. The blue and yellow tiled roof of the California Tower rises behind the garden wall, offering irresistible photo opportunities. A walk through the garden is the perfect way to clear your mind both before and after attending a production in the **Old Globe Theatre** complex (see "Secret Theater"), just across the street.

The **Quail Botanical Gardens** (Quail Gardens Drive, Encinitas, California, 760-436-3036) is about as hidden as a garden can get. There is no way you'd trip over this place on your own. The entrance is unassuming and gives no hint of the flora within. But a hike through it reveals just about everything San Diego offers in terms of plant growth. Lush green lawns with a gazebo and tropical flowers one moment, desert scrub the next, beach grasses further down the trail, and a waterfall with ferns and mosses in the center of it all. Nearby, you'll find an adobe house with cacti nestled against garden walls and greenhouses nursing young plants. Additionally, a two-story, open-sided observation tower at the farthest end of the garden offers views of meadows, pine forests, and the Pacific Ocean. The paths are steep — a vigorous walk through the entire garden can easily take the place of your daily workout. Open 9 AM to 5 PM daily.

The **Tribute Garden** at **San Diego Hospice** (4311 3rd Avenue, Hillcrest, 619-688-1600) offers a space to take in the panorama of Mission Valley from high atop a bluff. The distant gold and sky-blue dome of the Immaculata Cathedral on the campus of San Diego University across the valley contrasts with the deeper blue of the Pacific that fills the horizon. The plants are generic and unobtrusive, allowing this godlike view of the teeming humanity beneath to fill your perspective. I-8 and Highway 163 intersect far below, and the flow of traffic around the convoluted cloverleaf looks like those models of the future you see in old World's Fair film reels from the 1940s and 1950s. Funds raised through the purchase of "tribute stones" benefit San Diego Hospice programs and services for the terminally ill.

Surfers gave the nickname "Swami" to a stretch of beach 20 minutes north of downtown San Diego, in the city of Encinitas. Perched high above the pounding surf there, atop crumbling sandy cliffs, is a white stucco-walled compound with meandering, shady garden paths, miniature waterfalls, goldfish ponds, and stone benches tucked into quiet, hidden niches. Parmahansa Yogananda, author of *Autobiography of a Yogi* and an early proponent of meditation in the US, used to live on the property. Hence the garden's name, "Swami's," sprang to life. **The Self-Realization Fellowship Retreat and Hermitage Grounds** (215 K Street, Encinitas, California, 760-753-1811) owns the site. The complex is easy to find — its towers, capped by massive gold-painted cement lotus blossoms, are highly visible from the Highway 101 side of the property. A visit to these tranquil gardens has made more than one visitor consider giving up the 9-to-5 life, if only to sit cross-legged in white gauze robes and contemplate the universe. And the view of the Pacific Ocean and California coastline can persuade the most die-hard New Yorker to become a permanent resident of the Golden State. The gardens are open to the public from 9 AM to 5 PM, Tuesday through Saturday, and from 11 AM to 5 PM on Sundays.

The unreachable price of land in San Diego made a prop man at the **La Jolla Playhouse** (2910 La Jolla Village Drive, La Jolla, 858-550-1010) decide that his dream of owning a garden was about as probable as a Republican administration hosting a fundraiser for the National Endowment for the Arts. But a hillside next to the theater called to him, and he answered by planting it with cuttings of cactus and succulents from his own small home, as well as scattering generous sprinklings of wildflower seeds. What sets this garden apart, however, is the art. Tucked carefully throughout are items that properties artisan Ian Grant designed and built for various Playhouse productions, lending new meaning to Shakespeare's famous phrase, "all the world's a stage." Among the most unusual pieces you'll find are two casings from aircraft engines used in the "Rosie the Riveter" scene from the musical *Tommy* — which, by the way, originated at the La Jolla Playhouse (see "Secret Theater"). Half the fun is looking for the props; the other half is guessing which productions they came from. Look for a coat of arms, a weather vane, foam topiaries, and bamboo wind chimes. You'll find the garden under a grove of eucalyptus trees about 100 yards past the Mandell Weiss Theatre box.

If you're clipping along I-5 through the coastal town of Carlsbad in March or April, you will likely get a split-second glimpse of what looks like candy-striped terrain sloping upward from the east side of the freeway. Keep on driving, and you'll be left wondering how these brilliant colors got there. Or exit at Palomar Airport Road, and the mystery is solved. The **Carlsbad Flower Fields** (760-431-0352) explode with 200 million ranunculus blooms annually. The flowers are grouped by color in wide bands that stretch horizontally across the 53-acre hillside. Dirt footpaths allow visitors to stroll through this mind-boggling spectacle, which is nurtured by **Carltas Company** (760-930-9123), a commercial flower-growing business that acquired the property from a private owner in 1993.

S E C R E T
GLASS

I was completely shocked the first time I gazed up at the high shelves inside **Saffron Noodles & Sate** (3737 India Street, Mission Hills, 619-574-0177) and discovered them filled with original glass objects by famous artiste Dale Chihuly. I had just recently lusted over his twisty, colorful works in an elaborate exhibit he presented at the spacious **California Center for the Arts** (340 N Escondido Boulevard, Escondido, California, 760-839-4100). And I suspected immediately that these pieces were blown with that unmistakable level of ingenuity. Chihuly's fantastic creations are showcased in more than 200 museums worldwide, yet this venue, better known for its Thai chicken egg rolls and jasmine rice, happens to house 16 pieces of ponderous value. How did they land here? Restaurant owner Su-Mei Yu is a good friend of Chihuly, who personally chose the pieces he decided to loan her three years ago. Most customers don't make the connection, despite a photograph of Yu and the Washington state artist hanging at eye level in the entranceway.

SECRET
GLASS PIPES

If you reveal to store clerks at **Vishions Smoke Shop** (705 Turquoise Street, Pacific Beach, 858-488-7473) that you're purchasing one of its many hand-blown glass pipes for anything other than tobacco, you'll end up leaving empty-handed. California law prohibits vendors from selling pipes, bongs, and rolling papers to customers who speak openly about illegal substances. The shop carries one of the most extensive lines of pipes by Jerome Baker, known globally for redesigning the hardware that burns green-leaf matter better than it does tobacco. Other merchandise sold here fits the unmentionable theme: air sanitizers, gram scales, and how-to books for passing employer drug tests.

SECRET
GOLD MINES

There's gold in them thar hills. Well, that's the legend, anyhow. Thomas L. Smith (1801–1866), better known as "Peg Leg," was a mountain man, a prospector, and a spinner of tall tales. Local legends about his lost gold mine have grown over the years. Lots of folk have poked around in the desert looking for the immense wealth it supposedly holds. A monument to Peg Leg resides on Henderson Canyon Road, 1,000 feet north of Pegleg Road, in the **Anza-Borrego Desert State Park** (200 Palm Canyon Drive, Anza-Borrego, California, 760-767-5311). It's believed the gold could be within a few miles of the monument. Anza-Borrego is the largest state park in the lower 48 states. It is about 80 miles east of downtown San Diego off I-8 and is an ideal place to get a real feel for the true diversity of life found in the desert Southwest. If the fever grips you to go digging for the gold, remember this is desert country — bring lots of water and scorpion repellent.

If you're seeking a gold-mining experience but aren't keen on actually digging, then head out to the rural historic town of Julian, about a 90-minute drive northeast of San Diego. Just a few blocks off the main street you will find the **Eagle and High Peak Mine** (north end of c Street, Julian, California, 760-765-0227). It's an authentic 1870s-era gold mine, with tunnels you can explore, and authentic tools, machinery, trucks, and cars of yesteryear on display. There is a gold-panning demonstration, and hour-long guided tours of the mine are available daily (10 AM to 3 PM). Back in town, Main Street gives you a feel for the flavor of the Old West with its collection of false-front stores and wooden sidewalks, as well as the historic Julian

Hotel (2032 Main Street, Julian, California, 760-765-0201). The town is famous today for its apples and resulting pies. It is also one of the few places in the region that regularly gets snow in the winter.

SECRET

GONDOLAS

No, there aren't any Venetian *palazzos* to awe you with their Italian grandeur, but you can gawk at $6-million estates instead. And the fragrance in the air is a lot more pleasant than the foul-smelling canals of Venice. **The Gondola Company** (4000 Coronado Bay Road, Coronado, California, 619-429-6317) offers hourly tours of the exclusive Coronado Cays community aboard authentic six-passenger Venetian gondolas, complete with a gondolier in traditional striped shirt and ribbon hat. Taped Italian music plays in the background and complimentary antipasto appetizers or chocolate-covered strawberries sit at your fingertips. Cruises depart (11 AM to midnight) from the marina docks at Loews Coronado Bay Resort (same address). **Coronado Cays** is a ritzy development on the Silver Strand peninsula, just south of the **Hotel Del Coronado** (1500 Orange Avenue, Coronado, California, 619-435-6611). There are boat slips for almost every house, and the "villages" within the development have names like Trinidad, Montego, and Grand Caribe Island. One of the homes featured recently in an architectural magazine boasts a 34-foot-high ceiling with glass rotunda and skylight — and that's just in the entrance foyer! The Gondola Company is operated by two California natives who trained for years on the canals of Venice. Their experience prompted them to replicate the gondola concept as precisely as possible. A one-hour cruise for two people runs $60. Additional guests cost $15 per person. Blankets, an ice bucket, and wine glasses are provided. Guests are invited to bring their own beverages.

SECRET
GROCER

Since 1920, the building that is now **Royal Food Mart** (3401 1st Avenue, Bankers Hill, 619-295-7666) has remained a modest-sized grocer in the charming residential neighborhood of Bankers Hill, located between Hillcrest and Downtown. It's somehow easy to imagine horse-drawn buggies parked in front as you mosey through the few short aisles, or await your pastrami sandwich from the old deli counter. Cold beverages are displayed in large wooden coolers, a modern convenience added in the 1940s that replaced some of the glass-bottle soda machines. Old stained-glass windows, with their original moldings, separate the store from the adjoining **Chatterbox Café** (same address), a modern coffeehouse with sunny yellow walls and Internet access.

SECRET
HAMBURGERS

Camouflaged among the city's burgeoning number of fast-food eateries are several notable mom-and-pop burger joints, which in my opinion cook up fresher and tastier burgers that the ones you can buy for 99 cents at drive-through windows.

Flame-broiled patties for some odd reason are getting harder to find these days. Perhaps it's because of the wayward fumes that charcoal grills emit into our low-humidity atmosphere. At **Phil's BBQ & Ice Cream** (4030 Goldfinch Street, Mission Hills, 619-688-0559), for example, a contentious cloud hangs over the neighborhood as its owner battles an expensive nuisance violation brought against him by Air Pollution Control and neighboring business owners. I personally find the smell outside this sidewalk shop intoxicating. And the burgers, along with the ribs and chicken, are infused with a good woodsy mesquite flavor that can't be beat. (Closed on Mondays.)

I dare most people to fully consume the giant charbroiled burgers at gay-popular **Hamburger Mary's** (308 University Avenue, Hillcrest, 619-491-0400). Chew to the cadence of disco and techno tunes while idling on the lively patio that features a full-service bar and beefy bartenders.

My favorite griddle-cooked burgers are flipped in the beach communities of Ocean Beach and Pacific Beach, commonly referred to as "OB" and "PB." The mini, single, and double-decked patties at **Hodads** (5010 Newport Avenue, Ocean Beach, 619-224-4623) have practically reached cult status among OB laggards. And there's something mysteriously alluring about the spices used in the beef at **Rocky's Crown Pub** (3786 Ingraham Street, Pacific Beach, 858-273-9140), situated about eight blocks from the ocean in PB.

One of the best-kept secrets at **The Waterfront** (2044 Kettner Boulevard, Downtown, 619-232-9656) is that it holds the oldest liquor license in San Diego, obtained immediately after Prohibition ended in 1934. The kitchen's greasy half-pound burgers with sweet grilled onions are better known. Since opening in the early 1900s, this modest structure has been livened up with fresh paint jobs and refitted front windows that open onto the street. It lurks just outside the shadows of Downtown, and attracts everyone from lawyers and office workers to fishermen and boat owners.

The ambiance is pure Old West at the **Hamburger Factory** (14122 Midland Road, Poway, California, 858-486-4575), where beef and buffalo burgers are served on picnic tables surrounded by stretches of Old Poway Park, northeast of San Diego. There's a variety of styles to choose from: the Gringo is topped with fresh avocado; the British comes with Swiss cheese and bacon; and the cowpoke features barbecue sauce, grilled onions, bacon, and cheddar cheese. And yes, that buffalo head you see mounted on the wall inside moves and blinks its eyes periodically, seemingly searching for the steam-engine train that encircles the park on weekends.

My cholesterol count must have spiked 100 points after chomping down on the decadent Rory burger at the bustling, '50s-style **Corvette Diner** (3946 5th Avenue, Hillcrest, 619-542-1001). Nowhere else in town will you find a beef patty garnished with peanut butter, bacon, mayonnaise, and lettuce. Ask your doctor about Lipitor after eating this.

Secret lingo is required when ordering specific types of burgers that aren't listed on the menu board at **In-N-Out Burger** (multiple locations, 800-786-1000, www.in-n-out.com). Aside from fries and shakes, this popular retro franchise carries a limited selection of single or double burgers, with or without cheese. But those in the know can increase their options. Ask for a "wish burger" and you'll get a bun with all the fixings sans the meat patty. Or request "protein style" for a bun-free burger wrapped in lettuce. The "2 x 4" is sheer evil to the arteries. It comes with two meat patties and four slices of cheese. The "animal burger" is more manageable — a single patty cooked with mustard and topped with grilled onions. No telling why these aren't listed on the menu.

S E C R E T
HAUNTINGS

Build your house on a former gallows, and you'll be asking for trouble. Add to the equation a group of former residents whose lives were fraught with gangster theft, illnesses, and a child's accidental strangulation, and things really start going haywire. Welcome to the **Whaley House** (2482 San Diego Avenue, Old Town, 619-297-7511), California's first two-story brick dwelling, built in 1856 by Thomas and Anna Whaley. During their on-again, off-again occupancy, the family leased the living room to the county to serve as a courthouse and gathering spot for political debates. During those times, official records were stolen from an upstairs office; one of the couple's offspring died of scarlet fever; and a playmate of the Whaleys' children fatally struck a low-hanging clothesline while running through the yard. Today, the so-called ghosts of Thomas, Anna, and the little girl, plus a convicted horse thief hanged on the property before the house was built, have joined forces in the afterlife. Claims of paranormal occurrences include the sudden odor of cigar smoke that can't be traced, strange orbs and shadows appearing on walls, and a meat cleaver that swings ominously from a utensil rack in the kitchen. Others report strange constrictions in their throats when they stand on the ninth stair leading up to the bedrooms.

The mysterious 1892 death of con artist Kate Morgan remains an open file, and to some, a source of shivers. Staff and guests at the historic **Hotel Del Coronado** (1500 Orange Avenue, Coronado, California, 619-435-6611) have long attributed her ghost as the source behind strange murmurings and sudden cold breezes that occur in room 3312 — where Morgan was last seen before she was found on a nearby stairwell with a gunshot wound to her head. The San Diego coroner believed the beautiful 24-year-old killed herself because she became pregnant by a man of whom her brother disapproved. Others have speculated that it was her brother who pulled the trigger because Kate wanted no more part in their team effort to swindle money through shady gambling ventures. Whatever the case, housekeepers regularly report seeing her ghost roaming the hallways. An electrician claims that light bulbs along the stairs where she died burn out just minutes after they're installed. But even those with doubts agree that her legend at least remains rooted in a good place with luxury amenities and ocean views.

Depending on whom you talk to, there are at least two prankster ghosts overstaying their welcome at the Victorian-style **Horton Grand Hotel** (311 Island Avenue, Downtown, 619-544-1886). The nefarious Roger Whittiger, who ran up several gambling debts, has taken up residence in room 309. He was shot to death inside Seven Buckets of Blood, a saloon that stood on the property before the hotel was built in 1886. Today, Roger likes to lock doors from the inside and shake beds. Ida Bailey, a well-known madam at a brothel that is now the hotel's bar, began hanging out in room 209 after her death. Her ghost is a flirtatious one, often knocking on doors and briefly becoming visible only if a man answers. Then there are Harry and Gus, two adolescents who died of fever and now run the halls at night.

Hunting down restless spirits is always more fun after sunset. **Old Town Trolley Tours of San Diego** (619-298-8687) conducts two-hour "Ghosts and Gravestones" excursions every evening except Tuesdays (6:30 PM). You'll visit several haunted properties around town, including the **William Heath Davis House** (4th and Island streets, Downtown, 619-233-4692) and **Villa Montezuma** (1925 K Street, Chollas View, 619-239-2211). Tours originate from the ghost-inhabited **Horton Grand Hotel** (311 Island Avenue, Downtown, 619-544-1886).

SECRET

HEAVENLY BODIES

Not to be confused with the bronze-skinned wonders you see stretched across the beaches, these extraordinary entities pertain to the astral matter lounging in space: the Whirlpool Galaxy, the Lagoon Nebula, or Jupiter and Saturn. You don't need your own telescope to join the star parties led by astronomers at the **Oceanside Photo and Telescope Astronomical Society** (1024 Mission Avenue, Oceanside, California, 800-483-6287), because the group comes well equipped with several high-powered lenses. It converges monthly on weekends closest to the new moon at **Little Blair Valley** in the **Anza-Borrego Desert**, about a 90-minute drive from San Diego. Getting there requires a map and directions provided by the society.

S E C R E T
HERBS

If California's burning hot sun or bubbly Valley Girl talk has given you a rash, there may be a cure just around the corner! You've arrived in a magical land that reveres herbal remedies almost as much as it does suntans and book deals with movie options.

Gen Min Acupuncture and Herb Center (2841 University Avenue, North Park, 619-297-0446) is the right half of twin storefronts, offering Asian goods in an atmosphere thick with the mystique of an old-time Chinese curio shop in a B-movie. Catching the flu? Ancient lore recommends taking some *gan mao ling*— but you've got to take it within 24 hours of your first symptoms. Or perhaps your love life has lost some steam? Ask about horny goat weed (*yin yang huao*). If you're looking to wander around a small shop crammed with exotic oddities and hear the bright cadence of the Chinese tongue all around you, this is the place.

Longevity Herbs (3753 6th Avenue, Hillcrest, 619-220-4815) is a somewhat yuppified version of the Chinese apothecary. Located in the predominantly gay section of town (see "Secret LGBT"), the shop offers herbal expertise in quiet, posh surroundings, and recently added chiropractic therapy and Ayurvedic skin care to the menu of well-being services. The soothing atmosphere inside offers welcome respite from the hustling traffic outside, although that tranquil atmosphere didn't exactly happen by accident. A recent remodeling of the store took place after the owners had a professional, 10-hour *feng shui* analysis done. Now you can feel calm while you learn how to add tang to your ginseng, or where you should put that crushed black walnut. Afterward, you can always reward yourself for making a healthy purchase by eating at the lovely **Lotus Thai Cuisine** restaurant (3761 6th Avenue, Hillcrest, 619-299-8272) right next door.

Jimbo's Naturally (12853 El Camino Real, Del Mar, California, 858-793-7755; and 1633 S Center City Parkway, Escondido, California, 760-489-7755) is the command center for the granola set. Among them, the store's name is spoken with a quiet and respectful tone of awe usually reserved for discussions about Jerry Garcia and the merits of hemp clothing. Technically, this is a health food store, carrying all varieties of organic produce. But the broad scope of naturopathic and homeopathic herbal cures on its shelves makes this mom-and-pop company the granddaddy of herbal purveyors in the region.

This could turn into an all-day, get-in-touch-with-your-inner-oneness event if you let it. The **Pacific College of Oriental Medicine** (7445 Mission Valley Road, #105, Mission Valley, 619-574-6909) features an herb shop onsite, as well as teachers and students of acupuncture and other Asian medical arts. Because it is a college, the acupuncture is offered at a significant discount compared to fees at private practices. And with an herb shop handily located on the premises, the proper tincture to soothe nerves is just steps away — which may be worth remembering as you watch a first-time student aiming for your earlobe with acupuncture needles.

The folks at the **Ocean Beach People's Organic Food Cooperative** (4765 Voltaire Street, Ocean Beach, 619-224-1387) boast the "freshest and largest" herb selection in San Diego. Whether or not they can back that claim up, the one thing going for them is location. Ocean Beach is San Diego's last remaining throwback to the hippie era. And while bell-bottoms and flower-power body paint may have quietly vanished over the past few decades, the aura left behind is palpable. This tiny grocery store surely has the ghosts of old Cheech and Chong sketches haunting the aisles. The combination of an active and well-read community bulletin board plus customers trading recipes for favorite herbal face scrubs all around may just have you humming old Bob Dylan songs before you exit.

The **Herb Shoppe** (3618 El Cajon Boulevard, North Park, 619-280-5621) sells more than 400 different types of dried herbs in powder, capsule, and liquid forms. Here you will find a small selection of books to help you educate yourself in herbology. And while you're improving your insides, you can browse a selection of herbal cosmetics to enhance your outsides. Located five blocks east of the I-805, the store is open Tuesday through Saturday (10 AM to 5:30 PM).

SECRET
HOME FURNISHINGS

Start with one gallon of plaster. Fill a rubber mold shaped like an old Roman column. Let dry. Remove the cast. Then display the finished product in a storefront and watch the bucks roll in. This formula for success has worked for over a decade at **Column One** (401 University Avenue, Hillcrest, 619-299-9074). In fact, it's worked so well that the store had to take over the old coffeehouse next door to handle the expansion of its line. Wares include everything from plaster friezes of Michelangelo's *David* to gold-leaf mimics of ancient Egyptian sarcophagi. They range wildly in size, from little wall corbels no bigger than a doorbell button to massive fountains as big as Jacuzzis. The outdoor statuary is rather grand, but shippable. The owner's main key to success, aside from the clientele's renowned desire to accessorize, is the low cost. Plaster is cheap. Marble isn't. And to a skillful designer, ersatz is just as good as gold.

Some of the ladies who lunch in coastal North County do it along the bohemian sidewalks of **South Cedros Avenue** in the city of Solana Beach. Beginning one block inland from the coastal highway (Highway 101), this amalgamation of home furnishing stores offers a kaleidoscope of works by local artisans. I spent an entire afternoon ducking in and out of shops with a friend of mine, gawking at utterly unique items that were out of my price league. I normally hate shopping when I can't buy — but half the fun here is exploring the winding, twisting garden pathways, hallways, and staircases of the different buildings that house one-of-a-kind galleries and shops. You'll find Ethiopian carved wood benches, hand-printed blouses, handmade mermaids, and antique Irish pine. Make sure to check out **Leaping Lotus** (240 s Cedros Boulevard, 858-720-8283), where you will find 21,000 square feet of marketplace with 95 different vendors that carry an extraordinary array of home appointments, art, and apparel. Another welcome shop is **Icons** (444 s Cedros Avenue, 858-481-2266). Fashion legends such as Jackie o, Princess Diana, and Audrey Hepburn inspired the boutique's name. It offers elegant attire for middle-aged women seeking a well-rounded wardrobe. Down the street, an organic nursery called **Cedros Gardens** (330 s Cedros Avenue, 858-792-8640) displays a wide selection of flowers and garden necessities, adding to the whole Southern California feel. The owners coddle the site as if it were their first-born. And if you want to hang around until nighttime, the **Belly Up Tavern** (143 s Cedros Avenue, 858-481-9022), a North County legend down the street, features rock, reggae, and big band music. The place occasionally draws luminaries from Los Angeles: Keanu Reeves has played here with his band, Dogstar, and so has Kevin Bacon's group, the Bacon

Brothers. This isn't just home furnishing shopping: it's a theme park unto itself!

A string of privately owned home furnishing stores can be found along **Morena** and **West Morena Boulevards** in Bay Park, but the area severely lacks eye appeal. **Scan Furniture** (920 Morena Boulevard, 619-296-7875) sits at the entrance to this unofficial district, offering an impressive selection of teak and beech wood furniture from Scandinavia. Continue down the street, past the West Morena split, and you'll find at least a dozen shops that specialize in lights, including the illuminated showrooms of **Light Bulbs Unlimited** (1017 Morena Boulevard, 619-296-2454) and **The Light Bulb House** (1655 Morena Boulevard, 619-276-1500). One of the more exquisite stores is **Genghis Khan** (1136 Morena Boulevard, 619-275-1182), filled with fine antique Tibetan cabinets, herb chests, hutches with secret compartments, dressers, and ornate vases. Nearly everything is imported from different regions of China, with some pieces dating back to the early 1800s. In the showroom's right back corner, a small alcove conceals stacks of old courtyard doors made of various hardwoods. These beautifully carved gems were salvaged from stately properties in China, and come in many odd shapes and sizes. **Mex-Art Pottery & Home Accents** (1155 Morena Boulevard, 619-276-5810) sits across the street, but you can't see all the clay pots and *chimeneas* it offers unless you wander into the back courtyard. Most of the pieces are imported from Mexico's central states, such as Guanajuato, Jalisco, and Oaxaca. You'll also find one of the best collections of Talavera pottery here. And if you're looking for a summery patio set to go with your big clay pot, **Hauser Patio & Rattan** (1180 Morena Boulevard, 619-275-4770) is one block away.

S E C R E T
J A Z Z

❦

For the rest of the world, the name Croce is associated with "Bad, Bad, Leroy Brown." In San Diego, the name means good food, loud laughter, and a reliable offering of the best in traditional, contemporary, and Latin jazz. San Diego's version of live jazz usually amounts to the extremely watered down, easy listening kind at best. **Croce's Jazz Bar** (802 5th Avenue, Downtown, 619-233-4355) is a rare exception that gives die-hard aficionados of the genre an excuse to stay out late. The door to the bar is left open so the enticing blue notes silk their way onto the street and seduce pedestrians to peek in. Memorabilia and pictures of the late Jim Croce, who resided in San Diego, cloak the walls. The owner and hostess of the club is his widow, Ingrid Croce. She opened the adjacent restaurant, Croce's, in the late '80s. Immediate popularity allowed her to expand operations to the point where she is now a four-storefront music/bistro tycoon. Every night of the week, people arrive from all over Southern California to listen to the sounds going down. Croce's son, A.J., who has made a name for himself in the jazz music industry, frequently makes appearances. The cover is $10, but if you buy an entrée at **Croce's Restaurant** or **Ingrid's Cantina & Sidewalk Café**, then admission to the bar is free. **Croce's Top Hat**, also adjacent, completes the set of live music venues that Ingrid runs.

This is such an anomaly in San Diego that you may have to pinch yourself to believe it. **Dizzy's** (344 7th Avenue, Downtown, 858-270-7467) has little that the usual Friday night downtown crowd looks for, yet its owner, Chuck Perrin, has watched it thrive. Step inside and you'll hear *pure* jazz. You won't see music videos playing over the bar. You won't see neon everywhere. And you won't see any alcohol served. Yes, a jazz club with no booze. Somewhere in Louisiana, a thousand saxophone players are spinning in their graves. But the place works. And that's because Perrin stays true to his concept. He ran three coffeehouses in the '60s and yearned to create that kind of atmosphere again, but in a venue where jazz artists could receive the respect — and audience — they deserve. In a stripped-down warehouse with brick walls and a bare-beam ceiling, he has re-created a "collective" for artists, musicians, and film and theater folk, as well as a gathering place for everyday people who have opinions about things. And he's doing it on a shoestring. Perrin returns an astonishingly high percentage of the cover charges to the performers. His dedication has brought the biggest names in San Diego jazz to his doorstep, including Peter Sprague, Coral MacFarland-Thuet, and Jaime Valle. Oh, and one last very welcome exception to the rule: a jazz jam on Friday nights that starts at midnight and goes until 3 AM. In a town that rolls up much of its sidewalks before midnight, the man deserves sainthood for that alone.

I'm tossing this one in more out of nostalgia than for its current jazz bookings. **The French Gourmet at Elario's** (7955 La Jolla Shores Drive, La Jolla, 858-551-3620) was *the* place for jazz for nearly 25 years until it closed its doors in the early '90s. During its heyday, such renowned artists as Papa John Creach, Frank Morgan, Jeannie Cheatham, and Mundell Lowe performed there. New owners later reopened the lounge under a different name. And confused San Diegans were left in a daze trying to figure out where to go for a good jazz fix. Just recently, the new owners wised up and incorporated "Elario's" back into the name, which has begun bringing people back. The jazz has resumed, but the offerings run more toward the gutless, watered-down fusion fare that most locals passively accept. Still, the club's desirable location makes it worth a visit. Perched 11 floors up in the penthouse of the surprisingly bland Hotel La Jolla, the lounge offers sunset views that will blaze in your memory forever. The view of the La Jolla shoreline with its quaint cottage community is quite literally a billion-dollar view, especially with live music and upscale French cuisine behind it. From this bird's-eye vantage point, you're looking at some of the priciest real estate in the country. Try to get to the lounge in time to give yourself a couple of hours of daylight.

Its bayside location, overlooking a ritzy marina, has made **Humphrey's** (2241 Shelter Island Drive, Shelter Island, 619-224-3577) a favorite among locals for decades. The main outdoor stage features a slate of big-name acts throughout the summer months. Spirogyra, Hiroshima, Bruce Hornsby, and David Benoit (famous for covering Vince Guaraldi's *Peanuts* theme "Linus and Lucy") have all performed here, as have David Sanborn, the Herbie Hancock Quartet, and Al Jarreau. The indoor venue, **Humphrey's Backstage Lounge**, is a smaller, more intimate space that frequently allows for dancing to jazz, blues, funk, and R&B, while live, solid jazz is featured at least once a week. And the jerk-chicken quesadilla on the appetizer menu is a must.

S E C R E T
JEWISH DELIS

The name **DZ Akins** (6930 Alvarado Road, La Mesa, California, 619-265-0218) is spoken by some with the same tone of respect many reserve for prayers at Seder. The corned beef and cabbage is lean and

generously served. Thick seeded rye bread, huge kosher pickles, chopped liver appetizers, and poppy seed Danishes have customers driving from miles away to satisfy their need for authentic Jewish meals. There is a deli counter up front stuffed with breads, meats, sausages, and roasts. And if you come during Chanukah, you can get Star of David cookies. The menu lists more than 100 different sandwiches. Each one towers about six inches high and requires a plan of attack before eating. Knishes, pirogen, matzo balls, tongue — if you had to pick a kosher heaven in San Diego, this would be the place. Also recommended: the breaded deep-fried pickles. *L'chaim!*

If your idea of a deli is a tiny, noisy storefront jam-packed with customers and men in dirty white aprons scurrying to fill orders, then **Milton's** (2660 Via De La Valle, Del Mar, California, 858-792-2225) is going to be a shock to your system. Two natives of Chicago built this popular eatery in the very upscale community of Del Mar. The mere approach to the 15-foot-high glass-panel front doors sets my uvula dancing in anticipation of the treats waiting beyond. Inside there is a well-stocked take-out counter and full-service restaurant. The high ceilings and tons of natural light make the space seem roomy even on the most crowded weekends. The menu features barbecued chicken and ribs, burgers, pasta, and overstuffed sandwiches served on their own line of breads. Traditional Jewish deli favorites include lox, and old-fashioned chicken broth with noodles, matzo, or kreplach. In a nod to their West Coast location, you'll find vegetarian selections on the menu as well. The restaurant's original multigrain bread has become so popular that the owners are marketing it nationally. Made with honey, brown sugar, cornmeal, and sesame and poppy seeds, it has devotees who have waxed orgasmic, praising the loaves in more than 10,000 e-mails the proprietors claim to have received thus far.

In the eyes of many transplanted New Yorkers, San Diego appears a vast, empty desert when it comes to late-night eating. But one of the few delis that burns the midnight oil on weekends (2 AM) is the **City Deli** (535 University Avenue, Hillcrest, 619-295-2747), which has been around for more than 17 years. The place used to have the comfy, lived-in feel of a dated New York City diner until a recent remodeling. Now it is more colorful and the furnishings are contemporary. But the original booths remain, as do the little chrome jukeboxes at every table. The food is traditional East Coast deli–style and the menu runs six pages. If you're on any kind of a diet, either drop it or don't go. The potato latkes, fried to a golden crisp and drenched in sour cream, would make any Jewish mother's heart swell with pride — or perhaps angina! The regular diner food here tends toward the bland, so stick with the traditional high-fat deli food and you won't go wrong. There is also a large selection of cakes and pastries that I am powerless to resist every time I visit, particularly a decadent concoction called the chocolate pyramid. Desserts are kept in a rotating display case that warmly greets you upon entering. Parking in the area is tight, especially on weekends. But a validated lot is available one block away at the **Union Bank** building (5th and University avenues).

SECRET
JOAN CRAWFORD

The imposing, dark-wood shelving unit behind the bar at **Café 828** (828 6th Avenue, Downtown, 619-231-8282) holds untold stories from the days it graced screen legend Joan Crawford's second home in Italy. The polished antique mantelpiece was acquired by the former St. James Hotel after the actress died, and one can't help wonder what took place beneath it. Shrewd business deals? Quiet Hollywood sabbaticals? Grappa parties with Fellini and other European film types? The furnishing blends wonderfully with the building's circa-1910 architectural trimmings, which are well preserved within the restaurant but somewhat skewered inside the adjoining lobby that is now operated by **Ramada Inn and Suites** (619-531-8877). The café serves up the kind of sophisticated fare and fine wine that would make "Mommie Dearest" feel very much in her element.

S E C R E T

JUNK

⚜

Kobey's Swap Meet (3500 Sports Arena Boulevard, Loma Portal, 619-226-0650) is reportedly the third most visited attraction in San Diego, after the Zoo and SeaWorld. It's a bargain hunter's paradise staged in the vast asphalt parking lot of the **Sports Arena**, Friday through Sunday mornings (7 AM to 3 PM). But first-time visitors can easily become weighed down with their purchases or overheated by the sun before ever reaching the back rows, where used goods are peddled for negotiable prices. The front and middle sections brim with new merchandise of mediocre quality, ranging from poster art and clothing to electronics and household bric-a-brac. The back area, I've found, holds more surprises: old books, vintage toys and games, handy tools, and occasional pieces of rare, antique pottery, all schlepped in by locals who can no longer live with their dusty possessions.

SECRET
KALUA PIG

If you've never been to Hawaii, then you don't know about "plate lunches," which translate to cheap, fast, and tasty meals anytime of the day. **Da Kine's** (4120 Mission Boulevard, Pacific Beach, 858-274-8494) is the last geographic point on the mainland where you can get these traditional meals without having to trek over the Pacific. Located a few steps from the ocean, near the **Surfer Motor Lodge** (711 Pacific Beach Drive, Pacific Beach, 858-483-7070), it specializes in Kalua pig, a common Hawaiian plate lunch consisting of slow-roasted pork shoulder that is shredded and mixed with cabbage. Macaroni salad and two scoops of sticky rice complete the tropical concept. Even more exotic is lau lau, a schizophrenic yet appetizing mixture of cubed pork and fish wrapped in taro leaves. Walls are slathered in Hawaiian memorabilia, and the owners are island transplants.

SECRET
KITES

Reliable onshore breezes and scant rainfall make San Diego the perfect launching ground for kites. An expanse of lawn just south of the **Hilton San Diego Resort** (1775 E Mission Bay Drive, Mission Bay, 619-275-7920) in **Mission Bay Park** is a prime location for flying kites of every shape and size. On weekdays especially, novice hobbyists will find plenty of elbowroom to test their strings — or untangle them — without encroaching on the domains of picnickers and passersby.

The downtown skyline becomes your backdrop when flying at the **Embarcadero Marina Park North**, located alongside a hidden little store called **Kite Flite** (859 w Harbor Drive in Seaport Village, Marina District, 619-234-8200). It's the only kite retailer in the area that allows you to "fly before you buy." It sells more than 100 different models, from parafoils to high-performance stunt kites, all of which include free flight lessons from the staff. Open seven days a week (9:30 AM to 10 PM), including holidays.

Kites shaped like whales, bugs, and dragonflies, with single or multiple lines, or delta-shaped and six-sided, can all be found at **Kite Country** (3350 Sports Arena Boulevard, Unit J, Loma Portal, 619-233-9495). The store is concealed behind the **Black Angus** steakhouse (3340 Sports Arena Boulevard, Loma Portal, 619-223-5604) and staffed with expert kite builders and flyers who have been in the business for several decades.

SECRET

KNITTING AND FABRICS

Learn the ins and outs of interlocks, verticals, and stripes from German yarn master Helga Nienaber, who offers ongoing knitting classes for every skill level inside her quaint La Jolla shop, **Helga's Yarn**

Boutique (7660 Fay Avenue, La Jolla, 858-459-3700). Classes are held on Tuesdays, Fridays, and Saturdays (10:30 AM to 12:30 PM). You'll also find yarns in the latest colors and textures, plus custom-designed sweaters that quench La Jolla's thirst for one-of-a-kind fashions.

Denizens of the old Adams Avenue Theater could have never imagined 30 years ago that their neighborhood moviehouse would turn into a mini-bazaar of drapery and upholstery materials. **Sew Fine** (3325 Adams Avenue, Normal Heights, 619-280-1791) abounds in fabrics for making pillows, bedspreads, curtains, and auto upholstery. About six blocks down is the company's second shop, **Novelty & Crafts** (3580 Adams Avenue, Normal Heights, 619-282-6920), where you'll find buttons, threads, lace trims, and felts for making one hell of a party dress.

SECRET
LAWRENCE WELK

He was as common a sight on living room TV sets as Wonder Bread was on kitchen counters. An American pop-culture maestro, known by many as Mr. Wunnerful, his legend persists in a sprawling site north of San Diego. **The Lawrence Welk Resort** (8860 Lawrence Welk Drive, Escondido, California, 760-749-3448) is a veritable haunt for senior citizens who remember when machine-blown bubbles waltzed in synchrony to folksy bandstand music, both of which became staples of Welk's successful 25-year television show. Nearly 600 acres pay tribute to the late baton-waving musician, who bought a parcel of the land in 1965 before developers embellished it with a country club, restaurants, dinner theater, two golf courses, and a museum that boasts the "world's largest champagne glass." Sidewalks are studded with bronze musical notes and miniature concert instruments. And if that isn't enough to get you waxing sentimental, then nuzzle up to the life-size cardboard cutout of Welk perched on a re-created bandstand inside the museum. Studio lights and illuminated applause signs give the haunting impression that this icon of the Geritol set is breathing down your back in spirit.

S E C R E T
LGBT

San Diego's undisputed gay core is Hillcrest, home to the freshly renovated **Lesbian, Gay, Bisexual, Transgender Community Center** (3909 Centre Street, 619-692-2077), plus scores of bars, restaurants, colorful shopping plazas, trendy coffeehouses, pretty-boy gyms, and quaint boutiques that garnish its main thoroughfare (University Avenue). Like other gay-friendly communities throughout the city (North Park, University Heights, Kensington, and Normal Heights), the neighborhood's village-like center is distinguished by an 800-pound, circa-1940 Art Deco neon sign, which imparts an inviting nighttime glow over University Avenue between 4th and 5th avenues. Pedestrians love Hillcrest. But motorists find it less appealing because of limited parking and relentless meter maids.

The **San Diego Lesbian, Gay, Bisexual, Transgender Pride** parade (619-297-7683, www.sdpride.org) is the city's largest civic event, held on the last Saturday of July (11 AM) along a one-mile stretch of University Avenue between Normal Street and 6th Avenue. Attendance over the past few years has swelled to nearly 135,000. And the number of floats and contingents now exceeds 200 — a far cry from Pride parades of the early 1970s, when trickles of marchers traversed Broadway past jeering sailors and shoddy tattoo parlors. Today's victorious spectacle calls for some secret viewing points. Three commercial businesses have patios situated advantageously along the parade route: **Starbucks Coffee** (1240 University Avenue, Hillcrest, 619-298-8111), **Ben & Jerry's Ice Cream** (1254 University Avenue, Hillcrest, 619-294-4212), and **Heidi's Frozen Yogurt** (1290 University Avenue, Hillcrest, 619-574-1644). Get there early and nurse your purchases if you want to secure these front-row posts.

Pride's two-day festival at Marston Point in Balboa Park begins immediately after the parade. One of its three beer gardens, **Tavern on the Green**, is a grassy terrace hidden down a slope at the festival's south end, which overlooks the downtown skyline. And to the left of the main entrance is a bowl-like area for the main concert stage, a space where local gay activists staged their first rallies some 30 years ago.

San Diego's first gay bar, **The Brass Rail** (3796 5th Avenue, Hillcrest, 619-298-2233), dates back to 1960. It offers nightly dancing and a well-positioned sidewalk patio for people-watching. Arrive before 9 PM on weekends or else get stuck in the admission line. Perfect pectorals typically blanket the dance floors at **Rich's** (1051 University Avenue, Hillcrest, 619-497-4588) and the three-level **Club Montage** (2028 Hancock Street, Middletown, 619-294-9590). But smooth-bodied GQ types are an odd fit at two neighborhood leather bars, **Wolf's** (3404 30th Street, North Park, 619-291-3730) and **The Zone** (3040 North Park Way, North Park, 619-295-8072). **Greystokes Bar**

& Grill (1903 s Coast Highway, Oceanside, California, 760-757-2955) is like an outer planet in a gay solar system, found 30 miles up the coast in an area better known for its Marine Corps housing and girl-chasing surfer dudes.

Of the nearly 25 other gay bars scattered around town, only two are geared expressly to lesbians. **The Flame** (3780 Park Boulevard, Hillcrest, 619-295-4163), with its spirited dance floor and female go-go dancers, resides on the beaten track, one block north of the **San Diego LGBT Pride** office (1807 Robinson Street, Suite 106, Hillcrest, 619-297-7683). **Six Degrees** (3175 India Street, Middletown, 619-296-6789) is grittier and more remote in comparison, yet offers an expanded outdoor patio, dartboards, and a late-night snack menu.

Since 1982, **The Bisexual Forum** (www.bisandiego.org) has rolled out its welcome mat to thousands of locals and out-of-town visitors who identify as bisexual, gay, lesbian, transgender, straight, or "in question." The group meets for discussion on the second Tuesday of every month (7:30 PM) at the **New Creation Church of Christ** (115 Thorn Street, Bankers Hill, 858-259-8019).

Great strides have been made for LGBT Latinos and other people of color with the recent opening of **Bienestar San Diego** (3020 North Park Way, North Park, 619-295-2192), a human services drop-in facility that offers discussion groups, cultural events, HIV services, and writing and drama circles. Additionally, the **Ebony Pride** (619-296-3245) festival is held in late August at the old Naval Hospital parking lot (2125 Park Boulevard, Balboa Park).

SECRET
LODGINGS

You can always do the obvious when you come to San Diego — the Hiltons, the Hyatts, the Wyndhams, and the Radissons. And the major chains do have some beautiful hotels here. But if you want to get a more personal, less generic taste of the city, a couple of places fill the bill well.

Many hotels in town offer the resonance of ocean waves lapping on the beach. Yet at the **Crystal Pier Hotel** (4500 Ocean Boulevard, Pacific Beach, 858-483-6983), you can hear the sound of the ocean lapping right under the floor. Built in 1927, this landmark in the community of Pacific Beach has mini-cottages that are actually built on the pier, where guests can feel the surge of surf beneath their beds. In the morning, if the mood hits, you can toss a fishing line from the pier with rental equipment offered by the hotel. There are 23 separate units, but because the pier extends over a portion of the beach as well, you have to specifically request a cottage directly over the water if you want it. Architectural aesthetics are basic, although each cottage has little flower boxes on its shuttered windows. Reservations must usually be made six months in advance for summer stays, and at least four to five months ahead for the winter season. Restaurants and nightclubs are within walking distance, and the boardwalk scene is only steps away.

Sitting on the edge of Balboa Park and semi-hidden behind tall pines is the **Balboa Park Inn** (3402 Park Boulevard, Hillcrest, 619-298-0823), which spills over with quaint Spanish Colonial charm. There are 26 suites to choose from, each with its own distinctive theme. The owners must have tapped into some new water fetish, because almost all of the units seem to have separate mirrored rooms with Jacuzzi tubs. My favorite has to be the Orient Express room, just for the unfettered gaudiness of it. With deep-Chinese-red fabric everywhere, lacquered furniture, and Asian bellpulls, I feel like I just stepped into an old Charlie Chan movie. It is excessive, but without question pleasant and unforgettable. Other suites include the Jungle Nook, Paris in the '30s, Victoria's Secret, and the Tara suite with an oil painting of Vivien Leigh dressed up as Scarlet O'Hara.

There are a handful of hostels in San Diego, each with a very distinct flavor. **USA Hostels San Diego** (726 5th Avenue, Downtown, 619-232-3100), located in a historic Victorian building downtown, was built in 1887. Even if you're not staying here, it is worth a stop to peek inside at the grand staircase — straight out of a Jane Austen novel. The hostel sits in the heart of the Gaslamp District, which vies with Mission Beach and Hillcrest for the title of "most active night-life" in San Diego. Despite the building's classic architecture, the hostel attracts mostly young, independent travelers, many of them foreigners. It offers DSL Internet connections, cable television, free videos, and a complimentary all-you-can-eat pancake breakfast every morning. It's also very close to the Gaslamp trolley station, which makes getting to other destinations in town simple. Dorm rooms, with four to six beds, range from $18 to $20 a night. Single rooms with two twins or one double bed start at $46 a night.

Banana Bungalow Beach San Diego (707 Reed Avenue, Pacific Beach, 858-273-3060) boasts that it is the only hostel in the continental United States located directly on the beach. It sits in the heart of the very hip, very casual Pacific Beach scene. And in the summer, the skylarking extends late into the night, so if you're looking for major zzzs, bring earplugs or sleeping pills. You can't miss this place,

as it's painted a very vibrant yellow and frankly looks like a low-rent version of an MTV summer beach house. In another community it would cause an uproar. In this part of town, it's just another piece of the puzzle. Inside, there is a tropical jungle theme. Outside, the compound includes a barbecue and beachfront patio with thatched umbrella and lounge chairs. Beach bonfires, barbecues, and pub crawls are organized for guests on a regular basis. The place is set up to accommodate more than 70 guests. Shared rooms cost $16 to $20 per night, depending on the season.

Ocean Beach International Backpackers Hostel (4961 Newport Avenue, Ocean Beach, 619-223-7873) is in the heart of the last remaining vestige of the hippie scene in San Diego. Ocean Beach maintains that reputation among San Diegans, although flower children are few and far between these days. But the atmosphere is still funky in a carefree, thumb-your-nose-at-the-establishment kind of way. And the hostel plays on that with its catchy "no curfews, no lockouts, no chores" motto. The sands and Ocean Beach Pier (at the foot of Newport Avenue) are within walking distance. The weekly farmers' market on Newport (see "Secret Farmers' Markets") is a great place to pick up fresh food or make friends. Though run-down, the hostel is among the lowest priced in the region. A double room goes for $17 to $20 a night. Regular dorms run between $15 and $18 per night.

Many visitors to San Diego peek at the cute collection of period Victorian homes in Heritage Park (Harney Street in Old Town). But few are aware that they can bed down in lace and four-poster beds at the **Victorian Heritage Park Bed & Breakfast Inn** (2470 Heritage Park, Old Town, 619-299-6832). Located in the middle of the park, the inn is a fully restored 1889 Queen Anne mansion with appropriate period antiques that add to the quaint, highbrow feel. The property offers 12 rooms ($135 to $155) and three suites ($145 to $250). Full breakfast and afternoon tea are included.

The Cottage (3829 Albatross Street, Hillcrest, 619-299-1564), at $75 a night, is quite a bargain — and fairly hidden. Just blocks away from the heart of restaurant-jammed Hillcrest, it is a two-room cottage with a secret garden on a residential cul-de-sac. Both units are filled with antiques, including a 19th-century player piano. The surroundings are very quiet, disrupted only by occasional life-flight helicopters landing at nearby Mercy Hospital.

SECRET
MARTINIS

Gone are the days when ordering a martini required two simple choices: gin or vodka, with or without olives. The drink that became popular among high-class lounge lizards of the 1950s and 1960s has returned with a vengeance in many flavors and colors. In fact, a martini in hand has practically become a fashion statement in chic nightclubs and restaurants ever since that fabulous foursome from HBO's *Sex in the City* series started sipping them.

San Diego has a fair crop of swanky martini bars that attract trendsetters and fad followers. Among them are the **Red Circle** (420 E Street, Downtown, 619-234-9211), a stunningly designed space bathed in tasteful red lighting and appointed with Russian accents and Red Army paraphernalia. The drink menu features more than 100 spiced vodkas from around the world. Also in Downtown's Gaslamp District is **Martini Ranch** (528 F Street, Downtown, 619-

235-6100), which attracts a younger singles crowd on weekends due to the recent addition of a dance area called "the shaker room." Around the corner at **The Bitter End** (770 5th Avenue, Downtown, 619-338-9300), designer martinis jibe with an elegant upstairs lounge that adheres to a strict and unusual dress code for San Diego: no jeans, gym shoes, baseball caps, T-shirts, or sandals are allowed.

Martinis come with many secrets at **Seven** (1421 University Avenue, Hillcrest, 619-297-0722), a Manhattan-style restaurant and lounge located on a vibrant commercial block in the community of Hillcrest. Depending on what drink list you look at, there are either 20 or 513 martinis to choose from. The bigger menu, called the "martini bible," is chained to the bar and offered only to patrons who ask to see it. Bartenders never reveal the recipes but will offer brief flavor descriptions. Recommended are the Vanilla Vogel, a sweet and soothing libation made with four different liquors; the sexy-looking Raspberry Moon, which tastes like a chocolate-raspberry truffle; and the clear Uptown Cosmopolitan. A full supper menu offers excellent mesquite-grilled meats and fish, and a tantalizing four-cheese fondue appetizer that pairs very well with the house's 007 martini.

SECRET
MASSAGE

It used to be that finding an erotic massage required knowing a few secrets. Now it's the legitimate ones that are hard to find. The sexy surprise you get with a massage at the **International Professional School of Body Works** (1414 Garnet Avenue, Pacific Beach, 858-490-1154) is a reduced price — at least 50 percent less than you'll pay in fancy spas or low-lit parlors. Students of the school administer the one-hour kneading sessions ($25) in eight rooms inside the clinic. Many of them are already adept at tackling chronic pain and sports injuries, even though they might still be months away from earning their licenses. The facility, nondescript from the outside, is directly across the street from **Play It Again Sports** (1401 Garnet Avenue, Pacific Beach, 858-490-0222). It is open seven days a week (9 AM to 9 PM). Make appointments at least one day in advance.

Conventioneers who can't peel away from their work and need the kinks worked out of their necks can order onsite chair massages through **San Diego Massage Professionals** (877-407-9173). They run $95 per hour or $2 per minute. Full body massages are available in a variety of Western and Asian techniques, such as deep tissue and *tui na*. But don't bother setting a romantic atmosphere in your hotel room, because all of the massage therapists stay fully clothed and draping for the clients is mandatory.

SECRET

MEAT MARKETS

An old-fashioned meat market with real Midwestern butchers in the middle of health-conscious San Diego? Yes, indeed. And it took me years to stumble upon the place because it's concealed within a stretch of fast-food restaurants and uninspired strip plazas in a cheerless section of Mission Valley. **Iowa Meat Farms** (6041 Mission Gorge Road, Mission Gorge, 619-281-5766) is like a learning center for barbecuing. The elongated display case is staffed with an army of apron-clad meat handlers who can explain the differences between rib eye and sirloin, filet and strip steak, or pork butt and shoulder. You'll also get advice on how to properly cook, marinate, or score the Iowa imports they sell. It's worth a visit if you find yourself playing grill master.

The dull, lifeless façade at **Sausage King** (811 w Washington Street, Mission Hills, 297-4301) explains why so many San Diegans have passed it by for the past three decades. It's one of the last mom-and-pop meat markets on the retail scene, offering a variety of homemade European-style sausages and cold cuts, such as bratwurst, Polish sausage, freshly cured bacon, and about as many different varieties of bologna as the number of flavors you'd find in an ice cream shop.

Removed from the tourist beat, about 12 miles east of the city, is **Kaelin's** (1435 E Main Street, El Cajon, California, 619-440-1423), an independently owned grocery store with a 60-foot-long meat counter in the back. The offerings include nearly 40 different cuts of meat commonly used in traditional Mexican recipes such as carne asada, pollo asada, cecina, carnitas, and fajitas, to name a few. The breakfast steaks and voluminous center-cut pork chops are particularly popular.

S E C R E T
MEMORIALS

The 1978 crash of Pacific Southwest Airlines Flight 182 into the residential neighborhood of North Park is an event forever seared into the memories of San Diegans who lived here at the time. One hundred and thirty-two lives were lost, including all the passengers and crew, plus several people on the ground, when a small private plane collided with the 727 in midair. The neighborhood, which was devastated both structurally and emotionally, has long since been rebuilt. A small plaque has been placed beneath a memorial tree planted on the property of the **North Park Library** (3795 31st Street, North Park, 619-533-3972), located only blocks from the actual crash site. The bronze-on-stone memorial, dedicated on September 25, 1998, reads simply: "This tree grows in caring memory of the passengers and community residents who perished in the crash of PSA Flight 182 on Sept. 25, 1978. This tree grows in the spirit of North Park and the residents who rebuilt their community." A larger plaque, listing the names of all those who perished, is located in the **San Diego Aerospace Museum** (2001 Pan American Plaza, Balboa Park, 619-234-8291), just off the entry rotunda, next to the doors leading to the Theodore Gildred flight rotunda.

The list of names of those who set out to sea from a harbor on San Diego Bay and never returned is surprisingly long. The **Tunaman's Memorial** (Shelter Island Drive, Shelter Island) is both stunning and morbid. Located along the peaceful waterfront at the western tip of Shelter Island, a marble slab furnishes the names of dozens of tuna boaters lost at sea between 1971 and 2001. Curiosity burns over what exactly happened out there. On the other side of the slab are tall bronze figures of three men, tilted back uniformly with fishing poles extending from their waists. Their lines are hooked to the mouth of a frantic tuna that sticks out from a cement block several feet in front of them. The perils inherent in the commercial fishing industry are poignantly conveyed as you gaze out to the calm and serene waters of the bay.

In a town that takes its military heritage very seriously, the **Veterans Memorial Center and Museum** (2115 Park Boulevard, Balboa

Park, 619-239-2300) is a strikingly human remembrance to our country's fighting forces. It is unique among military memorials because it honors all branches of the service in one building. It also features a rotating show of artworks by veterans and other artists that range from the traditional and patriotic to the more abstract and jarring. Featured exhibits include World War I, World War II, Pearl Harbor, the Korean and Vietnam conflicts, Desert Storm, and Women in the Military. The first American flag to fall in the Philippines during World War II is also on display. The center is located in the chapel building of the former Balboa Naval Hospital, across the street from Balboa Park. Veterans of recent wars conduct "living history" docent tours. And the collection of military books, brochures, yearbooks, and videotapes available for viewing make this a significant resource for visiting families of those who served in defense of the country.

The US **Navy Aircraft Carrier Memorial** is near Downtown on Harbor Drive, two blocks south of Broadway, at the site of the historic Old Fleet Landing. Nestled quietly amid deciduous trees and overlooking San Diego Bay, a dignified nine-foot, polished-black granite obelisk commemorates the US Navy's aircraft carriers, and all who have served on them and flown from their decks. Engraved on the obelisk is the name of every US aircraft carrier built since 1922 — from the USS *Langley* to the USS *Harry S. Truman*, plus America's newest nuclear-powered craft. Appropriately, you can gaze across the bay from the site and see the carriers docked at North Island Naval Air Station. The memorial was funded by donations from friends of the Navy and from former carrier shipmates. Two life-size bronze sculptures of a naval aviator and a sailor stand beside the obelisk. Created by artists T.J. Dixon and James Nelson, they depict a part of the Pacific Fleet's fighting team that has called San Diego Bay home port since the beginning of naval aviation.

SECRET

MINI-CABS

So what if they don't go faster than 25 MPH? They can at least scoot you to places that are too close for taxicab service, yet too far to walk. **Mini Cab Company** (619-234-1818, www.minicabco.com) is a young transportation outfit that escapes most visitors merely because it hasn't massively advertised. Nearly 20 battery-powered vehicles that resemble deluxe golf carts comprise the company's fleet, each capable of transporting up to three customers at a time between various locales, such as Downtown, Little Italy, Hillcrest, and Coronado. The doorless cabs come with storage space, DVD dashboard, and vinyl panels used to seal the interiors during rare rainstorms. Pickups are ordered by phone or online. Flat fees start at $3 for one to four blocks and climb to $10 for 20 to 30 blocks.

SECRET

MISSIONS

Every child in the fourth grade in California has to do a report on the historic Spanish missions in the state. The report usually includes a school field trip to one of the original 21 missions founded by Father Junipero Serra in the latter half of the 18th century. The missions cover the entire length of the state, and their locations were determined simply by making sure no mission was more than one day's walk from the next.

One state mission that doesn't get visited as much as some of the others do is the **Mission San Antonio de Pala** (Pala Mission Road off Highway 76, Pala, California, 760-742-3317). Situated east of I-15 in North County, it is tucked away behind avocado groves in the town of Pala. The bell tower, modeled after one in Juarez, Mexico, is separate from the main building and overlooks one of the oldest graveyards in California. An oddity is the cactus plant growing out of the top of the bell tower next to the cross. Also check out the original school, which native Americans attended more than 180 years ago. The long chapel, with an adobe floor and native American paintings on the inside walls, is the original structure. This building is a rarity in the state, as most missions today are re-creations of ones that were vandalized and plundered in the last half of the 19th century and the early 20th. Nonetheless, time did take its toll on Pala. In the 1950s, the resident friar started a grassroots campaign to restore the mission. Today, the Pala Indian tribe still resides on the reservation and visitors can observe ancient ceremonies during certain seasons.

You may have stayed at one time or another in a Ramada Inn, but do you know what a *ramada* is? I used to think that it was somebody's name. Turns out that it is a structure made of brush, open on all four sides, but with a roof to keep the sun and the rain off you. I learned this little factoid some years ago when visiting the **Mission San Diego de Alcalá** (10818 San Diego Mission Road, Mission Valley, 619-281-8449), where a ramada still stands near the chapel. Established on July 16, 1769, it was the first of the 21 missions founded by Father Junipero Serra. Historians refer to it as the "mother of the missions." The ramada was used to shelter native American laborers who baked adobe bricks in an outdoor oven. The mission itself still holds Mass and has a very active parish. And, in case you were wondering, the name of the mission — and not coincidentally our city, San Diego — means Saint Didacus, who hailed from Alcalá, Spain.

The **Mission San Luis Rey** (4050 Mission Avenue, Oceanside, California, 760-757-3651) is the big fat Cadillac granddaddy of the missions. It was also one of the richest. Stretched out in the sun like a gleaming white mansion, it includes a portico with multiple arches that architects have hailed for its grace and proportion. Amazingly, the original structure was even longer than its existing frame. Visit the sunken gardens to get a sense of being whisked away to an earlier time in California's history. The courtyard quadrangle, which was originally 500 square yards, hosted bullfights. That takes a lot of visitors by surprise, since this was once a religious sanctuary! Also of note: California's first pepper tree is here, planted in 1830 from seeds brought by Peruvian sailors. And don't miss the crudely carved gargoyles that once spouted water along the tiled stairway leading to the former site of the San Luis Rey River. They look like close cousins of carved stones you see in Mayan temples.

SECRET
MOVIE SCREENS

San Diego isn't far behind most other metropolitan areas that are steadily losing their old neighborhood movie palaces to giant multiplex cinemas. Theaters with plush stadium seating and convenient mall locations have grown here like dandelions. The newest complexes can be found at **Fashion Valley Mall** (7007 Friars Road, Mission Valley, 619-688-9100), where 18 AMC **Theaters** screens (619-296-0333) were added to the mall's most recent expansion. In 1997,

Pacific Theaters (701 5th Avenue, 619-232-0400) introduced to Downtown's historic Gaslamp District a four-story Goliath with a convincing Art Deco façade. The 78,000-square-foot venue encompasses 15 screens, all devoted to Hollywood's current releases. The project proved to be a successful redevelopment tool for Downtown. But if you're looking for a refreshing alternative, you need only step off the beaten track.

Two vintage movie theaters in San Diego remain. Both are owned and operated by **Landmark Theaters**. The oldest is the **Ken Cinema** (4061 Adams Avenue, Kensington, 619-283-5909), built in 1946. It was the first screen in San Diego to bring subtitled foreign films into vogue during the mid-1970s. And it's the only local theater that still runs movies on reel-to-reel carbon arc projectors. As promoted quarterly in the well-circulated *Ken Filmcalendar*, the cinematic fare regularly includes independent, experimental, and obscure foreign films. The venue also plays host every summer to a week-long gay and lesbian film festival, called OUTFEST.

As San Diegans developed a greater thirst for art films, Landmark Theaters tried its hand at the multi-screen approach — and succeeded. **Hillcrest Cinemas** (3965 5th Avenue, Hillcrest, 619-299-2100) represents the largest theater complex in San Diego County dedicated to art films. But don't be confused when you locate the address, because the theater's second-floor entrance and lobby are shrouded by a hospital, a gym, and restaurants that all share space in the modern stucco **Village Hillcrest** shopping complex.

New to the independent film scene is **Madstone Theaters** (7510 Hazard Center Drive, Mission Valley, 619-299-4500), which recently moved into a seven-screen theater complex formerly occupied by **Mann Theaters**. Gone are the commercial Hollywood blockbusters and hackneyed concession food. The company instead offers moviegoers a community-oriented cinema experience through varied film series, engaging discussions, a café, and gourmet concessions. Independent and foreign film titles share the marquee with time-honored classics such as *Citizen Kane*, *Some Like It Hot*, or *Breakfast at Tiffany's*. And shortly after its grand opening in 2002, it hosted the annual Cine Mexicano Film Series. The theater's entrance is behind the low-profile **Hazard Center** shopping center in Mission Valley.

So *this* is what it feels like to have a private screening in some fancy movie producer's sprawling mansion. The first time I walked into the Joan and Irwin Jacobs Theater in the **Museum of Photographic Arts** (1649 El Prado Way, Balboa Park, 619-238-7559), I felt like I had been transported into an exclusive showroom of the future. The plush carpeting, muted indirect lighting, arched white-stucco ceiling, and stadium-style seats tell you this isn't your typical 20-screen multiplex. What made me ooh and ahh like a fool, though, was the surreal deep-blue light cast over the ceiling to make it look like late dusk. Tiny bright lights peer out of pinholes in the ceiling, making it seem more like a planetarium. Words can't convey, so just go see it. The recently renovated and expanded museum is housed in one of the park's Spanish Colonial buildings, so the contrast between the old and the new is even more striking. To make the trip even more enticing, the offerings in the theater are a mix of obscure art films and major Hollywood films from the past that haven't been shown on the big screen in ages. San Diego Cinema Society director Andy Friedenberg handpicks the season's offerings, giving each season its own theme — as in the summer of 2002, which he branded "The Revenge of the Long Cult Summer." The series featured Bernardo Bertolucci's *Last Tango in Paris*, Stanley Kubrick's *Dr. Strangelove*, Mel Brooks's *Blazing Saddles*, and John Waters's *Desperate Living*, to name a few. The mix of titles is controversial, and the movies are never ordinary.

SECRET

MUSEUMS

Every city has them: those esoteric, understated museums that might take only 30 minutes to see, but which house unexpected and sometimes quirky exhibits that are no less fascinating than Egyptian mummies or paintings by the masters.

A relic commonly overlooked because of its lonesome placement is the Millionaire Calculator at the **Computer Museum of America** (640 C Street, Downtown, 619-235-8222). Weighing in at a not-so-portable 120 pounds, it was one of the first adding machines to hit the market between 1895 and 1935. Only 4,000 of them were manufactured by a Swiss company named Hans Egli. They were promoted with the promise of giving businesses and entrepreneurs an upper hand over their competition, since speedier number crunching meant a faster road to riches. The gizmo was made with only four basic math functions, but it was more than enough capability to wow consumers back then. It's hidden in a small alcove on the museum's second floor. After exiting the elevator, walk through the mezzanine and turn left. Other old clunkers include a Hollerith manual card punch from the 1950s; a Royal Precision vacuum tube computer from 1963, representing the end of the vacuum tube era; a rare, single-board Apple I computer, plus dozens of interactive exhibits that eminently frame the continuous evolution of computers. Open Tuesday through Sunday (10 AM to 5 PM).

It's a meal for the right brain and candy to the ears when you visit the **Museum of Making Music** (5790 Armada Drive, Carlsbad, California, 760-438-5996), which offers a nostalgic walk through the past 100 years of American music and its fabrication. The timeline of educational exhibits begins in the 1890s, when player pianos outsold every consumer product in the United States except bicycles. It trails along to the invention of the electric guitar, some 20 years before rock and roll made it famous, and on to the introduction of synthetic drumheads in the late 1950s — and beyond. A century's worth of musical artists and groups are celebrated through audio and video displays. But don't breeze over the placards that mark nearly 500 vintage instruments, because you can easily miss some of their celebrity connections. There's a guitar autographed by Peter, Paul, and Mary; another by Stevie Ray Vaughn; and an accordion left at the South Pole by Admiral Richard E. Byrd on one of his famous expeditions. The instrument was miraculously recovered 30 years later in full working order. Open Tuesday through Sunday (10 AM to 5 PM).

From the time that George Freeth brought the magic of surfing to California in 1907, early photographers sought to capture the exciting images of wave and rider. You'll find many of them at the **California Surf Museum** (223 N Coast Highway, Oceanside, California, 760-721-6876), an international repository and resource center devoted to surfing. Exhibits from around the world roll into the museum every 18 months, usually paying respect to legendary wave riders such as John "Doc" Ball, the California dentist who became a surf documentarian in the 1930s; or Duke Kahanamoku, considered by most the father of surfing. Founded in 1986, the museum can hold many unexpected surprises, depending on when you visit.

Perhaps one of the most overlooked exhibits inside the **San Diego Model Railroad Museum** (1649 El Prado Way, Balboa Park, 619-696-0199) is an expansive 3-D topography map illustrating every inch of railroad in San Diego and Imperial counties. Visitors naturally gravitate to the interactive toy train gallery and numerous operating models — all spread over 24,000 square feet. But it is the map that actually provides the best overview of the region's vast network of track and stations. Cities and towns are illuminated by lights, which will help even the most inept map readers understand the geography. The Pacific Desert Line model is also noteworthy. It's based on blueprints from the early 1900s, showing a railroad that was supposed to begin at San Diego Harbor and hug the Mexican border into Arizona. But the line was never constructed, due to the rugged terrain between here and there. The model is 160 times smaller than actual scale. The painstaking piece of work was started by hand in 1986, and it continues taking on miniature freight yards and sidings. Open Tuesday through Saturday (10 AM to 4 PM).

Chug along tracks leading through secret Indian backcountry on steam or diesel locomotives kept polished and preserved at the **San Diego Railroad Museum** (Highway 94 and Forrest Gate Road, Campo, California, 619-595-3030). The passenger cars are relics from the 1950s and 1960s, with their original lighting fixtures and luggage racks still intact. Conductors, dressed in old-fashioned railroad attire, are quick to offer narratives on the foothills and ranches you see during your ride through the remote **Milquatay Valley**. Few San Diegans are aware of the museum, probably because it's located 61 miles from downtown — the end of the earth to most weary freeway drivers. The 90-minute rides conclude with an optional tour of the facility's car barn and restoration area. Trains run on various days of the week (11 AM and 2:30 PM). Dinner excursions are available on selected Saturdays (6:30 PM) and there's brunch on selected Sundays (11 AM).

Unearthed toothbrushes, combs, kitchen utensils, and teapots are among the artifacts originating from a secret Chinatown that existed in the early 1900s along the Downtown streets of Third, J, and Island. Excavation in the area took place about 50 years ago, during a mini wave of urban expansion. The items that surfaced, along with

yellowing photographs, are on permanent display at the **San Diego Chinese Historical Society Museum** (404 3rd Avenue, 619-338-9888), which occupies a modest Spanish-style mission that once schooled Chinese children. Its location is peaceful — about five blocks southwest of Downtown's commercial Gaslamp District. Open Tuesday through Saturday (10:30 AM to 4 PM) and Sundays (noon to 4 PM).

People come to see the hook-and-ladders. But what they don't expect to find are antiquated, hand-drawn pumpers that required the labor of 20 firemen when they were deployed to extinguish large blazes. It used to be Station 6. Now it's the **Firehouse Museum** (1572 Columbia Street, Little Italy, 619-232-3473), which also displays fire gear from around the world, plus wooden miniatures of fire-fighting equipment. And yes, there are big red fire engines — four of them dating back to the early 1900s — as well as a staff of friendly neighborhood firefighters to answer all your questions. Open Thursdays and Fridays (10 AM to 2 PM), and Saturdays and Sundays (10 AM to 4 PM).

In a nondescript building just south of Gillespie Field airstrip is the **World War II Flying Museum** (1860 Joe Crossin Road, El Cajon, California, 619-448-4505), which boasts an impressive collection of panoramic prints and memorabilia from those who fought in the war. Go behind the museum, just outside the back hangar, to find an A-26 Invader and an A-6 Sarah Nancy Jane two-seat, propeller trainer plane. A secret Stinson L-5 observation aircraft hides within the hangar. An imposing selection of static planes attached to pillars sits outside the **Flying Leatherneck Museum** (Building T-2002, Miramar Marine Corps Air Station, Miramar, 858-693-1723). A rare, permanent exhibit commemorating the history of women marines can be found inside. More publicized, but worth a visit, is the **San**

Diego Aerospace Museum (2001 Pan American Plaza, Balboa Park, 619-234-8291). The entire historical saga of flight is captured here, from the 15th-century experiments of Leonardo da Vinci to the construction of the International Space Station. You'll wonder how they squeezed more than 80 air and spacecraft inside the building, like boats in a bottle.

Before you traipse through the historic **Hotel Del Coronado** (1500 Orange Avenue, Coronado, California, 619-435-6611), you should pay a visit to the nearby **Museum of History and Art** (1100 Orange Avenue, Coronado, California, 619-435-7242). Numerous displays and photographs make it easier to visualize what life was like in the vicinity of the hotel following its construction in 1888. Those on travel budgets camped in tents on the beach. And those with the really nice bodies covered much of them up.

SECRET
NECESSITIES

Forget your underwear? **Traveler's Depot** (1655 Garnet Avenue, Pacific Beach, 858-483-1421) carries stuff that people forget to pack — or might need if they are continuing on to other destinations. Among the goods you'll find readily available are all-weather travel clothing, converters for AC and DC outlets, telephone plugs, compact hair dryers, irons, money belts, daypacks, and more. **Le Travel Store** (739 4th Avenue, Downtown, 619-544-0005) in the Gaslamp District offers a similar array of products and is more accessible if you happen to be staying Downtown.

Even if you do remember to pack all of your essentials, other calamities can strike the intrepid traveler. Recently I returned to San Diego from a trip that took a final toll on my luggage. Having been dragged down pebbly asphalt and cobblestone streets, the wheels on my valise became nothing more than shredded plastic nubs. Should you find yourself with popped zippers, broken pulley handles, or missing wheels, a handful of leather goods and shoe stores offer repair services for luggage. Among them is **John's 5th Avenue Luggage** (3833 4th Avenue, Hillcrest, 619-298-0993; and 690 Fashion Valley, Mission Valley, 619-574-0086), a high-end retailer that is also an authorized repair center for Zero Halliburton luggage. **A Walker's Luggage and Shoe Repair** (2697 Mission Village Drive, Serra Mesa, 858-278-2420) will also mend your woes. **Chito's Shoe Repair** (2911–A University Avenue, North Park, 619-298-2506) does all types of leather repair. And **Anthony's Shoe Repair** (Carmel Mountain Ranch Town Center, 11885 Carmel Mountain Road, #902, Solana Beach, California, 858-673-7207) promises professional repairs done on the premises for zippers, golf bags, handbags, briefcases, and buckles. And finally there is **Independent Luggage Repair** (7909 Silverton Avenue, #211, Miramar, 858-566-7749), offering a full repair service for all types of damage.

SECRET
NEIGHBORHOOD BARS

You want secrets? Then plant your caboose on a barstool inside one of San Diego's casual neighborhood bars. The locals like to talk in these environments. And they'll give you an earful about the ups and downs of living in San Diego, where they came from, and what they do for kicks. Better yet, you can easily end up with a new chum over a rousing game of pool.

If the regulars at **NuNu's** (3537 5th Avenue, Hillcrest, 619-295-2878) knew this was going in the book, they would probably have me banned for exposing one of the most cherished and surreptitious watering holes in San Diego. From the outside, the place looks like a boxy, closed-down steakhouse. Like many people, I drove by it for years before discovering its cozy lounge atmosphere, usually filled with hip neighborhood types. It's fiercely outdated, so it's easy to imagine a young Doris Day or Andy Williams crooning Christmas carols by the fireplace. Semi-circular red booths and drab lighting set the mood for stiff martinis and whiskey sours. A small patio in the back accommodates smokers and lends itself to easy chitchat with strangers. Near the jukebox is a shoddy door counter from which you can order bar snacks, although a hand-written sign on a paper plate tells you to shout for the cook. It's the kind of ambiance that makes you want to stay awhile.

In bar years, it's as old as the hills. **The Alibi** (1403 University Avenue, Hillcrest, 619-295-0881) was established in 1925 and operated as a speakeasy during Prohibition. Its dingy, windowless exterior remains in sharp contrast to the neon-lit businesses that flank it. Unless a gaggle of smokers is standing out front, you would never think there were living, breathing people rubbing elbows inside. I like this bar for a number of reasons. The crowd is eclectic and friendly. The jukebox carries a great selection of classic rock tunes. Bar service is quick. And the 23-ounce draft beers, called big dippers, are frosty and cheap ($2).

With a name like **Kelly's** (2222 San Diego Avenue, Old Town, 619-543-9767), you might think that it's one of those fun and rowdy Irish pubs. But step inside and you'll see that it's nothing more than a dressed down neighborhood bar that happens to serve Guinness. When the local population is out en masse on weekend evenings, this bar manages to evade the crush of people soaking up space in other places. That's because it sits several blocks outside the hubbub of Old Town, at the southerly end of the neighborhood's main street where businesses start to die out. As a result, parking is easy; bar stools and tables are always available; and the crowd is pleasantly mellow. Oddly, bar snacks are served only on weekday evenings.

Two bars that appear to be battling for San Diego's dive trophy are **The Morena Club** (1319 Morena Boulevard, Bay Park, 619-276-9109) and **O'Connell's** (1310 Morena Boulevard, Bay Park, 619-276-5637). Each stares bleakly at the other from opposite sides of the street, leaving you no choice but to try out both. The former clearly represents the underbelly of the nightlife scene — a barren interior with a few pool tables, blaring rock music, and the smell of cheap alcohol embedded in the floor. But it provides an adequate escape when you feel the world has grown too pretentious. From the outside, O'Connell's looks like a restaurant until you step inside and see nothing but beer bottles under everyone's chins. If there was ever a kitchen here, it's long been paneled in. The crowd ranges from the just-turned-21 set to the newly retired. Karaoke and live music somehow link them all together.

The Lamplighter (817 w Washington Street, Mission Hills, 619-298-3624) attracts a pure party crowd — people who like to perch at the bar to drink, and others who can't sit still when the karaoke stage opens every night (9 PM). I've seen many talented voices unleashed here by folks who might be better off spending their time at casting calls. Or is it the amateurs performing in between that make them sound so exquisite? A big square bar in the middle of the room allows for easy socializing. When hunger strikes, the **Mission Hills**

Café (808 w Washington Street, Mission Hills, 619-296-8010) is directly across the street. The atmosphere is slightly upscale, and the prix fixe dinners are always outstanding.

S E C R E T

NEW ORLEANS

I love going to stores and restaurants that make me feel as though I've been beamed down into another land the moment I walk through the door. Whether it's an Italian deli or a British market, I want to see genuine products and imported staff from the places they supposedly represent. Phony facades won't do.

Since making a few memorable trips to New Orleans, I periodically long for the flavors of Louisiana — a po'boy sandwich, traditional shrimp Creole, a sugar-dusted beignet — or any munchie that brings me back to beer-drenched Bourbon Street. With the exception of cheap voodoo sticks and party beads, **Mardi Gras Café and Market** (3185 Midway Drive, Loma Portal, 619-223-5501) has served me well. The store is small and set back from the street in an unnamed strip plaza, but it manages to pack in a slew of products and a few lunch tables. Browse the shelves for canned okra, Creole mustards, étouffée sauce, or frozen frog legs while feasting on an alligator sub sandwich or red beans and rice. The po'boys taste straight out of those French Quarter delis. And the chicory coffee and beignet mixes are shipped directly to the shop from the famous Café du Monde.

Chateau Orleans (926 Turquoise Street, Pacific Beach, 858-488-6744) has all the trappings of a French Quarter supper club — live jazz musicians; warm, dim lighting; and signature dishes expertly constructed with tasso ham, gulf shrimp, and tangy Creole sauces. The atmosphere is cultivated, although prices are surprisingly moderate. Included with the entrées are big, balloon-like popover breads, served piping hot with a side of honey butter. Everyone asks for the recipe. And you will too. The restaurant is found in Bird Rock, a mini-business district in the community of Pacific Beach, about eight blocks north of the neighborhood's main commercial hub. Reservations are recommended. (Closed on Sundays.)

Several blocks outside Downtown's historic Gaslamp District is **Bayou Dining & Jazz** (329 Market Street, Downtown, 619-696-8747), which keeps its ovens running into the wee hours of the night (1 AM). The big secret here isn't the imported gulf shrimp or pecan bread pudding or classic hurricane drinks. It's the old record player that sits at a far end of the large polished-wood bar along with the owner's vast album collection. Patrons can play the role of disc jockey by choosing albums and loading them onto the archaic turntable. Stories have been told about young Generation xers, and how they fumble with the equipment and marvel at the record covers.

If you've partied in the French Quarter and left with some memory intact, then you know about all those festive, open-air patios hidden in the backs of bars. That same architectural feature is what makes **Bourbon Street** (4612 Park Boulevard, University Heights, 619-291-0173) so popular. First-time visitors, however, will need to walk past the central indoor bar and head toward the paned-glass doors toward the back to discover this lively veranda. Though the clientele is primarily gay, the bar manages to draw in neighborhood folk of all persuasions.

SECRET
NIKI DE
SAINT PHALLE

Although the internationally beloved artist died in May 2002, her giant, whimsical sculptures live on throughout the city. De Saint Phalle, whose projects include *Noah's Ark* in Jerusalem and the sprawling *Tarot Garden* in Tuscany, resided in San Diego until her death at age 71. For the last several years of her life, she was working on a California-themed sculpture garden in **Kit Carson Park** (3333 Bear Valley Parkway, Escondido, California, 760-839-4691). The project is slated to be complete by the end of 2003 and will include a 400-foot serpentine structure surrounding a mythical "Queen Califia." But in the meantime, there are plenty of the artist's sculptures perched around town for you to see, if you're paying attention. Drive by the **Solana Beach Train Station** (corner of Lomas Santa Fe Drive and Cedros Avenue, Solana Beach, California), and you'll see one of de Saint Phalle's *Nana* sculptures, voluptuous female figures started in the mid-'60s and inspired by the pregnancy of one of her close friends. At the **University of California at San Diego** (Gillman and La Jolla Village drives, La Jolla, 858-784-0323), the towering *Sun God* serves as an unofficial mascot for the campus and the reason for a festival each spring. At the south end of the **San Diego Convention Center** (111 W Harbor Drive, Marina District, 619-525-5000) is *Coming Together*, a two-sided face with a mosaic and ceramic skins. Outside Balboa Park's **Mingei International Museum** (1439 El Prado Way, Balboa Park, 619-239-0003), where a large exhibition of de Saint Phalle's work was on display in 1998, two pieces remain: *Nikigator*

and *The Poet and His Muse*, which children love — and are encouraged to climb. The sculpture garden at the **Museum of Contemporary Art, San Diego** (700 Prospect Street, La Jolla, 858-454-3541) is graced by *Ganesh*, a huge elephant accompanied by a little dog looking up at it. And in front of the **East County Performing Arts Center** (210 E Main Street, El Cajon, California, 619-440-2277) are 10-foot-high sculptures of famous jazz musicians Miles Davis and Louis Armstrong. Trot across the street to the Prescott Promenade (on East Main Street) to see *Blue Obelisk with Flowers*.

S E C R E T
NUDITY

Clothing-optional beaches require a special mix of ingredients before they become tolerated or established: wide sands hidden from public view; low interference from municipal codes that prohibit nudity; and free-spirited denizens who couldn't give a damn about protecting their private parts when playing volleyball or loafing in the sun.

Those standards are duly met at **Black's Beach**, a two-mile sandy strip at the base of eroding, majestic cliffs, with a glider port perched 300 feet above. The beach was formerly known as Torrey Pines City Beach and Torrey Pines State Beach, because the city and state jointly own it. At the south end, below the glider port, it's mostly heterosexuals who occupy the sands. Walk further north, where the cliffs diminish slightly in height, and the demographic gives way to gay males. The winding trail leading down to the beach is a spectacular hike. Makeshift stairs and occasional dirt steps lend footing when you need it most. The path begins from the glider port's large, dusty parking lot, a few hundred yards past the entrance to the Salk Institute (10010 N Torrey Pines Road, La Jolla).

The **Swallows Sun Island Club** (1631 Harbison Canyon Road, El Cajon, California, 619-445-3754) is the area's oldest nudist colony, located about 30 minutes east of San Diego in sun-baked El Cajon. Families pull in recreational vehicles and mingle around the pool with northern "snowbirds" who trickle in between November and April. The facilities are of backcountry caliber, offering a clubhouse with pool table, tennis and volleyball courts, a children's playground, and a snack bar. About 10 rooms are available ($28 to $40), plus one private cottage ($76).

SECRET
OBSERVATORY

It all began in 1928, when the **California Institute of Technology** in Pasadena was awarded a generous grant by one of the Rockefeller foundations to build an eye-popping, 200-inch research telescope. An assiduous hunt followed for a site with perfect atmospheric conditions, while voyeuristic astronomers remained locked in excitement over the prospect of chasing down unsuspecting new galaxies. By 1934, a decision was finally made to position the instrument on a 6,126-foot peak of **Palomar Mountain** in the northeast corner of San Diego County. But the biggest task rested on the shoulders of engineers at Corning Glass Works in New York State. The 20-ton glass disk they managed to create took eight months to cool before it was ready for polishing. It wasn't until 1948 that the telescope and all its state-of-the-art components came together within a rotating dome that is now the **Palomar Observatory** (35899 Canfield Road, Palomar, California, 760-742-2119). Visitors can lay eyes on — but not through — the telescope any day of the week (9 AM to 4 PM). Since the facility is devoted to full-time research, nighttime tours are offered only on occasion through the **Reuben H. Fleet Science Center** (1875 El Prado Way, Balboa Park, 619-238-1233). The drive to Palomar takes about two hours, and the scenery at the mountain is stunning. Cool-water streams keep the area green most of the year. And the landscape is lush in ponderosa pines and bracken ferns. From the north coastal city of Oceanside, take Highway 76 to County Road s6, which leads directly to the gate of the observatory.

Gaze at the evening sky in the middle of a sunny morning on an IMAX dome screen, located inside the **Reuben H. Fleet Science Center** (see details above). Star shows are held every Saturday (10:30 AM). They depict our planet's movement through the cosmos and give audiences a peek at the seasonal sky as it appears above San Diego. Visitors will also get a behind-the-scenes look at the technology that so accurately re-creates these nighttime skies on indoor ceilings.

SECRET
OLD RIDE

This San Diego landmark recently faced an uncertain future. Tucked away beneath spreading eucalyptus trees near the carousel in Balboa Park, the **Miniature Train** (Zoo Place, off Park Boulevard, Balboa

Park, 619-239-0512) is a diminutive locomotive that tows 48 passengers around in open coach cars on a three-minute, half-mile trip through four acres of the park. It is also right next to the San Diego Zoo. When the zoo announced plans to expand into the train's territory, San Diegans roared louder than the lions; thus, zoo officials quietly revised their plans. The locomotive is one-fifth the scale of the diesels that pull the Santa Fe's Super Chief liners. It is a rare antique, with possibly fewer than 50 of its kind left in the world. The ride has resided in the park since it was introduced in 1948, and conductors still wear railroad caps and overalls. The train operates on Saturdays and Sundays, and daily during school vacations (11 AM to 5 PM).

SECRET
OLYMPICS

San Diego isn't scheduled to be the site of the Summer Olympic Games until at least . . . well, it's not even in the running. But until that day comes — or doesn't — fans of the games can watch Olympians-in-training at the ARCO/US **Olympic Training Center** (2800 Olympic Parkway, Chula Vista, California, 619-656-1500). The year-round facility in southern San Diego County is the first of its kind in the US to be master planned from the ground up. It supports nine Olympic venues: archery; rowing; canoeing and kayaking; soccer; softball; field hockey; tennis; track and field; and cycling. Free guided tours are conducted every hour, Monday through Saturday (10 AM to 3 PM), and Sundays (11 AM to 3 PM). Guests to the center can thrill to the idea that an estimated 4,000 serious athletes a year come to the 150-acre complex to receive coaching and support.

SECRET

OUTLET MALLS

It used to be that factory outlet stores had about as much architectural sheen as tin-roofed tractor barns. Shoddily displayed merchandise and minimal customer service seemed a fair exchange for deep discounts on slightly flawed goods. But in the past several years, San Diego's outlet stores have grown into cheerful-looking malls, complete with food courts, waterfalls, and luxuriant landscaping.

Carlsbad Company Stores (5620 Paseo Del Norte, Carlsbad, California, 760-804-9000), for example, offers the quintessential Southern California shopping experience for label-minded consumers, appearing not much different from the city's outdoor retail malls — **Fashion Valley** (7007 Friars Road, Mission Valley, 619-688-9100) or **Mission Center** (1081 Camino Del Rio s, Mission Valley, 619-296-7236). The 300,000-square-foot Carlsbad outlet center features more than 90 designer stores, including Donna Karan Company, Ralph Lauren, Coach Factory, Samsonite, and the famous catalog company, Harry and David. Manufacturer discounts range from 30 to 70 percent. Several eateries are also sprinkled throughout this Mediterranean-style complex, such as the upscale **Bellefleur Winery and Restaurant** (760-603-1919) and the retro-inspired **Ruby's Diner** (760-931-7829). One of the unique amenities hidden in the mall's foliage displays are "poopy bag" dispensers, which tell you that it's okay to tow along your pooch. And a breast-feeding room in the main public restroom offers a soothing, private space for new moms.

The **San Diego Factory Outlet Center** (4498 Camino de la Plaza, San Ysidro, California, 619-690-2999) is conveniently located near the Mexican border for those who want to keep on shopping after spending a day in Tijuana. The plaza recently underwent a remodeling and features 35 outlet stores, including Levi's, Carole Little, Jockey, and OshKosh B'Gosh. And in the eastern outskirts of the county, alongside the Viejas Casino (see "Secret Bingo"), the Kumeyaay Indians have built a high-end outlet mall in a colorful pueblo-village motif. Compared to other outlet malls, discounts don't run deep at the **Viejas Outlet Center** (5005 Willows Road, Alpine, California, 619-659-2070). But names such as Jones New York, Liz Claiborne, London Fog, and Koret offer considerably more stock than what you'll find in popular department stores.

SECRET
OVER THE LINE

To visitors who find themselves on **Fiesta Island** (Mission Bay) in the middle of July, the annual **Over the Line Tournament** (619-437-8788) makes no sense. Scantily clad teams consisting of three players each bat and catch balls over lines drawn in the sand amid a Super Bowl–like atmosphere fueled by enthusiastic beer-drinking dudes and babes. It's the prefect recipe for occasional bare breasts and colorful revelry. The games loosely resemble back-lot softball, except that they attract 1,150 teams that compete in 2,200 games over two consecutive weekends. Started over 50 years ago by the **Old Mission Beach Athletic Club** (3990 Old Town Avenue, Old Town, 619-688-0817), it is one of the last pure Southern California recreational games untouched by commercialism. That's an amazing phenomenon when you consider that the event attracts nearly 50,000 people.

SECRET
PEANUT BUTTER

My longtime wish of finding a restaurant where everything is made with peanut butter finally came true when I stumbled upon **Nutter's** (428 C Street, Downtown, 619-239-7075). Owners Andrew Schiff and Robin Miller arrived at the idea while analyzing a slew of everyday food products that no longer present straightforward choices. If potato chips, orange juice, and condiments can be sold in myriad flavors and blends, then why not create 25 new varieties of peanut butter? Their restaurant offers homemade nutty butters that include mint-chocolate, cinnamon-raisin, carob, super-honey, M&M, and more. Make your pick, then decide on a sandwich that complements your peanut butter. There are about 12 to choose from, including the Grilled Elvis, made with bacon, honey, and bananas. Less adventurous palates can stick with the Classic, which comes with strawberry, grape, or "mystery jelly." Or how about a power-boost salad instead? The Happy Together features your choice of two peanut butters, garnished with apple slices, celery sticks, bananas, and raisins. Nostalgic board games and Dr. Seuss books create an interactive atmosphere that brings out the kid in everyone. The eatery is located next to the 5th Avenue trolley station, about three blocks outside Downtown's Gaslamp District.

SECRET
PERSIAN

It's the size of a college dorm room, but the food and service earn the raves of neighborhood residents who find it. **Café Caspian** (4636 Park Boulevard, University Heights, 619-298-2801) caters well to vegetarians and carnivores alike. Spicy hummus, baba ghanouj, strawberry tabbouleh salad, and abgousht lamb stew are among the delectable Middle Eastern treats served up by an Iranian mother and her two daughters. The biggest table seats six — a mammoth group in a place this size. But there's only one of those, which means a reservation is required if you're visiting with a full clan.

For a reasonably priced lunch in a highly elegant setting, go to **Bandar** (825 4th Avenue, Downtown, 619-238-0101). For only $8, you'll come out feeling like you just had dinner with a shah. The beef, chicken, and lamb kabob plates are generously portioned with lots of deeply marinated meat, and two different types of fluffy basmati rice: one plain, the other embellished with lentils, raisins, and dates. You also get a hefty green salad, enough for two people, dressed up with feta cheese, olive oil, and fresh lemon juice.

SECRET
PET TREATS

Pets on vacation need luxuries too. So when you're sipping an icy margarita or wolfing down a fish taco, why not toss your furry friend a delectable treat as well? In the Uptown District's **Pet Pleasers Bakery** (1220 Cleveland Avenue, Hillcrest, 619-293-7297), pampered dogs and cats can share the goodies with their generous owners, because everything in the store is edible by humans, too. How does apple-walnut "barklavah" sound? Or peanut butter mousse cake? The "dogolate" chip cookies and non-dairy vanilla yogurt are particularly luscious. Felines have less to choose from. Dehydrated "skittles" of calamari, chicken, and liver, packaged as Itty Bitty Kitty Treats, keep cat grudges at bay if you return home with these in your luggage. The store occasionally throws pet birthday parties and "barkmitzvahs." Open Monday through Friday (10 AM to 6 PM), Saturdays (9 AM to 6 PM), and Sundays (10 AM to 4 PM).

Pet Me Please (3401 Adams Avenue, Normal Heights, 619-283-5020) doesn't hold bakery status, but serves the surrounding neighborhood with all-natural foods for dogs and cats, sans the hormones or preservatives. Among the rarer items is Perfect Servings — dried meat stew that you prepare by adding hot water.

SECRET
PIANO BARS

Black leather booths, red carpeting, and Rubenesque paintings of nudes on the walls set the stage for a lively, sing-along piano bar that attributes 40 years of success to word-of-mouth advertising. Unless you're staying in one of the small budget hotels along the street, otherwise devoid of nightlife, chances are great that you won't stumble upon **Albie's** (1201 Hotel Circle South, Mission Valley, 619-291-1103). The antiquated lounge has an underground feel to it — about 10 chairs encircle the piano in a dining room packed with adults who come itching to sing. The house pianist shows up Tuesday through Saturday (6:30 PM to midnight). Weekdays generally attract single and married revelers over 40, although the age demographic runs the gamut on weekends, when jazz and contemporary numbers get mixed in with popular show tunes. Full dinner menus are available.

The fireplace and Tudor paneling bear the date 1642. They were hauled over from England 35 years ago, along with wood-carved figures of people that peer from behind the bar at **The Red Fox Room** (2223 El Cajon Boulevard, North Park, 619-297-1313). The longstanding love affair between piano music and steak suppers is celebrated nightly in this dimly lit neighborhood restaurant. Pianist Shirley Allen adds a sense of permanence to the place; she's played here for 13 years and is joined sometimes by a drummer and horn player. Reasonable dinner prices attract mixed age groups. And the archetypal dark-red booths add coziness to the wonderfully outdated ambiance.

The Caliph (3100 5th Avenue, Hillcrest, 619-298-9495) is a popular neighborhood haunt for mature gay men who remember when plush piano bars competed with the hedonistic disco scene. This little cocktail parlor is a throwback to the '70s — still cozy and well maintained. It pulls in pianists (Mondays, Wednesdays, and Fridays) who are adept at interacting playfully with the customers by occasionally handing them the microphone.

SECRET
PICNICS

If there are more than five other picnickers in eyeshot, then it's really not a secret picnic — is it? San Diego has plenty of open park grounds for plopping down a blanket and spreading out the sandwiches. On almost any given weekend, for example, the grasses along **East Mission Bay Drive** near the **Hilton San Diego Resort** (1775 E Mission Bay Drive, Mission Bay, 619-275-7920) are overlaid with wiener-roasting folk who arrive early to stake out tables close to the water or under shady trees. Scores of other spots are scattered throughout **Mission Bay Park**, a 4,600-acre aquatic wonderland filled with jigsaw-shaped inlets and verdant shores offering tables and fire pits. Families with children especially love the ample grounds at the northwest section of **Balboa Park** (between 6th Avenue and Balboa Drive). The area is stocked with plenty of tables and children's playground equipment. And if you're lucky enough to land one of the few picnic tables in **Scripps Park** at **La Jolla Cove** (1100 Coast Boulevard, La Jolla), you can peek down the sandstone cliffs and spy on snorkelers while your burger cooks.

My favorite secret place for a picnic is on top of a grassy knoll overlooking the western end of Mission Valley. If you're okay with sitting on the grass on this tiny patch of park space, you can look across I-8 to the white, Moroccan-like buildings of the **University of San Diego** (5998 Alcalá Park, Linda Vista, 619-260-4600). Just a few yards away are two picnic tables, set back from the edge of the hill down a few antiquated stone stairs. You'll lose your view but gain additional shade from an umbrella of fat old palm trees. Steps away, you'll discover some little-used hiking trails that meander into the

deep, green canyon separating this hill from an adjacent one known as **Presidio Park**. That side is clearly marked by the **Junipero Serra Museum** (2727 Presidio Drive, Mission Hills, 619-297-3258), a chalk-colored, mission-style building that was built in 1929. The museum serves as your landmark for getting to the picnic spot. From its base on Taylor Street, look for an unmarked, paved road that resembles a steeply graded private driveway. It's about 50 yards west of the I-8 on-ramp. Take it to the top, where it ends at a parking lot. Then walk toward the edge of the hill and turn left.

Few picnickers take advantage of the long, narrow strip of grass that runs between **Shelter Island Drive** and the waters of **San Diego Bay**. The grounds are located on yacht-infested **Shelter Island**, an elongated sub-peninsula of Point Loma that sticks into the bay like a small hook. Picnic tables appear about every 50 yards, beginning from the popular restaurant-resort-concert venue, **Humphrey's by the Bay** (2241 Shelter Island Drive, Shelter Island, 619-224-3577). They continue to the western tip, past a small pier, to the point where the road loops back east at the **Japanese Friendship Bell**. The bell, by the way, was presented to San Diego in 1958 by our Japanese sister-city, Yokohama, as a symbol of eternal friendship. The picnic tables at that end are much quieter. But no matter where you plop down, the environment offers occasional sightings of brown pelicans, great blue herons, and harbor seals. California gulls are guaranteed.

If you walk toward Downtown from the ticket windows at **Harbor Excursions** (1050 N Harbor Drive, Marina District, 619-234-4111), the street soon turns into a promenade leading into the colorful, touristy shopping plaza of **Seaport Village** (Kettner Boulevard and W Harbor Drive, Marina District, 619-235-4014). Halfway between is a succession of underutilized concrete tables and benches that make for a perfect urban picnic, provided you can co-exist with a few homeless stragglers. The area is set far enough away from street traffic to make it a relatively peaceful spot for a casual lunch, with the bay in full view.

SECRET
PIMP
❀

Normally, when people rent limousines, they want handsome cars with exquisite amenities that make them feel like rich tycoons or glamorous Hollywood celebrities. They want to outclass their friends, just as the limousine companies strive to outdo their competition with more luxuries and better white-glove service. But all those formalities fly straight out the sunroof when you hop into a purple stretch vehicle from **Pimp Daddy Limos** (866-876-7467, www.pimpdaddylimos. com). Right down to the cheetah-print seats, these garish stretch limos look like customized pimp suits from the 1970s. Red pillows shaped like lips, white fur roofs, interior fog machines, and flashing disco lights amount to nothing less than a party on wheels. Each car also comes equipped with 13-inch flat-screen televisions, Sony Playstations, a bar, and, of course, those long-forgotten disco balls.

SECRET
PIZZA
❀

Ask any "back east" transplant (and there are many) about a good place to go for pizza, and you'll get an answer fraught with 0expletives. San Diego has a lot going for itself in the way of culinary offerings, but pizza isn't one of them. I'm originally from Buffalo, New York, a town with as many Italian restaurants as snow blowers. And I think that I've figured out the recipe problem over the past two decades while searching for that perfect slice. A low-humidity climate makes for cardboard crusts. And for some reason, oregano is usually lacking in the sauces. But don't become completely discouraged until you visit a few of the places that bake up excellent pizza pies — and defy the Southern California standard.

The restaurant's name is the first clue that the pizza is terrific. The smell outside is the second. **Bronx Pizza** (111 Washington Street, Hillcrest, 619-291-3341) is owned and operated by Bronx natives, some of whom outgrew careers in professional boxing, as evidenced by photos of their ring matches covering the walls. Since opening in 1997, the single-structure eatery (not much bigger than a neighborhood dry cleaner) has never been deserted. Seating capacity tops off at 30, with most customers relegated to the back patio. Pizzas come in various sizes, although people drop in mainly for the ever-present slices, displayed without pretense in the glass-faced order counter. Whole-milk mozzarella, plum tomatoes, and fresh yeast give these pizzas their New York flair. A word of caution about parking: spaces that are usually available at the Laundromat next door are tow traps. Luck and determination are needed to find a spot on the street.

You know there is a shortage of prize-winning pizzerias when a menu states that the pizzas are free of fake cheese, canned vegetables, and mock soybean meats. Modeled loosely after a police station, **New York Pizza Department** (6110 Friars Road, Mission Valley, 619-296-0911) restores culinary law and order with hand-tossed dough, whole mozzarella, and fresh meats and herbs. If you opt for delivery, expect your law-abiding pizza, albeit with its extra-thin crust, to arrive in a vehicle modeled after a police car.

Taste of Italy (1013 University Avenue, Hillcrest, 619-688-0336) isn't as hard to find as a table on weekend evenings is. Savory, bubbly pizzas include traditional mozzarella and pepperoni, as well as specialty types that incorporate cream cheese, Greek toppings, or jalapeño peppers. The big secret is that the dining room stays open until 2 AM, long after the lights go out in neighboring restaurants. Calzones, baked pasta dishes, and submarine sandwiches drizzled with an outstanding house dressing round out the menu.

Pizza always tastes better for some reason when it's served on red-and-white-checkered tablecloths. **Filippi's** (1747 India Street, 619-232-5094) is the godfather of San Diego's old-fashioned Italian restaurants, located appropriately in the heart of Little Italy. You're greeted first by the smell of aged cheeses and dried, salted codfish displayed in the restaurant's front store. The dining sections in the back bring you within eyeshot of the busy pizza ovens. And a thick canopy of old Chianti wine bottles dangles from the ceilings in defiance of the region's potential for earthquakes. The pies, along with classic spaghetti and meatball plates, receive no interference from contemporary food trends.

SECRET
POLISH

It took me several years to find homemade pierogies after moving to San Diego. Old Eastern European dishes common on the East Coast seem incongruous in this city's culinary landscape of trendy restaurants, Mexican taco huts, and fast-food joints. Say "pierogi" to a native and you'll be asked if it's some nouveau vegetarian dish. Or ask about the **Cottage Café** (2351 5th Avenue, Middletown, 619-696-0071), and you'll find that nobody's ever heard of it. The homey restaurant, owned by a Russian immigrant, offers two different kinds of hot, buttered pierogies: potato and cheese, and cabbage and mushroom. Better yet, a few of them get tossed into the restaurant's hearty Polish combo, along with one stuffed cabbage roll, a large Polish sausage link, garlic mashed potatoes, sauerkraut, and bread — all for $9.99.

SECRET
PROPHYLACTICS

In San Diego, there's no need to go to the drugstore and hem and haw and blush when you want to buy condoms. A quick stop at **Sensual Delights** (1220 University Avenue, Hillcrest, 619-291-7400) opens the doors to a variety of rubbery necessities that you may not even know exist. The staff will matter-of-factly discuss the features of various brands, and perhaps educate you on the uses of some of the exotic apparel and personal gratification devices on the shelves. A demure young friend of mine, who popped into the store with me on a lark, received a full narration about dental dams when she merely pointed at them out of curiosity. Their uses are also explained in some of the store's books that focus on safe foreplay. If such topics should ever come up at a cocktail party, my friend can now enter the conversation with confidence — and give advice.

SECRET
PUPPETS

Finding an art museum in Balboa Park isn't unusual — but a puppet theater is an unexpected discovery. The **Balboa Park Puppet Guild** (www.balboaparkpuppets.com), which performs regularly, is regarded as one of the best in the world when it comes to working with marionettes, as well as hand, rod, and shadow puppets. The troupe stages its shows in the **Marie Hitchcock Puppet Theater** (2130 Pan American Road West, Balboa Park, 619-685-5990), in the Palisades area of Balboa Park. The site frequently hosts visiting puppet companies from all over the globe. Morning and early afternoon programs are offered Wednesday through Sunday. The theater is named after a quirky but tireless woman who created and produced puppet shows for San Diego's children until she died in the '90s. The thriving theater and its ongoing shows are a fitting memorial to her vision.

SECRET
RANCHES

One of San Diego's greatest secrets is the large number of expensive and exclusive homes that are tucked far away from the public eye, camouflaged by craggy hills and deep canyons. But some you can find by zigzagging around the county. **Rancho Zosa** (9381 W Lilac Road, Escondido, California, 760-723-9093), a private estate high atop a mesa, fits the category well — and offers a few fun twists. The first one: 5,000 guava trees grow on the property, along with citrus and avocado trees, all mixed in with bougainvillea. Twist number two: weddings are regularly booked on the property — by very wealthy parents, I'm guessing. And the last twist: this is one San Diego ranch you can stay at overnight. A waterfall and arched bridge, a koi pond with water lilies, and the flower-perfumed breezes blowing in from the Pacific Ocean all add up to a hypnotic charm that may hold you hostage longer than you planned. Being in the heart of the Temecula wine-producing countryside adds further appeal. Those 5,000 guava trees, by the way, yield the fruit that appears on the ranch's breakfast tables every morning. Finally, rubbing elbows with the well-to-do in the Jacuzzi or pool might just give you that once-in-a-lifetime brush with fame. Rooms are priced from $125 to $250 per night.

Rancho Buena Vista Adobe (651 E Vista Drive, Vista, California, 760-639-6164) was one of the first structures erected in the North County area of San Diego, having been built over 150 years ago. This curious little slice of history is the best preserved of the fabled Mexican land-grant ranchos, originally deeded by Governor Pio Pico in 1845. It sits inside a small patch of verdant parkland right in the middle of the bustling commercial district of Vista. The hacienda inside offers a quiet taste of a slower-paced era. Originally part of a 1,184-acre land grant, it was a working ranch in its day, but it now hosts a gift shop with books about San Diego County history as well as artifacts from the ranch's earlier years of operation. A good friend of mine says she always takes out-of-town guests to see the ranch, and caps the day with a delicious Mexican feast at **La Paloma Restaurant** (116 Escondido Avenue, Vista, California, 760-758-7140), just steps away from the site.

Rancho Guajome Adobe (2210 N Santa Fe Avenue, Oceanside, California, 760-724-4082), also in the North County area, is a spectacular, restored 20-room adobe ranch house that was the area's center of social life during the 1800s. The Bandini family, well known in San Diego for their eponymous restaurant in the city's Old Town neighborhood, originally occupied the ranch. Now a national historic landmark, it was originally built with huge profits from the cattle boom of the 1850s. The house was vibrant in its day, hosting extravagant fiestas, lively rodeos, and a steady stream of visitors from all over Southern California. A noted author of the day, Helen Hunt Jackson, stayed here while she gathered material for her famous novel *Ramona*. The adjacent **Guajome County Park** also offers a natural riparian area, marshes, spring-fed lakes, picnicking, hiking, horseback riding, fishing, and camping.

SECRET
RETRO NOVELTIES

Betty Page clocks, nursery rhyme coloring books, and Mary Jane candies are among the bygone wares that evoke twinges of nostalgia when you browse the single-aisle shop **Dime Store Retro** (449 5th Avenue, 619-232-8080.) Always good for a laugh are those plastic smoking donkeys, which dispense cigarettes through their rear ends after you push down on the ears. The shop is located in Downtown's bustling Gaslamp District, but you'll have to walk to the far south end of 5th Avenue to find it.

One of my favorite places to shop for oddball greeting cards and kitschy gifts is at **Babette Schwartz** (421 University Avenue, Hillcrest, 619-220-7048). Named after its drag-queen owner, who performs at various nightclubs around town, the store stocks an inventory that changes often to keep up with pop-culture trends, both past and present. Everything from grow-your-own Sea Monkey kits and Spam cookbooks to bead curtains and colorful Mexicana makes the hunt for souvenirs a rather playful experience.

S E C R E T

ROTATING HOME

It took more than 100 specialty parts and a three-horsepower motor to get Al and Janet Johnstone's opulent home moving in a smooth, circular motion. The modern 8,500-square-foot residence known as the **Rotating Home** (4903 Mount Helix Drive, La Mesa, California) can be seen several tiers below the north side of **Mount Helix** when you're driving up the street from the base of the hill. The retirees designed the circular house themselves and have begun marketing the blueprints to others who want to their new homes to revolve too (www.rotatinghome.com). Just think — no more fussing over which rooms should face certain directions, because occupants get to see their favorite views from all major chambers. From an outside perspective, the dwelling imparts a startling contrast to the more conventional habitats dotting the hillside.

SECRET
SANDCASTLES

Some tower to nearly 40 feet. Others are so rich in medieval detail that you can't believe they were constructed with only trowels, buckets, and crafty bare hands. The three-day US **Open Sandcastle Competition** (Seacoast Drive, Imperial Beach, California, 619-424-3571) registers about 40 sand carvers each year between mid- and late July, when tides are at their lowest. Sand carvers are given 50 square feet to erect their fortresses and vie for the $10,000 grand prize. About 300,000 spectators turn out. One can't help but wish that these architectural wonders could grace the beach forever. But they're destroyed in a merry frenzy on the third day after judging.

SECRET
SCALPERS

Sports fans wishing to buy or sell coveted seats at **Qualcomm Stadium** (9449 Friars Road, Mission Valley, 619-641-3100) can usually find success about two miles west of the venue on Friars Road, between the Highway 163 overpass and Hazard Center Place. The scalpers come out in droves when the San Diego Chargers graduate to the NFL playoffs, or when opposing teams with strong fan bases roll into town. This long-tolerated mini–black market, only a block long, also springs up when the San Diego Padres are enjoying a winning season or when an occasional big-name music group tours through. The scalpers stand along the south side of the street, but there is no shoulder between the street and the curb, which means consumers must negotiate quickly amid the flow of traffic.

S E C R E T
SCHNITZEL

Don't be misled. Those little red A-frame food stands you're likely to see around town, called **Wienerschnitzel** (101 Washington Street, Hillcrest, 619-298-6483; or 1852 Rosecrans Street, Point Loma, 619-224-1197), do *not* serve the real thing. They're okay if you want a fast, cheap chilidog or burger. But the franchise pays no respect to the traditional German-Austrian schnitzel, which is a breaded pork or veal filet, pan fried in butter and served with lemon wedges. Since schnitzel isn't easily found here, it's no wonder so many San Diegans associate the word *schnitzel* with wieners.

The Kaiserhof (2253 Sunset Cliffs Boulevard, Ocean Beach, 619-224-0606) offers several varieties of schnitzel in pork or veal, all coated nicely with traditional breading but enhanced with different toppings. The imperial version, for example, comes with a mantle of grilled Black Forest ham and melted Swiss cheese; another is topped with mushrooms and rich German gravy. Wash it all down with an imported Paulaner pilsner in the restaurant's outdoor beer garden, and the enormous distance between Deutschland and San Diego starts to shrink.

The schnitzels are wider and thinner at **Old Country Restaurant and Deli** (7097 University Avenue, La Mesa, California, 619-460-

7942). They're especially fun to eat when accordion players take the stage Thursday through Saturday. The menu also features classic, slow-cooked sauerbraten, fresh apple strudel, German keg beers, and sweet white wines from the Rhine Valley. Imported sauerkraut, tangy mustards, and homemade spaetzle noodles can be purchased in the restaurant's adjoining store.

The labor that goes into pounding out veal and pork filets by hand is bypassed with the aid of a tenderizing machine at **Tiptop Meats** (6118 Paseo del Norte, Carlsbad, California, 760-438-2620). Located about 20 miles up the coast, it's part restaurant, part meat market. The automated equipment used to prepare the schnitzels makes them a little less authentic. Even some of the employees have confided that the dish is slightly Americanized. The red cabbage sauerkraut, however, doesn't cut corners. Seating is available on a flower-filled patio or in an indoor dining room replete with pictures of German castles.

SECRET
SCULPTORS

While you're driving on Torrey Pines Road along the campus perimeter of the **University of California at San Diego** (Gillman and La Jolla Village Drive, La Jolla, 858-534-2230), a mysterious red shoe appears as though it's loping through a grove of nearby eucalyptus trees. Colorful jewels lie in its wake, leaving spectators baffled as to where the shoe is headed, or how it got there. The cutting-edge sculpture is one of 15 sprinkled around the university's 1,200 acres as part of a bold art experiment known as the **Stuart Collection**.

Conceived in 1982 by the late visionary art patron James DeSilva, the ongoing project brings together site-specific works by leading artists, many of whom were better known for artistic achievements in other media before creating their first outdoor sculptures. The sculptures' backdrop includes natural chaparral-filled canyons, green lawns, urban plazas, and a potpourri of architectural styles ranging from California cottages and World War II barracks to structures built in the 1960s. At the university's Media Center, an installment called *Something Pacific* features several ruined television sets embedded in the landscape. Some are paired with Buddhas, and one with a tiny Sony Watchman.

SECRET
SECOND HELPINGS

You'll hear it blurted from every table: "Oh my God!" Shockingly huge portions of vertical cuisine are the towering trademarks of **Hash House A Go Go** (3628 5th Avenue, Hillcrest, 619-298-4646), where a simple breakfast of hash and eggs turns out to be your next two meals of the day. The menu subscribes to the "more is better" adage, as food portions become even more colossal into the lunch and dinner hours. Meat and fish entrées depend on fresh vegetables, potatoes, and wispy branches of fresh rosemary to obtain their great heights. Unfinished victuals are neatly boxed and placed into brown-paper, grocery-size bags for easy hauling.

S E C R E T
SHAKESPEARE

San Diego isn't home to a world-renowned Shakespeare festival, but it's a good place to find free plays by the famous bard in surprising venues, along with opportunities to try your own hand at iambic pentameter. To start with, I would be remiss not to say that the **Old Globe Theatre in Balboa Park** (1363 Old Globe Way, Balboa Park, 619-239-2255) offers at least two professional Shakespeare productions in the summer/fall season on one or more of its three stages (see "Secret Theater"). But the big secret is that there are a few places where you can take in Shakespeare productions at no cost. The **Coronado Playhouse** (1775 Strand Way, Coronado, California, 619-435-4856) presents its annual free **Outdoor Summer Shakespeare Festival** to the delight of playgoers who view the plays from folding chairs and blankets on the grass of this small outdoor theater. If you want to be more than just a common spectator, then pick up a script, brush up your English accent, and read the parts of Othello, Rosalind, and other famous characters with the **Semi-Spontaneous Shakespeare Society** (www.semishake.org). Visitors can let down their guard by reading scenes from selected plays with the help of a role master. The fun takes place at two locations in **Balboa Park** — the front lawn of the **Botanical Building** and at **Zoro Garden**, just west of the **Reuben H. Fleet Science Center** (1875 El Prado Way, Balboa Park, 619-238-1233). There are no rehearsals. Participation is free, with donations accepted. Enough said. Get thee to a play!

SECRET
SHAWARMA

The origin of shawarma remains in conflict. Restaurant proprietors who specialize in it will send you on a wild goose chase through Lebanon, Turkey, Israel, and even parts of India if you conduct a background check on these thin strips of marinated meat, tucked usually into thin pita bread. When it's made to my liking, I stop caring where it comes from. At **Falafel King** (3715 India Street, Mission Hills, 619-235-2627), the meat of choice is chicken, tenderized correctly in yogurt, lemon juice, and a fair dose of garlic. It's cooked appropriately in a rotating cage in front of an open flame, and served with a luscious homemade tahini sauce.

SECRET
SHOES

Sandwiched among a plethora of unique gift shops and restaurants in Hillcrest is a European-inspired shoe store called **Mint** (525 University Avenue, Hillcrest, 619-291-6468). It opened in the summer of 2002 to the delight of shoe shoppers looking for footwear that doesn't exist at average department stores — unique, trendy styles at prices ranging from $30 to $150. The long, tunnel-like design of the store is a big draw in itself. The shoes, divided with men's on the left and women's on the right, seem to float in the air from their aluminum peg perches against the store's soothing mint-green walls. Women will discover European brands such as NM70 and Miss Sixty, and all manner of Mary Jane styles, including sporty numbers with athletic racing stripes. Men will find a lot of the usual suspects from Adidas and Puma, but in limited editions not carried in malls or mainstream shoe stores. Owner Erik Kramer takes his cue from European shoe stores when he travels there for buying trips. The result is a tight line of merchandise reserved for shoes, meaning that nary an accessory, shoelace, or related shoe product can be found.

SECRET
SHORTCUTS

Most San Diego freeways run true to the four main compass points: north, south, east, and west. But motoring around on these five- and six-lane arteries could prove disorienting nonetheless. Craggy canyons slice through many neighborhoods. And lofty sun-baked bluffs impede views of territories that hide in the yonder. Rugged and sometimes confusing, it's the kind of topography that makes San Diego so visually arresting yet calls for a few good shortcuts off the hustling interstates.

Take **Harbor Drive** when traveling between Downtown and scenic Point Loma. From its northern end, the six-mile street cuts away from the city's urban hub past the square-rigged *Star of India* vessel, built in 1863 on the Isle of Man. A poor man's harbor dotted with shanty boats ensues. And a few miles past is San Diego's central commercial airport, Lindbergh Field. The drive ends conveniently at Rosecrans

Street in Point Loma, where you can connect to Highway 209 for quintessential views of the Pacific Ocean from 422 feet above sea level. Look east from the tip of this quiet peninsula, and the entrance to San Diego Harbor makes sense. Point Loma is also home to the Cabrillo National Monument, two historic lighthouses, and tide pools that fill up with squirmy marine life when the water recedes.

It was originally constructed for parking access and emergency use at the University of California at San Diego Medical Center. But local cyclists, walkers, and motorists couldn't resist the direct link **Bachman Place** provides between two popular areas: retail-rich Mission Valley and artsy Hillcrest. I've been sneaking up and down this steeply graded road for years, long before restrictions on public use were lifted. From its Mission Valley base at the Holiday Inn (595 Hotel Circle s), the pavement looks as though it ascends to nowhere. Three-quarters of a mile up, however, you land in residential Hillcrest. Make a left at Lewis Street, then a right on 4th Avenue to enter the neighborhood's colorful commercial center, which spans nearly 14 blocks along University Avenue.

You can avoid the freeways when alternating between Downtown and Hillcrest by taking a straight drive, or four-mile cakewalk, down some of the one-way numbered streets that offer quieter passage. If you're motoring to Downtown, go south on **6th** or **4th Avenues** from University Avenue. Drive north up **5th Avenue** from Broadway to return to Hillcrest.

SECRET

SINGLES

San Diego boasts a thriving singles community, and it has served as a sexy backdrop for countless reality TV dating shows because of its trendy restaurants, ethnically mixed nightclubs, and brightly colored theme parks. The scene is less fast track than Los Angeles's, and far more approachable than those you'll find in other secondary cities throughout North America.

For over 10 years, **Darlena's Turning Point** (858-259-6166) has been throwing late-night dance parties twice a week for singles over 30. They attract up to 200 single men and women per event. Casually dressed singles start blanketing the dance floor on Tuesdays (7:30 PM) at the **94th Aero Squadron** (8885 Balboa Avenue, Kearny Mesa, 858-560-6771), after mingling over a complimentary buffet. Or you can "dress to impress" at Darlena's Saturday bashes (8 PM) in the **Four Points Sheraton Hotel Skies Lounge** (8110 Aero Drive, Kearny Mesa, 858-277-8888). The music menu at both dances ranges from contemporary to "romantic slows." Admission for either event is $10.

The **San Diego Tall Club** (858-693-8255) organizes events around town where "lofty" guests can meet and socialize with other tall people. For those more bent on securing mutual food interests, the **Single Gourmet** (437 J Street, Suite 311, Downtown, 619-233-1661) brings single visitors together at hip, fine dining restaurants in Coronado, La Jolla, and throughout metropolitan San Diego. Prices range from $35 for happy hours to $85 for dinner or theater outings.

The **Athletic Singles Association of Southern California** (2725 Jefferson Street, Carlsbad, California, 760-434-4700; and 3435

Camino Del Rio s, #217, Mission Valley, 858-530-2114) has a very active chapter in San Diego, catering to active, sports-minded individuals. Activities include cycling, tennis, volleyball, softball, and more. About 12 events are held each week. Sporting equipment is provided.

A diverse roster of events is offered each month through **Unlimited Adventures** (1010 University Avenue, Hillcrest, 619-525-7892), which claims responsibility for 10 marriages since it was founded in 1997. Members and guests get acquainted through theater events, movies, karaoke bars, hiking excursions, and picnics.

SECRET
SLEEPING QUARTERS

Parents think they're cute wooden beds for kids to test out. But in actuality, they were the bunks designed for adult immigrants sailing from England to New Zealand during the late 19th century. The *Star of India* (1492 N Harbor Drive, Centre City, 619-234-9153), built in 1863, is the world's oldest surviving sailing vessel. It's berthed in San Diego Harbor along a walking promenade, just blocks away from the city's ever-growing downtown skyline. The rebuilt beds, one level below the main deck, are testimony to our own physical evolution; we've become noticeably taller than the 13-year-olds who today fit snugly into these historic sleeping spaces. Docked in the same location are two other antiquated vessels of note, all part of the **San Diego Maritime Museum** (619-234-9153): the *Medea*, built around 1903; and the *Berkeley*, constructed in the late 1800s.

SECRET
SMOKE

Smokers beware. San Diegans are generally the most intolerant people in the world when it comes to cigarette smoke. They'll cough, scoff, and even yell at you when you're puffing in wide-open public spaces. It's ironic when surfers and cyclists, who fry their skin in the California sun all day, become more threatened by a waft of high-flying smoke than by the ultraviolet rays they bathe in. I agree that their concerns over personal health may be incontestable — and I'm trying to avoid editorializing. But the state's ban on workplace smoking remains fraught with contradictory technicalities that allow smoking on some restaurant patios, yet prohibit it from others because of a few structural beams crossing overhead. Conversely, businesses that operate as tobacco vendors, and employ fewer than five people, can legally allow smoking indoors. My European friends in particular find the rules perplexing when they visit. Pointing them to various smoke shops around town has become a far easier task than explaining where they can't light up.

Tobacco is sold in all forms at **Holy Smoke** (1080 University Avenue, Hillcrest, 619-294-3529). The shop is set back from the street in a popular shopping plaza and doesn't allow smoking inside. It carries all major brands of cigarettes, loose tobacco, and imported cigars such as Dunhill, Don Thomas, and Romeo and Juliet. **Puff N Stuff Smoke Shop** (3837 Park Boulevard, Hillcrest, 619-574-0455) sells only designer-flavored tobaccos, such as cherry, chocolate, and clove. However, the biggest selection of domestic and European cigarettes is found at **Inhale** (548 5th Avenue, Hillcrest, 619-239-4253). It also carries ultra-fragrant clove cigarettes from obscure Indonesian vendors. Downtown, inside a narrow storefront, is the lounge-like **Gran Havana Cigar Factory** (560 5th Avenue, 619-338-0780), which rolls all of its cigars on the premises with imported Cuban tobacco leaves. Cigarette smoking is allowed inside.

Bargain hunters can evade the state's escalating tobacco tax at **Cigarettes Cheaper** (5665 Balboa Avenue, Kearny Mesa, 858-571-9271), where special promotions on brand-name cigarettes come and go. The **World Duty Free Shop** (5775 Camiones Way, San Ysidro, California, 619-662-2028), near the Mexican border, offers brand-name cartons for nearly 50 percent less than commercial retailers. But there are two catches: only one carton per person can be purchased, and you must cross into Mexico.

Trendy Turkish-style hookah lounges ruffle purist San Diegans for two reasons: they blatantly defy the city's anti-smoking mindset, and they generally attract 20-something folk, whom we assume don't know any better. Customers toke on flavored tobaccos from ornate tabletop water pipes called hookahs while lazing on couches with their coffee drinks. Tobacco is usually sold in three-ounce measures for $10, which take about an hour to burn. Disposable mouthpieces that attach to the tips of multiple suction hoses are included in the package. The atmosphere is decidedly hip and relaxing at **Xen Hookah Lounge and Coffee Shop** (1263 University Avenue, Hillcrest, 619-543-0984). But fuller food menus are available at both **Fumari** (330 G Street, Downtown, 619-238-4949) and **Sinbad Café and Hookah Bar** (1050 Garnet Avenue, Pacific Beach, 858-866-6006).

S E C R E T
SPAS

San Diego County is home to one of the most secretive and expensive spas in the country. It's so private and exclusive that the staff will not reveal the exact address until you have a confirmed reservation. But I already know it. The **Golden Door** (777 Deer Springs Road, Escondido, California, 760-744-5777) was established in the 1950s as a fitness getaway for the super rich and famous. Since then, patrons have continued popping in and out in private jets and limousines, many of them A-list celebrities and business moguls. For a little more than $6,200 per week, visitors are provided rooms with soothing Japanese-style décor, ample meditation time, body wraps, scalp treatments, and just about any service having to do with hairdressing. A friend of a friend who used to work at the spa's salon claims he washed and snipped Barbra Streisand's locks here several years ago. There is no need to tow along a clunky suitcase, because the facility provides customers with daily warm-up suits, T-shirts, shorts, and cotton *yukata* robes for dinnertime and evening activities.

Julia Roberts and Michelle Pfeiffer are nuts about the deep conditioning treatments for tresses. And Oprah Winfrey apparently loved the food so much that she lured away the chef. It's perhaps one of the most intimate high-end spa retreats in the western United States, where five employees are assigned to a single guest. **Cal-A-Vie** (29402 Spa Haven's Way, Vista, California, 760-945-2055) is located approximately 40 miles north of downtown San Diego, within a gated 200-acre property that allows a maximum of 24 guests at a time. Individual French country cottages looking out to mountainous vistas serve as the bunks. Visitors are lavished with spa meals, European body treatments, and individually tailored exercise programs. One of the unique services is the cranial sacral massage, meant to eradicate all that cranium pressure you checked in with. Three-day packages run $2,495 and one-week stays begin at $4,995. Complimentary ground transportation is provided to and from the airport.

In a noisy urban setting lies a remarkably quiet place where worn-down urbanites can rest their weary soles. **Anatomy Day Spa and Boutique** (1205 University Avenue, Hillcrest, 619-296-6224) is tucked into a trendy retail district among vintage clothing shops, furniture showrooms, legendary bars — even an upscale hardware store. At first glance it appears to be a small, chic establishment. But its size belies the eye. Behind the comfortable sitting area is a warmly lit corridor dressed in soothing sand and sage tones. It dips and curves, leading to a succession of treatment rooms that doesn't seem to end. The spa offers a menu of services based on its philosophy of beauty for body and spirit, the most enjoyable of which may be the spa pedicure. Sip Aveda comforting tea from a pristinely white china cup while one of the excellent staffers ministers to your tootsies with exfoliating scrubs and aromatic lotions. Toenails are then buffed to a natural, high-gloss finish. The foot massage, which uses reflexology, puts the pep back in your step. Other services include skin-cleansing treatments, facials, body wraps, and waxing. The spa is open Sundays (10 AM to 6 PM), Monday through Thursday (10 AM to 8 PM), Fridays (9 AM to 8 PM), and Saturdays (9 AM to 7 PM).

SECRET
SQUARE DANCING

San Diego may be the sixth largest city in the nation, but many of its residents still fancy themselves settlers in a frontier outpost. The **San Diego Circulators** (619-464-0135) could fall into that category. The group gets together every Friday evening at the **Recital Hall** in Balboa Park, across the parking lot from the **San Diego Hall of Champions Sport Museum** (2131 Pan American Plaza, Balboa Park, 619-234-2544). They promenade, alaman left, and do-si-do at the plus level, which means that you better know your stuff if you want to play with them. They do welcome the public, and they use a "single rotation board" to make sure non-partnered guests get a chance to hit the dance floor during the night.

The **Flying A Squares** (858-569-7810) host dances on Thursday evenings at 9:30 PM at the **War Memorial Building** (3325 Zoo Drive, Balboa Park). This is an advanced-level group. So if you know your dance calls and are ready to boogie with the big boys, then stop by for lessons (6:30 PM to 8 PM).

When the caller shouts, "grab your partner and promenade," it's boys with the boys and girls with the girls at **San Diego's Finest City Squares** club (619-223-8746). Serving the LGBT community in the San Diego area, the club conducts classes for all skill levels at **The Flame** (3780 Park Boulevard, Hillcrest, 619-295-4163) on Wednesday evenings from 6:30 PM to 8:30 PM. New sessions start periodically, so call ahead. The group also holds monthly dances on the second Saturday of the month from 6:30 PM to 9:30 PM at the **Kensington Community Church Recreation Hall** (4773 Marlborough Drive, Kensington, 619-284-1129). Admission is $6.

SECRET
SURVIVORS

So often when we hear the word "cancer," we think only of pain and despair. Yet Richard and Annette Bloch wanted to share their experience of not only surviving, but also thriving in a big way after Richard's battle with what was thought to be terminal cancer. Their message: "Don't equate death with cancer." And they have put up $850,000 to shout it to the world. Their donation created the **Cancer Survivors Park** (eastern edge of Spanish Landing, off North Harbor Drive, Downtown) with the support of the San Diego Unified Port District's public art program (619-686-6200). A sculpture by Mexican artist Victor Salmones sets the theme for the park. Eight life-size figures pass through a maze representing cancer treatment and success. A meditation path features 14 plaques; four are inspirational, and 10 are specific suggestions for fighting cancer. A huge multi-colored tile dome by artist Marlo Bartels and a 40-foot fountain help to create a space that is both inspiring and joyful. The Blochs have built cancer survivor parks in other cities, as well. San Diego's is the only one that includes a fabric-covered tension structure sheltering the "Positive Mental Attitude Walk" and a colorful tile mandala created by Bartels that is visible beneath the dome. The whole feeling of the park is an exuberant "Yes, we can!"

SECRET
SUSHI

Close your eyes, spin around three times, and throw a shrimp in the air. Chances are that it will land on the doorstep of one of San Diego's many sushi bars.

Sushi on the Rock (7734 Girard Avenue, La Jolla, 858-456-1138) is currently the trendiest place to visit. As the name implies, it is located in the part of La Jolla known as The Rock. The music is contemporary and kept a notch louder than in most sushi bars because owners Paul and Celeste Johnston like to keep things lively and a little tongue-in-cheek. In addition to traditional sushi dishes, you'll find oddly named creations like the Don Juan and the Kitchen Sink. The quality is first class, and the fish is ordered fresh daily from all over the world. If you aren't the raw fish type, go for the Hong Kong noodles, served with grilled hoisin shrimp and mixed vegetables in a soy-sesame cream. It's top-rated and guaranteed not to bite back.

Locals from the community of Pacific Beach tout **Sushi Ota** (4529 Mission Bay Drive, Pacific Beach, 858-270-5670) as the best in town. Like many storefronts along this street, aesthetics have never been the prime goal here. But it remains a destination spot for sushi diners. And it's always busy, so call before you go.

The hip professionals of La Jolla flock to **Cafe Japengo** (The Aventine, 8960 University Center Lane, University City, 858-450-3355), a place where platinum chopsticks almost seem possible. The restaurant is hard to see from the street because it is accessible only from the enclosed square of the Aventine complex. The atmosphere is bustling. And the sushi is highly artistic.

Leopard-print barstools and booths are the first clues that **Ono Sushi & Pacific Spice** (1236 University Avenue, 619-298-0616) isn't your typical sushi haunt. The restaurant is a popular nightspot in trendy Hillcrest with its lineup of specialties that include the Smokin' Roll, made with smoked salmon and jalapeño mustard; and ahi poki, a salad of raw tuna and spicy sesame seaweed. Spanish tapas and unusual raviolis add a curious twist to the menu. A special dessert treat is the tempura-fried bananas topped with fresh fruit and cream sauce. The word *ono* is Hawaiian for "delicious." And the adjective aptly describes the food here.

Ichiban (1449 University Avenue, 619-299-7203), which means "number one" in Japanese, is a modest-looking sushi restaurant that resides in the less-than-glamorous east end of Hillcrest. It attracts everyone from Goth teenagers to neatly suited professionals. There is no bar and the place is pretty kicked-out looking, but the line runs out the door most evenings. Ask for the Uptown Roll. It's not on the menu, but it has four kinds of sushi topped with either salsa or a mayo-wasabi dressing, depending on which chef is working. For dessert, the plum wine and green tea ice creams are big hits.

Nestled among the many yacht brokers that line tropical-looking Shelter Island Drive is the sleekly designed **Umi Sushi** (2806 Shelter Island Drive, Point Loma, 619-226-1135). Modern Japanese décor corresponds visually to the colorful sushi rolls and sashimi salads displayed behind the glass at the eating bar. Window booths and tables provide additional seating. The extensive menu offers prettily arranged plates of chilled, cooked, and tempura rolls for under $11. Entrées jump significantly in price. The Love Boat is a vessel-shaped, wooden plate loaded up with at least six different rolls ($39). But economical options for parties of two or more are the combination sashimi plates made in small, medium, and large servings ($39 to $89).

SECRET
SWIMMING POOLS

A noon dip in the great Pacific could feel more like a cold morning shower if you're visiting outside the summer months. Even then, the coastal waters off San Diego rarely climb above 70 degrees. And, let's face it, not everybody likes the feeling of seaweed sliding between their toes. There are more than 15 public swimming pools in the county, although the older urban ones are generally bigger and have more character.

Among the most charming and aged is the **Bud Kearns Memorial Pool** (2220 Morley Field Drive, North Park, 619-692-4920), built in 1928 and named after a devoted caretaker. Many of the original Spanish tiles used to adorn the cement deck are still in place. People particularly love the pool's jumbo dimensions: 22 yards wide by 40 yards long. It never seems crowded, considering it can legally accommodate 300 people. Special discount rates are available to seniors, children, and the disabled ($1.50). Regular admission is only 50 cents more, and includes the use of lockers, fins, kick boards, and other aquatic equipment.

The water gets bigger and warmer at **The Plunge** (3146 Mission Boulevard, Mission Beach, 858-488-3110), located within the **Belmont Amusement Park** near the **Giant Dipper Roller Coaster** (see "Secret Children's Stuff"). The mammoth pool, measuring 25 by 58 yards, glistens from an enclosed structure with arched, cathedral-like windows that look out to the boardwalk and ocean. Visitors can leap in easily, because the water is kept at a comfy 83 degrees. Built in 1925, the facility is clean and well maintained, providing enough space for both lap swimmers and waders. Open 5 AM to 8 PM Monday through Thursday; 5 AM to 6 PM on Fridays; and 7 AM to 6 PM on weekends. Admission is $3.50 for adults and $2.50 for children under 12.

You'll find three brand-new pools under one roof at the **Ray and Joan Kroc Corps Community Center** (6737 University Avenue, Rolando Park, 619-287-5762), which opened in June 2002 as a result of an $80-million donation given to the **Salvation Army** by San Diego philanthropist Joan Kroc. The non-profit organization used the funds to purchase a 12-acre parcel of land and build a multi-purpose recreational center that also includes an indoor skateboard park, an ice skating rink, a gymnasium, and heated pools designated for different purposes. A shallow therapy pool is used to limber up the knees. Another is designated for lap swimming and water polo, while the third pool gives way to aerobic mayhem. The facility is big and clean, and also functions as the Salvation Army's primary warehouse and distribution center for the annual Christmas food and toy drive.

The City of San Diego operates a **swim hotline** (619-685-1322) that provides up-to-date information on a number of facilities open to the public for lap and recreational swimming.

S E C R E T
TEA

Scratch a wealthy San Diegan and you'll find a British wannabe underneath. Even the not-so-wealthy seem to have this weird secret desire to call elevators "lifts" and use the word "actually" too many times. One of the ways we satisfy this curious craving is with the most cliché of English traditions: high tea. Contrary to popular notion, high tea is no dainty affair with tiny finger sandwiches and lace doilies. That is afternoon tea. High tea is actually a pig-out fest, with hearty sandwiches and hot soups and entrées, all topped off with a thick slice of cake. A few places in San Diego pull out all the stops for either high or afternoon tea.

The Grant Grill at the **U.S. Grant Hotel** (326 Broadway, Downtown, 619-232-3121) had excluded women during lunchtime business pow-wows for as long as anyone could remember. A small handful of indignant women boldly smashed that barrier in the early '70s. One of them, Kay Jarvis-Prokop, was a reporter who worked for the former *San Diego Tribune* at the same time I did. The lobby of this four-star hotel reflects that politically incorrect history as a grand bastion of masculine snobbery, with highly polished mahogany furniture and dark wood paneling everywhere. But tasteful art and massive crystal chandeliers today help offset it all. Afternoon teas are served Fridays and Saturdays (2 PM to 5 PM). The hotel is located directly across Broadway from the **Horton Plaza** (4th Avenue and Broadway, Downtown, 619-238-1596), making it an ideal spot for reclaiming civility after the savage sport of mall shopping.

For French flair, the lobby of the **Westgate Hotel** (1055 2nd Avenue, Downtown, 619-557-3650) is the spot to check out. Eighteenth-century antiques, French tapestries, and Persian carpets warmly glow under Baccarat crystal chandeliers. The opulent lobby shimmers with tons of gold accents. It's enough to make you feel like you're in the court of the Sun King himself. Here you'll find San Diego's elite taking traditional high tea service (2:30 PM to 5 PM) every day except Sunday. Reservations are strongly suggested, as seating is limited.

The **Hotel Del Coronado** (1500 Orange Avenue, Coronado, California, 619-435-6611), located across the Coronado Bridge from downtown San Diego, is a sprawling 19th-century Victorian oddity. The pair of brothers hired to design and build it used no blueprints. They just decided each day what they wanted to add to the structure and simply started building. The result is a gargantuan delight. The tea here goes by other names, but it is still the real thing. They call one of their offerings Del Tea. It features watercress and cucumber sandwiches, smoked salmon with dill crème fraîche, butter cookies, and mini cream puffs. The other offering, closer to a true high tea, is called the Royal Tea. This is indulgence on a sublime level. Kir royale, a mixture of champagne and Chambord liqueur, starts things off. After the sandwiches, assorted Belgian truffles and tuxedo strawberries dipped in white and dark chocolates arrive. Yes, it takes decadence to regal heights.

Back in the early 1900s, the Gaslamp District in Downtown San Diego was a lawless area of prostitution, gambling, and general thuggery. The most famous, and some say classiest, of madams was Ida Bailey. When the mayor of San Diego and three councilmen were inadvertently nabbed in the surprise "Great Raid" of brothels in 1912, Bailey's days in the "comfort" business quickly drew to a close. Her place in local history is remembered, however, with the restaurant bearing her name at the **Horton Grand Hotel** (311 Island Avenue, Downtown, 619-238-1818). On Saturday afternoons (2:30 PM to 5:00 PM), you can partake of a classic English afternoon tea or a traditional high tea. The former features petit fours; finger sandwiches; scones with butter, cream, and homemade preserves; and English Breakfast tea. The high tea includes the works: a glass of sherry; gourmet sausage rolls, scotch eggs; a variety of finger sandwiches; scones with butter, cream, and homemade preserves; petit fours; and truffles. Earl Grey and Darjeeling teas are also available. If you're feeling a little whimsical, the restaurant will provide you with dress-up hats. Be a Lady Bracknell or just look like one. Reservations are suggested.

SECRET
TEDDY BEARS

I'll let the staff at the **Basic Brown Bear Factory** (2375 San Diego Avenue, Old Town, 619-497-1177) tell you the quirky story about the connection between these furry stuffed playthings and the late President Theodore Roosevelt. Bring the kids along to hear it during the store's Sunday walk-in tours (1 PM). Afterwards, they can machine-stuff their own teddy bears, expel their fuzz with an air-compressed bath, then embellish them with hats, stars, and ribbons. A mini-manufacturer of sorts, the shop sells more than 30 different types of teddy bears that you won't find in major department stores, including the original "basic brown bear" designed by owner Merilee Woods some 20 years ago.

SECRET
THAI

Celadon Royalty Thai (540 University Avenue, Hillcrest, 619-297-8424) reopened recently in this new location in the very heart of

Hillcrest. The quiet interior is complemented by a broad picture-window view of the bustling avenue out front. The food is without compare, especially the salads. You'll find generous portions and a wait staff that pays great attention to detail. Lunch specials, which come with soup, fried wonton, and steamed rice, are an attractive bargain ($6).

I haven't yet tried **Karinya Thai** (825 Garnet Avenue, Pacific Beach, 858-270-5050), but I hear nothing but raves from everyone who's been there. Word is that the curries are very kicky and there are a lot of vegetarian dishes to choose from. A nice touch is the way you customize the meals to suit your taste by mixing ingredients and determining the intensity of the seasoning. If you're feeling spontaneous, you can opt for traditional floor seating.

Whenever I have company in town, it is a prime directive that at least one dinner shall be eaten at **Royal Thai Cuisine** (467 5th Avenue, Downtown, 619-230-8424). This large, cushy dining room, with subdued indirect lighting and soft linen furnishings, makes you feel like a diplomat dining in a posh hotel in Bangkok. The food is some of the best I've tasted anywhere, with prices that are extremely reasonable. Highly recommended: the naked shrimp appetizer and the basil-fried rice with chicken.

From the outside, it looks like a lunch canteen for the surrounding office park. But inside, **Try Thai** (407 Camino Del Rio s, 619-692-9300) has all the non-corporate trappings of any other sophisticated Asian restaurant in town. Small, bright, and airy, it's located halfway down a cul-de-sac in Mission Valley, with **El Torrito Mexican Cantina** (445 Camino Del Rio s, 619-296-6154) at one end, and TGI **Friday's** (403 Camino Del Rio s, 619-297-8443) at the other. Upstaged as it is, people pass it by all the time. The Thai toast topped with minced chicken and shrimp is a tasty and uncommon appetizer.

And the tom khar galangal soup rivals them all. Dinner prices are low to moderate, and complete lunches are available Monday through Friday for only $5.

Saffron Chicken (3737 India Street, Mission Hills, 619-574-7737) owner Su-Mei Yu proudly displays a picture of herself arm in arm with the most famous chef of the modern era, Julia Child. Yu attended several cooking seminars with the quavering-voiced Child, and her restaurant has been written up in just about every four-star guidebook imaginable. I have yet to find anyone who can make peanut sauce the way Yu does. In fact, I have purchased it many times as a party dip for skewered meats and crudités. Half of the shop is for take-out only; the other half provides ample seating (see "Secret Glass"). My favorite middle-of-the-day treat is to stop here for chicken egg rolls. They're stuffed solid and come with your choice of peanut or sweet-and-sour sauce. With the exception of garden spring rolls, you'll find only meat dishes on the take-out side.

SECRET
THEATER

Theater in San Diego walks a tough road. Still largely conservative, the population is willing to support middle-of-the-road, easy-to-swallow fare. The city's allure and warm climate, however, attract an influx of young artists eager to push the boundaries. Thus, smaller spaces have sprung up to allow yearning voices to pierce the air. Lacking a true theater district per se, San Diego is home to a quixotic mix of major theaters wishing they could present more daring works, and smaller ones dreaming of funds to fuel their edgy productions up to the grand designs they wish. As in many other metropolitan areas, the majority of the spaces are squeezed into a fairly tight radius around downtown.

Located some 20 minutes from Downtown is the **La Jolla Playhouse** (University of California at San Diego campus, 2910 La Jolla Village Drive, La Jolla, 858-550-1010). In 1947, when San Diego was still nothing more than a small West Coast port for the Navy, hometown boy–turned–megastar Gregory Peck, along with acting pals Dorothy McGuire and Mel Ferrer, enticed a coterie of Hollywood's notables down the coast from the soundstages of Los Angeles. It was a coveted opportunity to do live theater in a small-town atmosphere. The La Jolla Playhouse was born of that effort and began San Diego's longstanding love affair with the live stage. The city has since sprouted productions that frequently land with a splash on Broadway, such as Pete Townsend's musical version of his rock opera *Tommy*. More recently, the prestigious **Old Globe Theatre** (El Prado Way, Balboa Park, 619-239-2255) sent the theatrical version of *The Full Monty* on its way to the Great White Way. Stephen Sondheim's *Into the Woods* first saw light here too. And the off-Broadway hit *Suds — A Rock 'n' Roll Musical* played several theaters in San Diego before and after successful runs in New York City.

One of the biggest companies in town, the **San Diego Repertory Theatre** (see below), got its start in a truly secret location: a funeral chapel that looks for all the world like a small church. **St. Cecilia's Playhouse** (1620 6th Avenue, Downtown, 619-544-1484) housed the troupe until the mid-1980s. When the Rep hit the big time and moved out, the edgy **Sledgehammer Theatre** eventually moved in to call the once religious space home. Forewarned is forearmed. With a name like Sledgehammer, the company ensures its patrons do not sit through productions with pleasant little suburban smiles. Facial tics and puzzled looks are de rigueur for exiting audience members. This company was born to be the electric cattle prod that shakes up and wakes up a sleepy laid-back beach town. Among its other odd claims to fame is the fact that it once staged a five-hour nude production of *Hamlet* in an abandoned factory before most ravers were even born. And with St. Cecilia's entire interior painted jet black (yes, the religious incongruity jars you — and savvy producers use it), other fledgling and fringe companies find it the ideal place to try out the new as well.

The aforementioned abandoned factory, once a production facility for Carnation Milk Products, was gutted and refurbished in the '90s as the Reincarnation Project. It now houses the equally offbeat **Sushi Performance and Visual Art** (320 11th Avenue, East Village, 619-235-8466). This is the prime spot in the city to find visiting, small-scale productions; nationally acclaimed performance art pieces; and a maze of studios for moneyed artists crafting in various media.

Hunkering down oddly underground, almost hiding from San Diego's burning sun, the **San Diego Repertory Theatre** company is ensconced beneath the Disney-like, multi-colored Horton Plaza in the **Lyceum Theatre** (79 Horton Plaza, Downtown, 619-235-8025). In its early years, the company boasted the talents of an unknown Whoopi Goldberg. The move to more posh digs hasn't changed the Rep's penchant for presenting offbeat and lesser-known fare — something of a rarity for a major theater in San Diego. A small experimental stage beside the main one allows the company to remain true to its original spirit. Its annual production of *A Christmas Carol*, which dates back to the company's founding, rarely looks like the confection you find elsewhere. Sporting a set reflecting different environs each year, the Yuletide classic has been placed in a Mexican *colonia* and a homeless side street, as well as traditional Dickensian London.

You get the feeling that you ought to tie your horse to the old hitchin' post and ask the saloon barkeep to pour you a tall sarsaparilla when you first see the **Theatre in Old Town** (4040 Twiggs Street, Old Town, 619-688-2491). The rustic, whitewashed, rough-hewn wooden face of the building suits the image of the Wild West that old MGM films planted in our brains. And its location — squeezed between the festive **Bazaar del Mundo** (2754 Calhoun Street, Old Town, 619-296-3267) and a large parking lot — may make you doubt your choice of entertainment for the night. But once you pass through the doors, plush modern comfort rules the day. This intimate, steeply tiered, semi-circular theater has housed some of the most popular and archly satirical productions in San Diego. Operated by Miracle Theatre Productions, it maintains a reputation among locals for flawless comic direction — which usually translates into extended runs for its musicals and comedies. Its intimate size does mean that it fills up fast. Booking tickets early is wise.

San Diego's theater cognoscenti will tell you that among the fringiest of the fringe is **The Fritz Theatre** (operating in various venues around town, 619-233-7505). I love this company because it occasionally makes me cuss at the arrogant, artsy confusion inherent in some of the productions. But it feels good to get heated up over a play in a town that still considers *Annie Get Your Gun* risqué. Noted for its innovation, the company presents the annual Fritz Blitz each summer, boasting the largest collection of new plays by California playwrights staged on the West Coast. The Blitz was originally presented in a one-room, bare-brick storefront downtown. But the annual extravaganza recently graduated to the Lyceum Theatre. Expect the greatest range of the unexpected from this group. In conservative San Diego, the

Fritz and its older cousin, the Sledgehammer Theatre, are the longest-running pinpricks to the establishment.

Open-air theater is practically a legal requirement in a climate like San Diego's. And two companies wrestle for the crown. The most well known is the **Starlight Musical Theatre** (Starlight Bowl, Balboa Park, 619-544-7827), staging four to five shows per summer season. Located in Balboa Park, directly under the flight path for Lindbergh Field, its unusual claim to fame lies in the way actors freeze on cue while low-flying jets pass overhead. Once the roar dies down, the performers start from where they left off as though someone just pressed "play" on the VCR. I love watching visiting actors who are not used to the phenomenon trying to mask their irritation through the process. You'll find the most reliable of the old standard Broadway musicals presented here each season. Locals pack a picnic dinner to enjoy in the park before the show.

A less disjointed experience can be found at the top of residential Mount Helix, minutes east of San Diego in La Mesa. Here, the **Christian Community Theater** (619-588-0206) presents roughly the same menu of time-tested musicals, lavish enough to please most, and clean enough to bring grandma and the kids. It's the kind of family fare that makes Pat Boone look edgy, but lack of grit is compensated for by solid performances and surprisingly high-quality sets and costumes. And the adjacent small stone amphitheater, replete with cross and small garden, will have you absentmindedly humming "Jesus Christ, Superstar" despite yourself.

Closer to sea level, but much farther from a PG-rating, is the **Diversionary Theatre** (4545 Park Boulevard, University Heights, 619-220-0097). San Diego's large and active gay community provides the energy that keeps this troupe in front of the footlights year-round. Works consistently include gay, lesbian, bisexual, or transgender content, and draw frequent raves from mainstream critics. Local and regional talent walks the stage, and productions range from original works to more established plays. Founded in 1985, it has become the recognized leader in "legitimate" theater in the gay niche.

6th @ Penn Theatre (3704 6th Avenue, Hillcrest, 619-688-9210) offers a gritty jag to its cutting-edge productions. The theater abuts a dry cleaner on a tiny commercial corner — and it's easy to drive past. Stage shows are the stuff you'll never see in larger theaters around town. Nudity in productions is commonplace. And in true avant-garde spirit, the theater has been known to present special evenings to select audiences wishing to attend *au naturel*. Comedies with broad sexual innuendo are its mainstay. And literary genius is not a prerequisite. Like most of the smaller venues in town, as it gains in longevity it will acquire a veneer of respectability.

SECRET
THRIFT

Thrift stores have never been my thing, but there are devotees who scour them to unearth that one-of-a-kind ceramic duck doorstop for their aunt's third-floor study. **Action Thrift** (2525 Clairemont Drive, Clairemont Mesa, 619-275-3503), near Mission Bay, is very close to the I-5 freeway. It's housed in an old supermarket building, offering plenty of space for endless treasure hunting. You'll find everything from car parts to jewelry, as well as sporting goods, clothing, antiques, and record albums. Profits help battered, abused, pregnant, and homeless women in San Diego County. The staff says that a lot of people donate pricey, quality goods on a fairly regular basis. On Tuesdays, the store offers a 20-percent discount to seniors, students, and active military. (Open seven days a week.)

Thrift Korral (525 E Main Street, El Cajon, California, 619-593-9695) surprises some visitors who aren't aware that it's a thrift store. Clean and well arranged, it appears more like a boutique. The emphasis is on clothing and small collectibles. It also features a notable collection of toys, jewelry, and knickknacks, and some antique furniture. You may stumble upon an occasional gem, such as an old school desk or antique trunk in reasonably good shape. Grossmont Hospital Auxiliary volunteers staff the store.

Auntie Helen's (4028 30th Street, North Park, 619-584-8438) is a medium-sized thrift store that uses its profits to benefit men and women with AIDS. Inside, you'll find lots of household items, including glassware, mixers, records, tapes, books, and art, as well as men's and women's clothing, some furniture, and occasional antiques and collectibles.

A restored house in North Park holds six rooms full of goods ranging from quality artwork and crystal to a wide variety of dining room tables, dressers, occasional desks, and night stands. Oriental and area rugs are to be found, along with armoires, vintage clothing, and kitchenware. The prices are higher here at **St. Vincent's Specialty Shop** (3137 El Cajon Boulevard, 619-624-9701), but the likelihood of finding something unique is better, too.

This is more like stepping into granny's attic. At **St. Bartholomew's Thrift Shop** (12845 Poway Road, Poway, California, 619-486-2110), you can find Depression-era glass, old radios, sewing machines, collectible art, rare books, antique pencil sharpeners, and Art Deco bric-a-brac. There is also a lot of jewelry, some from the '30s and

'40s. Used records, books, linens, and vintage clothing abound. And you'll find a separate room filled with good-quality clothing for men and women.

At **Brother Benno's Thrift** (3965 Mission Avenue, Oceanside, California, 619-967-7505), it's frequently difficult to tell whether an item of clothing here is new or recycled. The stock changes often, and also includes a special Christmas collection with ornaments, lights, and such. Look for glassware, crystal, linens, dishware, knickknacks, paintings, and records. Prices are low on most items, fair on others. On Thursdays, visitors will enjoy a 20-percent discount on all merchandise and 50 percent off selected items.

SECRET
TIJUANA
❖

If it weren't for immigration checkpoints and dissimilar currencies, Americans and Canadians would have a hard time pinpointing exactly when they crossed their shared border. But walk into **Mexico** from San Diego and the land suddenly feels full of secrets. With just the push of a turnstile, radically different sights, smells, and sounds come rushing at you. From I-5, the border is only 25 minutes south of downtown, or a 40-minute ride on the **San Diego Trolley** (619-233-3004). Day trips are doable. But the safest and easiest way to visit is by walking across the border once you arrive at it. Most car rental companies do not allow their vehicles to be taken into Mexico. Insurance laws there are convoluted. And looping roads marked by Spanish signage are sure to confuse first-time visitors. Instead, take the freeway off-ramp marked "last exit before the border" and bear to your right into the expansive parking lot, which costs about $10 for the day. From there, the walk to the border takes only a few minutes. Taxis lie in wait on the other side to take tourists to Tijuana's main commercial street, **Avenida Revolución**. My advice is to determine the fare with the cab driver before embarking on the five-minute ride. Anything over $8 is too high.

The beaten track is lined with shopping arcades, margarita bars (many with balconies), cavernous restaurants, food stands, and colorful merchandise that will test your bartering skills. Nearly all vendors accept American currency, so there is no need to exchange money beforehand. But if you want to shop in an open-air market that few tourists know about, then walk five blocks east of Revolución to **Mercado Hidalgo** (Avenida Independencia and Sanchez Taboado). Prices are actually cheaper, and the wares more interesting — herb candles, potions, Mexican chocolates, and some very fashionable sandals.

If there is a secret code of etiquette to follow when visiting here, I would have to advise showing respect to vendors and homeless people; this advice is based on the arrogant behavior I have witnessed occasionally by ignorant tourists. While bartering is a way of life for most merchants, they will walk away before you do if they feel exploited by unreasonable offers. Pointing cameras in the faces of impoverished families is shameful. And throwing coins to the wind just for the sake of creating reaction is hardly necessary.

Among the many guided tours that go into Tijuana, **Contract Tours** (1720 Wilson Boulevard, National City, California, 619-477-8687) offers the best glimpse of the city, covering most historical points and the Moorish-style Palacio Fronton (Revolución and Calle 8), a quasi sports center where *jai alai* is played. Tour operators are bilingual.

Charter buses of various sizes leave daily (8 AM) from most major hotels and return by 3 PM. Prices range from $26 to $38.

SECRET
TIME CAPSULE

Two centuries of artifacts and manuscripts reflecting the evolution of San Diego lie buried beneath the soil in a small clearance of trees behind the parking lot of the **Junipero Serra Museum** (2727 Presidio Drive, Mission Hills, 619-297-3258). Resting peacefully at the top of **Presidio Hill**, a bronze plaque in the ground marks the spot where the time capsule was inhumed — and where it will be unearthed on July 16, 2069. The date is significant because it corresponds to the date that Father Junipero Serra founded the area's first mission on the site in 1769. San Diego was declared a town then, having started out as an ancient Indian village that budged after the arrival of Old World sailors, soldiers, and missionaries. But in case you're wondering where the mission went, Roman Catholic padres moved it six miles east in 1774. A red-brick cross now stands in its place. Historians will have much to sift through when the time capsule is opened, because it includes materials from the city's Franciscan founding all the way up to December 31, 1969. Much to my dismay, basic math tells me that I won't be around to see what comes out of that container.

SECRET
TIMPANO

It's one of the hardest Italian dishes to find anywhere. The 17-layer baked timpano originated as a convenient dish for Fat Tuesday during the 1950s in Calabria, Italy. Catholics would expunge from their refrigerators the foods they were giving up for Lent and create monstrous, weighty loaves out of them. Starch from pasta holds it all together. Timpano served as a climactic prop in the 1996 art film *Big Night*. And it takes center stage at **Lotsa Pasta** (1762 Garnet Avenue, Pacific Beach, 858-581-6777). One-pound slices contain meatballs, sausage, hard-boiled egg, roasted red peppers, and spinach, plus penne and flat pastas. Eat your heart out for $11.95.

SECRET
TORTILLAS

Corn or flour? San Diegans choose their tortillas decisively. Visitors frequently waver. The rule of thumb is to try both, without any fillings or toppings to interfere with the judging process. Most Mexican eateries and taco stands sell trios of hot, buttered tortillas for under a buck. The best ones fly straight off metal grills directly into their yellow paper wrappings, allowing you to stroll, eat, and conclude simultaneously.

The last place one expects to find traditional, hand-rolled tortillas is in a remote corner of the **San Diego Museum of Man** (1350 El Prado Way, Balboa Park, 619-239-2001.) Since 1967, Diana Montoya has commuted back and forth from Mexico to her little ceramic-tiled nook at the museum, where she mixes up masa, corn flour, and water on a rustic stone *metate*. The resulting dough is baked on an authentic *comal*, producing individual tortillas that sell for only 25 cents apiece. After entering the main-floor gallery, walk straight to the back and turn right.

Hundreds of tortillas are churned out daily at **El Indio Mexican Restaurant** (3695 India Street, Middletown, 619-299-0333), where metal conveyor belts push them along in plain view of the front counter between 7 AM and 9 AM. Naturally, breakfast burritos don't get any fresher than this. And it's the only place where you'll find mordiditas, which means "mini-bites." But to understand what you're biting into, you must first grasp the meaning of taquitos, a word popularized by the restaurant in the 1940s that translates to "little tacos." Thus, mordiditas materialize when skinny, beef-filled taquitos are cut into thirds and covered with a good and goopy cheese sauce.

Corn and flour tortillas are free for the taking while you're waiting in the ever-present line outside **Casa de Pico** (2754 Calhoun Street, Old Town, 619-296-3267), a popular, colorful Mexican restaurant located within Old Town's **Bazaar del Mundo** (same address, 619-296-3161). The stand is adjacent to the restaurant and easy to miss if you're standing toward the front of the line at the restaurant's entrance.

SECRET
TRADER JOE'S

Whenever I receive company from points east, I take them for a shopping run to **Trader Joe's** (1092 University Avenue, Hillcrest,

619-296-3122; and five other locations in San Diego County). The store isn't a secret to Californians, considering there are more than 100 of them in the Southwest, but visitors take novel delight in the many imported foodstuffs and wines tagged with shockingly low prices. Stores vary in size, ranging from five to 10 aisles. Yet every section provides a sense of discovery: olive oils and prettily packaged pastas from Italy; sherries from Spain; chocolates from Germany and Switzerland; beers from Bavaria; wines from Chile. And if you're looking for cheese to go with that bargain bottle of wine, you'll find all sorts of it in the refrigerated section, at nearly half the prices charged in major supermarkets.

SECRET
TRAILS

Rarely do you find a vast network of rugged trails cutting through 5,800 acres of mostly undeveloped land within the boundaries of a major metropolitan city. What's stranger still is that I didn't even learn about them until 10 years after relocating here. And many San Diego natives I know still haven't set foot on one. **Mission Trails Regional Park** (1 Father Junipero Serra Trail, Tierrasanta, 619-688-3275) is only 20 minutes northeast of downtown, off a vacuous stretch of Mission Gorge Road that seems neither here nor there. The park offers 40 miles of trails ranging from easy to difficult, several of which begin at the visitors' and interpretive center at the park's entrance. The protected land beyond is slathered with history, having been used by La Jollan Indians, Spanish explorers, Mexican settlers, and early American farmers. The Old Mission Dam Trail is my favorite. It begins about two miles past the visitors' center near a 200-year-old dam built by Indians. But the San Diego River the dam once controlled is barely a trickle, allowing you to analyze every stone that went into its ancient construction. The trail continues 1.7 miles across easy grasslands, up rocky hills, and through tunnels of sagebrush. Parts of the trail are lined with yerba santa plants, used by native Americans to treat coughs and sore throats. Maps, bottled water, walking sticks, and a 90-seat theater that shows educational films about the area can all be found at the visitors' center — a wise place to start your visit to the park.

The trailhead at **Cowles Mountain** (Navajo Street and Golfcrest Drive, San Carlos) is where you'll find fit locals embarking on a path that leads to the highest point in San Diego. The reward at the top is a 360-degree view of the city from 1,592 feet above sea level — and a slimmer waistline, if you hike it a few days in a row. The trail is steep and rigorous in parts, cutting through brushy chaparral and offering little respite from the sun. It's a three-mile round trip to the summit and back, with about 1,000 feet of elevation gain and loss. During the winter solstice, bleary-eyed hikers trudge to the top before daybreak to glimpse a natural phenomenon — the appearance of two suns rising at the same time, but just for a nanosecond. The mountain, located in the eastern community of San Carlos, was named after pioneer George A. Cowles. And, for the record, it's pronounced "coals," although most locals insist on "cowls."

Visitors looking for informative, easy-paced hikes in and around San Diego can tag along with hikes sponsored by the **San Diego Natural History Museum** (1788 El Prado Way, Balboa Park, 619-232-3821). The walks are held on Saturday afternoons (times vary). The **Sierra Club** (3820 Ray Street, North Park, 619-299-1743) periodically schedules hiking and backpacking excursions throughout the city's outskirts. The organization is located behind the chapter's bookstore (619-299-1797), where you can find several updated hiking guides for sale. A full schedule of free hikes and walking tours is conducted every month through **Walkabout International** (835 5th Avenue, Downtown, 619-231-7463). The selection includes everything from light urban walks through neighborhoods and parks to difficult treks through rural foothills and valleys. **Guided Adventures in Nature** (760-434-0487, www.guidedadventures.net), headquartered in the northern coastal city of Carlsbad, conducts four-hour hiking tours of La Jolla Cove and Torrey Pines State Park, as well as overnight trips to areas outside the region. Call for schedules and fees.

S E C R E T
TREES

❧

You'll have to wander behind the **Natural History Museum** (1788 El Prado Way, Balboa Park, 619-232-3821) to fully observe the imposing stature of a Moreton bay fig tree that has been recognized as one of the biggest in the state by the California Register of Big Trees. Planted shortly before the city's Panama-California Exposition in 1915, it flaunts a girth of 486 inches, which aptly supports its 78-foot height and 123-foot canopy. It's amazing what nearly a century of persistent sunshine does for majestic timbers.

Equally notable is a rare, 50-year-old kauri pine in Balboa Park, located several yards south of the **House of Charm Building** (1439

El Prado Way, Balboa Park, 619-235-1100) and directly west of the El Cid statue. In their native New Zealand, these trees can tower to nearly 300 feet high and live up to 2,000 years. But this one seems a little homesick, since it has grown only 60 feet so far. Nonetheless, its light-colored, sinewy bark and deep-green crown make it easy to detect against the surrounding eucalyptus and palms.

Hot days especially warrant a stroll into **Palm Canyon** (off Pan American Road, Balboa Park), where a wooden footbridge leads you into a cool and lush ravine, filled with more than 450 palms of 58 varieties. The trees are mostly imports, dating back to the early 1900s. Among the tallest are the ever-swaying Mexican fan palms. With trunks so tall and slender, you get the feeling they'll come tottering down at the slightest whisper.

S E C R E T

TUNA MELT

I'm not normally nuts about the combination of warm tuna fish and cheese, but the grilled-tuna sandwich at the **Crest Café** (425 Robinson Avenue, Hillcrest, 619-295-2510) is the best in all of San Diego. Friends and I have eaten it so many times that we've yet to sample much else from the menu. The bread is big, grilled to a crisp and greasy finish, and packed thick with white albacore tuna and sliced cheddar. Colorful vintage Fiestaware catches whatever oozes out.

S E C R E T

24 / 7

&

At **Night & Day Café** (847 Orange Avenue, Coronado, California, 619-435-9776), hungry customers enjoy breakfast, lunch, or dinner (served any time) cooked from a grill that operates about four feet from their lunch-counter seats. There's a little bit of attitude here. The café sells T-shirts that read, "Shut up and take a stool" — yet the quality of the food is worth obeying such an abrupt command. This is diner food, true and true. The breakfast menu features standard fare, such as pancakes and more than a dozen kinds of omelettes. If you dare, try the "garbage omelette," a concoction of four eggs, ham, chili, veggies, and cheese. Lunch and dinner present a ton of choices, including New York steak, a Reuben sandwich and chips, or an excellent meatloaf sandwich with fries.

A visit to **Rudford's Restaurant** (2900 El Cajon Boulevard, North Park, 619-282-8423) is like walking into the year 1949, when the place first opened. Fishbowl windows, pink counter tops, lots of stainless steel, and an aqua-blue neon sign out front add to the retro-diner feel. Roast pork dinners are a favorite on Thursday nights, as are the old-fashioned roast turkey dinners on Sundays. And the famous chicken and dumplings are just like the ones mother used to make. Dinner entrées include soup or salad, potatoes, vegetable, hot roll, and a choice of pudding, ice cream, sherbet, or Jell-O.

Some locals still refer to **Brians' American Eatery** (1451 Washington Street, University Heights, 619-296-8268) as **Topsy's**, a name it held for years until two new owners, both named Brian, took over in 1999. The duo spruced up the place and made some minor menu changes for the better. Open 24 hours only on Fridays and Saturdays (until 10 PM the remainder of the week), the kitchen now offers a large selection of three-egg omelettes, including a big seller called the Acapulco — stuffed with shrimp, jack cheese, tomatoes, onions, and guacamole. It's served with salsa on the side, potatoes, and an English muffin. A popular lunch sandwich is the King of Clubs, made with turkey, bacon, tomatoes, sprouts, and Swiss cheese, all piled onto rye toast, and served with a choice of two sides. For dinner, try the chicken-fried steak, a wide filet of beef topped with country gravy and accompanied by a choice of potato or wild rice, vegetable, soup or salad, and dinner roll.

In the east neck of the county, **Tyler's Taste of Texas** (576 N 2nd Street, El Cajon, California, 619-444-9295) is my recommended destination for Texas-style catfish and mesquite-smoked ribs. The menu's "smoke aroma" dishes include a killer barbecue chicken dinner, which includes a juicy half chicken, plus salad or soup, spicy pinto beans, potato, and corn bread or biscuit. The pork rib plate comes with four ribs and the same sides. Beef rib dinners are also available. For a hearty breakfast, try Uncle Shorty's: two sausage patties over biscuits, with scrambled eggs, gravy, and potatoes.

S E C R E T
USED GARB

If it doesn't flaunt a purple tag, then you know it's been around the block a few times. Trendy raiment from the past three decades, both used and new, can be found at **Buffalo Exchange** (1007 Garnet

Avenue, Pacific Beach, 858-273-6227; or 3862 5th Avenue, Hillcrest, 619-298-4411). For aging baby boomers who still consider themselves hip, but can't pull off bell-bottom jeans and polyester shirts, the racks are loaded with factory-fresh apparel by Ben Sherman and Dragon Fly as well. Need gas money? Then bring in your outdated, outgrown clothing to sell here. The company buys just about any piece of used apparel that's fashionable, washed, and in worthy shape.

At **Flashbacks Recycled Fashions** (3847 5th Avenue, Hillcrest, 619-291-4200), it's more about finding a "look" than a specific time period. But the era from which vinyl records, big discotheques, and Pet Rocks sprang is hard to block out when rifling through piles of hip-hugging jeans and wide-lapel shirts. Step behind the leopard-print curtains into the dressing rooms and see for yourself. The selection is immense and fiercely retro, with styles and accouterments dating as far back as the 1950s.

SECRET
VAULT

You'll have no doubt that an impenetrable vault lurks somewhere beneath your feet while supping on kabobs at **Faz** (530 Broadway Street, Downtown, 619-446-3040). The Iranian-owned restaurant, situated within the lobby of the **Marriott Suites**, provides architectural clues that this was once a great marble bank of the 1920s. Brass teller cages are incorporated into the dining room's perimeter. And the Romanesque ceiling and walls smell of old money, the kind used for building structures that resembled ornate European opera houses.

What isn't obvious, however, is that if you're a well-behaved customer with a knack for schmoozing, the management will let you peek into one of the best kept secrets I've encountered in years — the mighty basement vault once belonging to **San Diego Trust & Savings**. Unlike the narrow vaults you see at branch banks, this is an ostentatious memorial to the wealth it once preserved. Hundreds of metal safety-deposit drawers line the room from floor to ceiling. Most of them are unlocked and barren, although we discovered three pennies in one, and an Italian edition of *Playboy* magazine in another. A shiny wooden conference table centered in the room harks back to the days when captains of industry hammered out deals while smoking their cigars. And the immovable door, about three feet thick, stands silent guard before a threshold with many stories. The room can be rented for dinner parties and special events.

S E C R E T
VEGAN

Ironically, vegetarians have a hard time finding restaurants in this health-conscious environment that cater exclusively to their diets. Most herbivores I know are leery about eating in places that list vegetarian meals on one half of their menus, and steaks and ribs on the other. Those saturated fats floating around kitchen grills and fryers can potentially sneak into other dishes, turning an innocent plate of braised tofu into something that tastes more like beef stew.

San Diego's oldest meat-free restaurant comes with a serene atmosphere and Indian flair that even most carnivores find tempting. **Jyoti**

Bihango (3351 Adams Avenue, North Park, 619-282-4116) expertly breaks down old stereotypes pertaining to vegetarian food by converting otherwise bland organics into flavorful concoctions laced with exotic spices and homemade curries. The vegetarian chili with cornbread is a must. And the "infinite blue" salad, topped with cooked rice and vegetables, plays auspiciously to those who don't mind ingesting a touch of dairy from the blue cheese dressing. Meatless meatloaf, smoothies, oversized burritos, and some fairly convincing dairy-free desserts are all worth trying. Pastel-painted walls and metaphysical publications strewn about tell you that you're definitely not in a steakhouse.

The menu at **Galoka Gallery and Restaurant Bar** (5662 La Jolla Boulevard, La Jolla, 858-551-8610) is 100-percent vegetarian. Neighborhood customers call it the "secret restaurant" because it is located in a residential coastal strip connecting the communities of Pacific Beach with La Jolla. Most people hop onto I-5 when traveling between the two, thus completely missing this pleasant district called Bird Rock. The menu abounds with mock meats such as savory fish, shrimp, and beef kabobs, all flavored with robust curries and Indian Ayurvedic healing herbs. Also recommended: Miss Fish Olivia, a grilled tofu filet that mimics whitefish. It's wrapped in seaweed and topped with an eventful Indian tomato sauce. Or try the aloo tikki — potato patties presented beautifully with tamarind-root chutney and sweet carrots. Now on to the gallery, which is actually the dining room itself. The family that owns the restaurant is artistically blessed. Its members include a painter, a musician, a dancer, and a poet. Visual art and improvisational music naturally become the core elements of the environment, every night of the week.

The staff at **Tofu House** (4646 Convoy Street, Kearny Mesa, 858-576-6433) insists that all vegan entrées are cooked separately from the meat dishes with different utensils and cookware. The tofu steak with secret sauce and mushrooms wins the blue ribbon for most flavorful dish, although pan-fried veggies with brown rice ranks a close second. Lines grow long during lunch hour as patrons vie for limited seating.

SECRET
VICTORIAN

Mrs. Burton's Tea Room (2465 Heritage Park Row, Old Town, 619-294-4600) isn't the kind of place where you feel comfortable wearing an Adidas jogging suit. There are simply too many reminders hanging around of the days when constricting rules of etiquette permeated England's population during Queen Victoria's long reign. But the hats, dresses, and home furnishings born from that era still hold great appeal to many. The shop operates from a classic revival home adorned with pediments, dentiled cornices, and lace curtains. Flowery fabrics, fine porcelain, and Victorian-style clothing, including wedding dresses, soak up the space in the front. In the back parlor, you'll find ladylike customers donning the store's ostrich-feather hats, mingling over Earl Grey tea and cookies. The tea parties are held daily (10 AM to 4 PM) for $6 per person. **Country Craftsman of San Diego** (www.country-craftsman.com) co-inhabits the house and sells unique three-in-one high chairs for kids. Constructed from quality pinewood, they covert into rocking chairs and children's desks as well. The vendor also sells Shaker furniture, homemade crafts, and Beanie Baby accessories.

SECRET
VIEWS

✧

A city without hills is a city without views — unless you find tall buildings with top-floor restaurants and observation decks in them. San Diego affords visitors numerous fine vantage points, both natural and manmade, for taking in views of its bays, ocean, mountains, neighborhoods, and skyline. Breathtaking panoramas often pop into sight when you're driving into valleys or down steeply graded streets. But those only last a few seconds. The best views require stationary visits, where you can stay long enough to contemplate the lay of the land. Believe me, our views are big. And they get even bigger on clear, sunny days, which means you'll need to spend some quality time with them.

How about several good views rolled up into one nice walk? Beginning at the west end of **Balboa Park**, head east on Laurel Street from 6th Avenue. Within minutes, you'll be crossing the **Laurel Street Bridge**, which imparts a dizzying look at the lushly landscaped stretch of Highway 163 below. The downtown skyline peeks through eucalyptus trees off the right side of the bridge. And a little further in the distance, you'll see the **Coronado Bay Bridge** arching gracefully over the bay. Inside the park, the street becomes **El Prado Way**, a pedestrian midway lined with ornate Spanish Colonial buildings that house several of the park's museums. Continue walking toward the imposing **Bea Evenson Fountain** at the end of the midway for an expansive view of **Florida Canyon** and the rugged, brown mountains that separate San Diego from the desert. On your return, after crossing back over the Laurel Street Bridge, make an immediate left onto Balboa Drive and walk to the tip of **Marston Point**. Here,

the city's skyline reveals its full glory while a steady stream of low-flying commercial jets overhead make their descent into Lindbergh Field.

If you're looking for that quintessential view of the spot where ocean meets land, you'll need to drive about 12 miles north of downtown to the Salk Institute (10010 N Torrey Pines Road, La Jolla). Turn onto Torrey Pines Scenic Drive, which skirts one side of the institute and ends in a dirt parking lot at the **Torrey Pines Glider Port.** The stretch of sand 300 feet below is **Black's Beach** (see "Secret Nudity"). Look left to see the affluent community of La Jolla jutting its nose into the ocean. Turn right and let your eyes wander up the coastline toward the city of Del Mar. Look straight ahead at the endless ocean and daydream.

It's San Diego's version of the Top of the Mark in San Francisco, except that it's about 50 years newer and 21 floors higher. The **Top of the Hyatt** (Manchester Grand Hyatt, 1 Market Place, Downtown, 619-232-1234, ext. 4914) is a cushy cocktail lounge where you can enjoy a few libations over one of the most awesome views San Diego has to offer. Plenty of windows face out to all directions: the Point Loma peninsula to the west; urban sprawl and quiet mountains to the east; Coronado and Mexico to the south; and all of downtown to the north. Upholstered couches and armchairs supply the seating. The snack menu is available until midnight.

Sweeping views of La Jolla and the Pacific Ocean await looky-loos at **The French Gourmet at Elario's** (Hotel La Jolla, 7955 La Jolla Shores Drive, La Jolla, 858-551-3620), where west-facing windows beautifully frame the hillside homes on Mount Soledad and the sweeping blue waters of the Pacific. Live jazz music (Wednesday through Saturday) and high-end, sumptuous suppers bring romance to the twinkling evening view.

The **Top of the Park** (525 Spruce Street, Hillcrest, 619-296-0057) restaurant and bar is located on the seventh floor of the historic **Park Manor Suites**, an elegant, dark-brick hotel that offers bright, spacious views of Balboa Park, Downtown, and the surrounding community of Hillcrest. It's open for weekday lunch only. There's never a waiting line, although the elevator is a sloth. The elongated dining room and outdoor balcony are home to an elbow-to-elbow gay crowd during Friday happy hour.

The secret behind **Mount Soledad** is finding the street that leads to the million-dollar view at the top. There are actually a few options, but if you start on Hidden Valley Road, off Ardath Road in La Jolla, you can gape at some of the area's most sensational hillside real estate on your ascent. A large cross is perched at the summit, where a panoramic view of San Diego steals your breath away. From Hidden Valley Road, about halfway up, make a left on Via Capri, and then another left onto Soledad Road.

SECRET
WAFFLES

Terryl Gavre takes waffles very seriously. As the owner of **Café 222** (222 Island Avenue, Marina District, 619-236-9902), she even taped one to her head and had a photographer shoot the image for an eye-catching billboard advertisement that sporadically appears downtown and at the University Avenue exit off Highway 163. The round golden-brown waffle, tipped stylishly over her brow like a pillbox hat, reflects the café's whimsical décor and gourmet breakfast fare.

Paintings of fried eggs cover the floor. Old pocket cameras protrude from the restroom walls. And the waffle selection is downright dreamy. Choices include pecan, sweet corn, five-grain, and a killer pumpkin waffle that landed on the pages of *Gourmet* magazine two years ago. And nowhere else will you find "scrapple" — a sausage and cornmeal cake that harks back to the 1960s. Open seven days a week (7 AM to 1:45 PM).

The fruit is *inside* the waffles at **The Waffle Spot** (1333 Hotel Circle s, Mission Valley, 619-297-2231). Small, cozy, and obscure, the restaurant is located inside the outdated Kings Hotel in Mission Valley. It certainly doesn't look like a place where you'd expect to find some of the best banana-nut waffles in town.

Breakfast becomes a chic affair within the gleaming boundaries of La Jolla. Belgian waffles at **The Cottage** (7702 Fay Avenue, La Jolla, 858-454-8409) are best enjoyed al fresco, on a garden patio filled with jasmine and bougainvillea. The waffles topped with toasted almonds and mango reign supreme.

SECRET
WATER TAXIS

The water taxis clipping around San Diego Bay are no secret. But that you can usually persuade pilots to drop you off at uncommon access points is worth mentioning. The touristy stops are well covered: Seaport Village, the Marriott Hotel and Marina, and the famous Hotel Del Coronado; $5 one-way. For the regular fare, however, you can also request a landing at several upscale restaurants around the bay: the Rowing Club, Bali Hai, or Peoria's on nearby Coronado Island. Call it San Diego hospitality. The taxis operate under the auspices of **San Diego Harbor Excursions** (1050 N Harbor Drive, Centre City, 619-234-4111). They originate from the company's North Harbor Drive address and numerous other points along the bay front.

SECRET
WEATHER

It's no secret that San Diego boasts one of the most ideal climates in the world. The city's annual average temperature is 70.8 degrees, with only 9.9 inches of rainfall. Surely, this is why you've come — isn't it? But what many visitors don't usually understand is an esoteric term used in local weather reports that describes a particularly warm, dry day: a **Santa Ana**. The condition usually occurs between September and May, when high-pressure cells build over the region, and surface air blows from the east to the ocean. The pattern can last up to a few days, sending humidity levels down to single digits, and temperatures over the 100-degree mark in their most extreme form. Visibility turns shockingly clear, to the point where communities look like plastic landscape models from an elaborate train set. If you're lucky enough to catch a Santa Ana during your visit, go to a high place (see "Secret Views") where you can gawk at mountains and distant neighborhoods that are otherwise invisible.

Less appealing to both visitors and locals are the climatic phenomena known as **May gray** and **June gloom**. Just as the rest of the nation enters bright summery weather, San Diego becomes plagued by a cloudy marine stratus that can darken the sky through midday. Its cause is disputable. Northerly winds that pick up in early summer produce an upwelling along the coast, bringing cold water to the surface and creating enough cool air to form fog. The other theory points to complicated pressure effects that bring about low inversions of air, trapping moisture from the ocean so that it can't escape. The number of gloomy days during this two-month period varies from year to year, but visitors should prepare for at least a few charcoal-colored afternoons.

S E C R E T

WHIRLPOOL

It's as though the Green Giant pulled the plug on his bathtub. Just off the coast of notorious **Black's Beach** in La Jolla (see "Secret Nudity") exists a puzzling phenomenon. A giant sucking whirlpool was discovered by a sightseer flying up the coast in a biplane in 1999. He had the presence of mind to videotape 37 seconds worth of footage, which has been examined by the **Scripps Institution of Oceanography** (9500 Gillman Drive, La Jolla, 858-534-1829). The footage shows a rotating whirlpool, hoovering up muck and debris very close to shore, with a spiral of foam rising up from the center. Local TV station KFMB aired the tape, which then immediately generated theories of underwater UFOs. Well, this *is* Southern California, after all. Oceanographers, however, have said they've never seen anything quite like it. Bill Schmidt, a scientist with the Scripps Institution, does a lot of work with ocean rip currents and thinks they may be responsible. We may never know, however, because the whirlpool comes and goes unpredictably. It's a strange page right out of Homer's *Ulysses*.

S E C R E T
WINE STORAGE

Long-term visitors need not rummage for cool dark nooks at their accommodations to store cherished vintages. **The Cabernet Cellar** (3820 Ray Street, North Park, 619-683-2221) does it for you in a basement kept at an ideal 55 degrees Fahrenheit. No movement and no light means your booty doesn't turn to vinegar inside these rental "lockers," which nurture privately owned wines ranging in value from $10 to $1,500 a bottle. The units are available in various sizes for storing single bottles or multiple cases. They range from $20 to $50 a month.

S E C R E T
WINE STORES

Wine connoisseurs can spend hours poring over the huge number of hard-to-find labels available at **The Wine Bank** (363 5th Avenue, Downtown, 619-234-7487). Once a pharmaceutical company, the drug vault now stores high-end wines from exclusive vintners such as the Bryant family and Karl Lawrence of Napa, and Sassicaia of Italy. A nice selection of Canadian and German icewines is also kept in stock. Two floors allow for a burgeoning inventory of more than 20,000 labels that come and go in any given year. The store's tasting room attracts sippers of all age groups (21 years and older) on Wednesdays (6 PM), and Fridays and Saturdays (3 PM).

The WineSellar (9550 Waples Street, Sorrento Mesa, 858-450-9557) is more difficult to find, but also offers boutique wines from around the world, plus an elegant, contemporary French restaurant upstairs. Rare and expensive Napa Valley treasures include reds from Screaming Eagle, Colgin, and the Grace family. Tastings are conducted on Saturdays (11:30 AM to 1:30 PM). The store is located behind a building in an industrial office park. A small sign at the mouth of the driveway leads you in.

S E C R E T
WING
✤

When the winds blow in from the desert and create clear, dry conditions, a giant silver airplane wing comes into focus from miles away, jutting 90 feet into the air from a remote grassy knoll at **Montgomery Waller Community Park and Recreation Center** (3020 Coronado Avenue, Otay Mesa, 619-424-0466). The appendage serves as a monument to John Joseph Montgomery, an aviation pioneer allegedly responsible for launching man's first controlled winged flight, achieved from this hilltop in 1883. Since no remnants remain of the original glider he flew, a World War II B-24 bomber wing was used instead to commemorate his success. It was erected by the San Diego Junior Chamber of Commerce in 1950, yet many San Diegans don't know why it's there. To see the wing up close, you have to drive several miles south of downtown on I-5 toward the Mexican border, and exit at Coronado Avenue. Continue east for about one mile, then turn left into the quiet park after crossing Beyer Boulevard. A distant view of the ocean looms beyond the dedication plaque. And the sun-baked hills of Mexico dominate the southern vista.

SECRET FUTURE

No tour guide can be definitively comprehensive, especially when the aim is to uncover those hidden places that have previously escaped notice. Undoubtedly, some worthwhile attractions have remained hidden even from our best efforts to ferret them out.

In the interest of our own self-improvement, we ask readers to let us know of the places they've unearthed that they believe warrant inclusion in future editions of *Secret San Diego*. If we use your suggestion, we'll send you a free copy on publication. Please contact us at the following address:

Secret San Diego
c/o ECW PRESS

2120 Queen Street East, Suite 200
Toronto, Ontario, Canada M4E 1E2

Or e-mail us at: info@secretguides.com

PHOTO SITES

FRONT COVER: Chapel of Immaculate Conception
BACK COVER: India Street in Little Italy

Page

14	Santa Fe Train Station
31	Coronado Bridge
41	India Street in Little Italy
53	Mormon Temple in La Jolla
62	India Street in Little Italy
68	Old Town
80	Santa Fe Train Station
86	Broadway
93	Botanical Garden in Balboa Park
105	Hotel del Coronado
116	Corvette Diner in Hillcrest
128	Santa Fe Train Station
137	Hacienda in Old Town
145	Firehouse at the Fire Museum
154	Niki de St. Phalle statue
158	Museum of Contemporary Art
167	Kate Sessions statue in Balboa Park
182	Old Globe Theatre
188	*Star of India*
213	San Diego Street
227	La Jolla

SUBJECT INDEX

Accommodations

Bahia Hotel 19
Balboa Park Inn 126
Banana Bungalow Beach San Diego 127
Carlsbad Inn Beach Resort 39
Cottage, The 130
Crystal Pier Hotel 126
Hilton San Diego Resort 120, 166
Horton Grand Hotel 106, 107, 200
Hotel Del Coronado 71, 100, 106, 147
Hotel La Jolla 115
Humphrey's 115, 168
La Costa Resort and Spa 74
Lawrence Welk Resort 122
Mariott Suites 222
Ocean Beach International Backpackers
    Hostel 129
Park Manor Suites 229
Ramada Inn and Suites 119
Spooky Sleepovers 18
Surfer Motor Lodge 120
USA Hostels San Diego 127
U.S. Grant Hotel 199
Victorian Heritage Park Bed & Breakfast
    Inn 129
Westgate Hotel 199

After Dark

See also Bars/Booze/Beer
4th and B 66
Abbey, The 13
Alibi, The 149
Albie's 165
Bayou Dining & Jazz 152
Belly Up Tavern 111
Bitter End 131
Brass Rail, The 124
Caliph, The 165
Croce's Jazz Bar, Restaurant 113
Dizzy's 113
Field, The 44
Flame, The 125, 193
French Gourmet at Elario's 114, 228
Humphrey's 115, 168
In Cahoots 67
Lips 74
Martini Ranch 130

NuNu's 149
Ould Sod 44
Princess Pub and Grille 43
Red Circle 130
Red Fox Room 165
Rich's 124
Six Degrees 125
Top of the Hyatt 228
Xen Hookah Lounge and Coffee Shop 190
Zone, The 124

Bargains and Freebies

See also Malls and Markets
4th and B 66
Action Thrift 208
Auntie Helen's 209
Avenida Revolucion 211
Budweiser Beer School 32
Carlsbad Company Stores 160
Cheap Rentals 72
Chicken Pie Shop 56
Chua Van Hanh Vietnamese Buddhist
    Temple 45
Designated Drivers Association 90
Freeflight 19
Hash House A Go Go 180
Hillcrest Farmer's Market 78
International Professional School of Body
    Works 131
Kobey's Swap Meet 119
Museum of Contemporary Art 20, 155
Museum of Man 54, 214
Open Sandcastle Competition 177
Pacific Islander Festival 89
Ray and Joan Kroc Corps Community
    Center 198
Salvation Army 198
San Diego County Farm Bureau 78
San Diego Factory Outlet Mall 160
San Diego Historical Society 20, 35, 58
San Diego Public Library 16, 88
San Diego Velodrome 72
Soon Lee Chinese Laundry 60
Spreckles Organ Pavilion 88
St. Bartholomew's Thrift Shop 209
St. Mary Magdalene's 33
St. Vincent's Specialty Shop 209

Thrift Korral 209
Tijuana/Mexico 79, 210, 211
Timken Museum of Art 88
Trader Joe's 215
Viejas Outlet Center 161
World Duty Free Shop 190

Bars/Booze/Beer

4th and B 66
Alibi, The 149
Avenida Revolucion 211
Bellefleur Winery and Restaurant 160
Belly Up Tavern 111
Bitter End 131
Bourbon Street 34, 152
Brass Rail, The 124
Budweiser Beer School 32
Caliph, The 165
Club Montage 124
Coronado Brewing Co. 42
Croce's Jazz Bar, Restaurant 113
Deer Park Winery and Auto Museum 23
Field, The 44
Flame, The 125, 193
Four Points Sheraton Hotel Skies Lounge
    186
French Gourmet at Elario's 114, 228
Greystokes Bar & Grill 124
Humphrey's 115, 168
In Cahoots 67
Kaiserhof, The 178
Karl Strauss Brewery 39
Kelly's 149
Kickers 69
Lamplighter, The 150
Martini Ranch 130
Morena Club 150
NuNu's 149
O'Connell's 150
Ould Sod 44
Princess Pub and Grille 43
Red Circle 130
Red Fox Room 165
Rich's 124
Rosie O'Grady's Irish Pub and Grille 45
San Diego Brewing Co. 42
Seven 131
Shakespeare's Pub & Grill 43
Tavern on the Green 124
Top of the Hyatt 228
Top of the Park 229

Trader Joe's 215
Wine Bank, The 233
WineSellar, The 234
Wolf's 124
Zone, The 124

Beaches and Boardwalks

Black's Beach 155, 228, 232
Carlsbad Inn Beach Resort 39
Children's Pool 29
Coronado Ferry 79
Coronado Island 70, 79
Crystal Pier Hotel 126
Dog Beach 75
Fiesta Island 70, 75, 161
Hilton San Diego Resort 120, 166
Hotel Del Coronado 71, 100, 106, 147, 200
La Jolla Cove 166
La Jolla Shores 70
Leucadia State Beach 30
Marine Street Beach 70
Mission Bay 70, 120, 166
Moonlight Beach 30
Ocean Beach 70, 78
Ocean Beach Park 75
Ocean Beach Pier 38
Plunge, The 197
San Diego Maritime Museum 187
Seaport Village 89, 168
Shelter Island 168
Silver Strand 72
South Mission Beach 70
Star of India 187

Books/Literary/Ephemera

5th Avenue Books 35
Blue Stocking Books 35
Bountiful Books 35
Buddha's Light Bookstore 46
California Surf Museum 143
Comics-N-Stuff 64
Controversial Bookstore 34
Galactic Comics 65
Lesbian and Gay Historical Society of San
    Diego 21
Museum of History and Art 147
Museum of Making Music 142
Museum of Man 54, 214
Museum of Photographic Arts 88, 141
North Park Library 134
On Comic Ground 65

Prince and the Pauper Collectible
    Children's Books 35
San Diego Automotive Museum 23
San Diego Chinese Historical Society
    Museum 146
San Diego Historical Society 20, 35, 58
San Diego Public Library 16, 88

Buildings/Missions/Temples
Botanical Building 181
Chua Van Hanh Vietnamese Buddhist
    Temple 45
El Cortez Hotel 64
Horton Grand Hotel 106, 107, 200
Horton Plaza 199
Hotel Del Coronado 71, 100, 106, 147, 200
House of Pacific Relations International
    Cottages 66
Hsi Fang Buddhist Temple 46
International Society for Krishna Con-
    sciousness Temple 88
Junipero Serra Museum 168, 212
Mission San Diego de Alcala 55, 138
Mission San Luis Rey 139
Museum of Man 54, 214
Our Lady's Chapel 52
Park Manor Suites 229
Rancho Guajome Adobe 175
Rancho Zosa 173
Reuben H. Fleet Science Center 88, 157, 181
Rotating Home 176
Saint Francis Chapel 54
San Diego Convention Center 64, 153
Spreckles Organ Pavilion 88
U.S. Grant Hotel 199
University of San Diego 166
War Memorial Building 193
Whaley House 104
William Heath Davis House 107

Cheap Eats
See also Bargains and Freebies
Andres' Patio Restaurant 69
Bandar 163
Brian's American Eatery 220
Bronx Pizza 170
Chicken Pie Shop 56
Conching's Café and Ice Cream Parlor 83
Corvette Diner 103
Cottage Café 172
Da Kine's 120

El Indio Mexican Restaurant 215
Falafel King 183
Hamburger Factory 103
Heidi's Frozen Yogurt 124
Hob Nob Hill 38
Hodads 102
In-N-Out Burger 103
Jimmy Carter's 37
Johnny's Family Restaurant 39
Lotsa Pasta 214
New York Pizza Department 170
Night & Day Café 220
Ruby's Diner 160
Rudford's Restaurant 220
Saffron Chicken 203
Tofu House 224
V.G. Donuts and Bakery 25
Waterfront, The 102

Children's Stuff
Asian Story Theater 21
Basic Brown Bear Factory 201
Belmont Amusement Park 59, 197
Children's Discovery Museum of North
    County 58
Children's Park 58
Children's Pool 29
Christian Community Theater 207
Corvette Diner 103
Fall Back Festival 58
Filipino Family Day 83
Firehouse Museum 146
Freeflight 19
Game Empire 92
Giant Dipper Rollercoaster 59, 197
Jarrett Meeker Foundation 18
Kite Country 121
Kite Flite 121
Knott's Soak City USA 59, 83
LEGOLAND California 57
Liberty Carousel 59
Marie Hitchcock Puppet Theater 173
Miniature Train 157
Nutter's 162
Pacific Islander Festival 89
Plunge, The 197
Prince and the Pauper Collectible
    Children's Books 35
Ray and Joan Kroc Corps Community
    Center 198
Rocky Point Preserve 17

San Diego Children's Museum 58
San Diego Zoo 18, 57
Seaport Village 89, 168
SeaWorld 17, 32, 57
Spooky Sleepovers 18
Swim hotline 198
Thunder Boats 59
Ultrazone 57
Wild Animal Park 18, 57

Coffee and Tea
A La Francaise 26
All Things Bright and British 44
Bit O'Britain 44
Café 222 229
Chatterbox Café 101
Cottage Restaurant, The 230
Daily News Café 39
David's Coffee House 60
Dietrich Coffee 60
Kensington Coffee Company 63
Mission, The 38
Mrs. Burton's Tea Room 225
Night & Day Café 220
Ocean Beach People's Organic Food
    Cooperative 108
Sinbad Café and Hookah Bar 190
Twiggs Coffeehouse 63
U.S. Grant Hotel 199
V.G. Donuts and Bakery 25
Xen Hookah Lounge and Coffee Shop 190

Confections and Sweets
All Things Bright and British 44
Candy Depot 50
Cookies by Design 27
Dudley's 26
Julian Pie Company 27
Nutter's 162
Pet Pleasers Bakery 164
Seaport Village 89, 168
Terra 76
V.G. Donuts and Bakery 25

Fashion/Apparel
See also Malls and Markets
Ballroom Boutique 28
Buffalo Exchange 221
Carlsbad Company Stores 160
Crossroads Gift Shop 26
Eat Leather 82

Fashion Valley Mall 139, 160
Flashbacks Recycled Fashions 222
G.I. Joe Army Surplus Store 47
Hazard Center 141
Helga's Yarn Boutique 121
Icons 111
John's 5th Avenue Luggage ???
Kobey's Swap Meet 119
La Mesa Village 44
Mint 183
Mrs. Burton's Tea Room 225
Ringold Alley 82
Sew Fine 122
South Cedros Avenue 111
Terra Brazil 36
Tijuana 79
University Towne Center Mall 71

Festivals/Celebrations/Events
Comic-Con International 64
Fall Back Festival 58
Red Mass 55
House of Pacific Relations International
    Cottages 66
Jarrett Meeker Foundation 18
Midnight Madness 73
Open Sandcastle Competition 177
Outdoor Summer Shakespeare Festival 181
Over the Line Tournament 161
Pacific Islander Festival 89
Philippine Cultural Arts Festival 84
San Diego LGBT Pride 123, 125
Semi-Spontaneous Shakespeare Society 181
Unarius Academy of Science 85

For Adults Only
6th @ Penn Theatre 208
Adult Depot 15
Crypt on Park 81
Eat Leather 82
F Street Adult Video and Gifts 16
Holy Smoke 189
Inhale 189
Midnight Adult Book and Video Centers 16
Puff N Stuff Smoke Shop 189
Ringold Alley 82
Sensual Delights 172

GLBT
Bienestar San Diego 125
Bisexual Forum 125

Bourbon Street 34, 152
Club Montage 124
David's Coffee House 60
Diversionary Theatre 207
Flame, The 125, 193
Greystokes Bar & Grill 124
Hamburger Mary's 102
Kickers 69
Lesbian and Gay Historical Society of San
    Diego 21
Lesbian, Gay, Bisexual, Transgender
    Community Center 123
Rich's 124
San Diego LGBT Pride 123, 125
Six Degrees 125
Tavern on the Green 124
Top of the Park 229
Wolf's 124
Zone, The 124

Haute Cuisine/Fine Dining

See also International Interests
Abbey, The 13
Aswan African Restaurant 75
Bayou Dining & Jazz 152
Bellefleur Winery and Restaurant 160
Café 828 118
Café Caspian 163
Café Japengo 195
Celadon Royalty Thai 201
Chateau Orleans 151
Croce's Jazz Bar, Restaurant 113
Emerald Chinese Seafood 77
Faz 222
French Gourmet at Elario's 114, 228
Humphrey's 115, 168
Liaison 90
Mission Hills Café 150, 151
Molly's 49
Rei do Gado 36
Royal Thai Cuisine 202
Seven 131
Terra 76
Top of the Park 229

Home Furnishings/Décor

Action Thrift 208
Babette Schwartz 176
Column One 110
Country Craftsman of San Diego 225
Dime Store Retro 175

Fashion Valley Mall 139, 160
Genghis Khan 112
Hauser Patio & Rattan 112
Kobey's Swap Meet 119
Light Bulb House 112
Light Bulbs Unlimited 112
Mex-Art Pottery & Home Accents 112
Morena Boulevard 112
South Cedros Avenue 111
St. Vincent's Specialty Shop 209
Thrift Korral 209
Uptown District 61

International Interests

A La Francaise 26
All Things Bright and British 44
Andres' Patio Restaurant 69
Asian Story Theater 21
Aswan African Restaurant 75
Bit O'Britain 44
Café Caspian 163
Caffe Italia 61
Chua Van Hanh Vietnamese Buddhist
    Temple 45
Conching's Café and Ice Cream Parlor 83
Convoy Street 77
Cottage Café 172
Emerald Chinese Seafood 77
Filipino Family Day 83
Filipino Press 83
Galoka Gallery and Restaurant Bar 224
Genghis Khan 112
Haar Ethiopian Restaurant 76
House of Pacific Relations International
    Cottages 66
International Society for Krishna
    Consciousness Temple 88
Japanese Friendship Bell 168
Japanese Friendship Garden 94
Kaiserhof, The 178
Melodia Brazilian Seafood and Vegetarian
    Kitchen 36
Mex-Art Pottery & Home Accents 112
Mexico (*see Tijuana*)
Momo 47
Nijiya Market 78
Ould Sod 44
Pacific Islander Festival 89
Philippine Cultural Arts Festival 84
Princess Pub and Grille 43
Rei do Gado 36

Samahan Dance Company 84
San Diego Chinese Historical Society
    Museum 146
Seafood City Supermarket 83
Shakespeare's Corner Shop 43
Shakespeare's Pub & Grill 43
Terra Brazil 36
Thomas Cook Currency Service Inc. 71
Tijuana 79, 210, 211

Malls and Markets
Avenida Revolucion 211
Bazaar del Mundo 206, 215
Carlsbad Company Stores 160
Coronado Farmer's Market 79
Exotic Limes and Fruits 24
Fashion Valley Mall 139, 160
Hillcrest Farmer's Market 78
Horton Plaza 199
Iowa Meat Farms 132
Jimbo's Naturally 109
Kaelin's 133
La Mesa Village 44
Mardi Gras Café and Market 151
Mission Center 160
Nijiya Market 78
Ocean Beach Farmer's Market 78
Ocean Beach People's Organic Food
    Cooperative 108
Rancho Fruit Market 24
Royal Food Mart 101
San Diego Factory Outlet Mall 160
Seaport Village 89, 168
Seafood City Supermarket 83
South Cedros Avenue 111
University Towne Center Mall 71
Uptown District 61
Village Fair Shopping Center 58
Village Hillcrest 50, 140

Museums/Exhibits/Galleries
Botanical Building 181
California Center for the Arts 98
California Surf Museum 143
Children's Discovery Museum of North
    County 58
Chuck Jones Studio Gallery 48
Computer Museum of America 142
Deer Park Winery and Auto Museum 23
Firehouse Museum 146
Flying Leatherneck Museum 146

Galoka Gallery and Restaurant Bar 224
House of Charm 218
House of Pacific Relations International
    Cottages 66
Japanese Friendship Bell 168
Junipero Serra Museum 168, 212
Lawrence Welk Resort 122
Mingei International Museum 153
Mission San Antonio de Pala 138
Mission San Diego de Alcala 55, 138
Mission San Luis Rey 139
Model Railroad Museum 88, 143
Montgomery Waller Community Park and
    Recreation Center 234
Museum of Contemporary Art 20, 155
Museum of History and Art 147
Museum of Making Music 142
Museum of Man 54, 214
Museum of Photographic Arts 88, 141
Navy Aircraft Carrier Memorial 135
Palomar Observatory 157
Reuben H. Fleet Science Center 88, 157, 181
Saffron Noodles & Sate 97
San Diego Aerospace Museum 134, 146, 147
San Diego Astrological Society 22
San Diego Automotive Museum 23
San Diego Children's Museum 58
San Diego Chinese Historical Society
    Museum 146
San Diego Hall of Champions Sport
    Museum 193
San Diego Historical Society 20, 35, 58
San Diego Maritime Museum 187
San Diego Natural History Museum 88,
    217, 218
San Diego Railroad Museum 144
Santa Ysabel Indian Mission 27
Star of India 187
Stuart Collection 179
Timken Museum of Art 88
Victorian Heritage Park Bed & Breakfast
    Inn 129
Villa Montezuma 107
William Heath Davis House 107

New Age/Spiritual
Buddha's Light Bookstore 46
Chopra Center 74
Chopra, Deepak 73
Controversial Bookstore 34
Feng Shui Warehouse 81

Gen Min Acupuncture and Herb Center 108
International Society for Krishna Con-
    sciousness Temple 88
Longevity Herbs 108
Pacific College of Oriental Medicine 108
San Diego Astrological Society 22
Self-Realization Fellowship Retreat and
    Hermitage Grounds 96
Unarius Academy of Science 85

Organizations/Societies
Absolutely Dancesport 28
Athletic Singles Association of Southern
    California 186
Balboa Park Puppet Guild 173
Bienestar San Diego 125
Bisexual Forum 125
Carltas Company 97
Christian Community Theater 207
Country Craftsman of San Diego 225
Designated Drivers Association 90
Guided Adventures in Nature 218
International Professional School of Body
    Works 131
International Society for Krishna Con-
    sciousness Temple 88
Jarrett Meeker Foundation 18
La Mesa Women's Club 29
Lesbian and Gay Historical Society of San
    Diego 21
Oceanside Photo and Telescope Astronomi-
    cal Society 107
Pacific Beach Town Council 56
San Diego Astrological Society 22
San Diego Historical Society 20, 35, 58
San Diego LGBT Pride 123, 125
Semi-Spontaneous Shakespeare Society 181
Single Gourmet 186
Unlimited Adventures 187
Walkabout International 218

Outdoor Activities and Sights
See also Views and Vistas; Parks/Gardens;
    Sporting Venues and Events
Alcazar Garden 94
Anza-Borrego Desert State Park 99, 107
Aqua Adventures 18
Balboa Park 92, 166, 181, 226
Belmont Amusement Park 59, 197
Bikes and Beyond 71
Black's Beach 155, 228, 232

Bud Kearns Memorial Pool 197
Cactus Garden 94
Carlsbad Flower Fields 97
Cheap Rentals 72
Children's Pool 29
Coronado Ferry 79
Cowles Mountain 217
Del Mar Thoroughbred Club 89
Dolphin Interaction Program 17
Eagle and High Peak Mine 99
El Prado Way 22, 226
Giant Dipper Rollercoaster 59, 197
Gondola Company, The 100
Guided Adventures in Nature 218
Hillcrest Farmer's Market 78
Jarrett Meeker Foundation 18
Kite Country 121
Kite Flite 121
Knott's Soak City USA 59, 83
Liberty Carousel 59
Little Blair Valley 107
Midnight Madness 73
Milquatay Valley 144
Mission Trails Regional Park 216
Montgomery Waller Community Park and
    Recreation Center 234
Ocean Beach Pier 38
Oceanside Photo and Telescope Astronomi-
    cal Society 107
Open Sandcastle Competition 177
Outdoor Summer Shakespeare Festival 181
Over the Line Tournament 161
Pacific Islander Festival 89
Palm Canyon 219
Palomar Mountain 156
Philippine Cultural Arts Festival 84
Quail Botanical Gardens 95
Rotating Home 176
San Diego Harbor Excursions 19, 168, 231
San Diego LGBT Pride 123, 125
San Diego Mycological Society 91
San Diego Velodrome 72
San Diego Zoo 18, 57
Seaforth Boat Rentals 19
Seal Rock Mammal Reserve 30
Seaport Village 89, 168
SeaWorld 17, 32, 57
Self-Realization Fellowship Retreat and
    Hermitage Grounds 96
Sierra Club 217
Silver Strand 72

Swim hotline 198
Thunder Boats 59
Torrey Pines Glider Port 228
Trainer for a Day 17
Tunaman's Memorial 134
Walkabout International 218
Walk on the Wild Side Tour 18
Wild Animal Park 18, 57

Parks/Gardens
Alcazar Garden 94
Anza-Borrego Desert State Park 99, 107
Balboa Park 92, 166, 181, 226
Cactus Garden 94
Cancer Survivors Park 194
Carlsbad Flower Fields 97
Cedros Gardens 111
Children's Park 58
Embarcadero Marina Park North 121
Guajome County Park 175
Japanese Friendship Garden 94
Kit Carson Park 153
Mission Trails Regional Park 216
Ocean Beach Park 75
Pioneer Park 49
Presidio Park 168
Quail Botanical Gardens 95
Self-Realization Fellowship Retreat and
    Hermitage Grounds 96
Tavern on the Green 124
Tribute Garden at San Diego Hospice 95
Wild Animal Park 18, 57

Publications and Periodicals
Brazilian Pacific Times 37
Buzz Magazine 11
Caffe Italia 61
City Beat 11
Daily News Café 39
Downtown News 11
Filipino Press 83
Gay and Lesbian Times 11
Night & Day 11
Reader, The 11
San Diego Union-Tribune 11
Update 11

Restaurants
See also Bargains and Freebies; Cheap Eats;
    Haute Cuisine/Fine Dining; International
    Interests

94th Aero Squadron 47, 186
A La Francaise 26
Abbey, The 13
Albie's 165
Andres' Patio Restaurant 69
Aswan African Restaurant 75
Bandar 163
Bayou Dining & Jazz 152
Bellefleur Winery and Restaurant 160
Ben & Jerry's Ice Cream 124
Big Kitchen 51
Black Angus 121
Bread and Cie 26
Brian's American Eatery 220
Bronx Pizza 170
Café 222 229
Café 828 118
Café Caspian 163
Café Japengo 195
Caffe Italia 61
Casa de Pico 215
Cecil's Café 38
Celadon Royalty Thai 201
Chateau Orleans 151
Chatterbox Café 101
Chicken Pie Shop 56
Chuck E. Cheese's 57
City Deli 118
Coco's 37
Conching's Café and Ice Cream Parlor 83
Coronado Brewing Co. 42
Corvette Diner 103
Cottage Café 172
Cottage Restaurant, The 230
Crest Café 219
Croce's Jazz Bar, Restaurant 113
Da Kine's 120
Daily News Café 39
David's Coffee House 60
Dietrich Coffee 60
DZ Akins 115
El Indio Mexican Restaurant 215
El Torrito Mexican Cantina 202
Emerald Chinese Seafood 77
Falafel King 183
Faz 222
Field, The 44
Filippi's 170
French Gourmet at Elario's 114, 228
Galoka Gallery and Restaurant Bar 224
Greystokes Bar & Grill 124

Haar Ethiopian Restaurant 76
Hamburger Factory 103
Hamburger Mary's 102
Hash House A Go Go 180
Hob Nob Hill 38
Hodads 102
Humphrey's 115, 168
Ichiban 196
In-N-Out Burger 103
Jimmy Carter's 37
Johnny's Family Restaurant 39
Jyoti Bihango 223, 224
Kaelin's 133
Kaiserhof, The 178
Karinya Thai 202
Karl Strauss Brewery 39
Kelly's 149
La Paloma Restaurant 174
Liaison 90
Lips 74
Lotsa Pasta 214
Lotus Thai Cuisine 109
Melodia Brazilian Seafood and Vegetarian
    Kitchen 36
Milton's 117
Molly's 49
Momo 47
New York Pizza Department 170
Night & Day Café 220
Nutter's 162
Old Country Restaurant and Deli 178
Ono Sushi & Pacific Spice 196
Ould Sod 44
Phil's BBQ & Ice Cream 102
Princess Pub and Grille 43
Red Circle 130
Red Fox Room 165
Rei do Gado 36
Rocky's Crown Pub 102
Rose Creek Cottage 55
Rosie O'Grady's Irish Pub and Grille 45
Royal Thai Cuisine 202
Ruby's Diner 160
Rudford's Restaurant 220
Saffron Chicken 203
Saffron Noodles & Sate 97
San Diego Brewing Co. 42
Seven 131
Shakespeare's Pub & Grill 43
Sinbad Café and Hookah Bar 190
Sushi on the Rock 195

Sushi Ota 195
Taste of Italy 170
Terra 76
Terra Brazil 36
Tiptop Meats 179
Todai 47
Tofu House 224
Top of the Hyatt 228
Top of the Park 229
Try Thai 202
Twiggs Coffeehouse 63
Tyler's Taste of Texas 221
V.G. Donuts and Bakery 25
Waffle Spot, The 230
Xen Hookah Lounge and Coffee Shop 190

Sporting Venues and Events

ARCO/US Olympic Training Center 159
Athletic Singles Association of Southern
    California 186
Del Mar Thoroughbred Club 89
Midnight Madness 73
Montgomery Waller Community Park and
    Recreation Center 234
Old Mission Beach Athletic Club 161
Over the Line Tournament 161
Qualcomm Stadium 177
Ray and Joan Kroc Corps Community
    Center 198
San Diego Brewing Co. 42
San Diego Hall of Champions Sport
    Museum 193
San Diego Velodrome 72
Shakespeare's Pub & Grill 43
Sports Arena 15, 119
Torrey Pines Glider Port 228

Tours

Aqua Adventures 18
Contract Tours 211
Guided Adventures in Nature 218
Old Town Trolley Tours of San Diego 107
Palomar Observatory 157
Quail Botanical Gardens 95
San Diego Convention and Visitors'
    Bureau 11
San Diego Harbor Excursions 19, 168, 231
San Diego Railroad Museum 144
San Diego Visitor Information Center 11
Seaforth Boat Rentals 19
Unlimited Adventures 187

Walk on the Wild Side Tour 18
Walkabout International 218

Theaters and Stages
4th and B 66
6th @ Penn Theatre 208
Asian Story Theater 21
Belly Up Tavern 111
California Center for the Arts 98
Christian Community Theater 207
Coronado Playhouse 181
Diversionary Theatre 207
Dizzy's 113
East County Performing Arts Center 155
Fritz Theater 206
Humphrey's 115, 168
La Jolla Playhouse 96, 204
Lyceum Theater 22, 205
Marie Hitchcock Puppet Theater 173
Old Globe Theater 95, 181, 204
Outdoor Summer Shakespeare Festival 181
Reuben H. Fleet Science Center 88, 157, 181
San Diego Repertory Theatre 204, 205
Semi-Spontaneous Shakespeare Society 181
St. Cecilia's Playhouse 204
Starlight Musical Theatre 207
Sushi Performance and Visual Art 205
Theatre in Old Town 206
Viejas Casino 33, 34

Travel Essentials
A Walker's Luggage and Shoe Repair 148
Anthony's Shoe Repair 148
Independent Luggage Repair 148
John's 5th Avenue Luggage 148
Le Travel Store 147
Play It Again Sports 132
Sew Fine 122
Thomas Cook Currency Service Inc. 71
Traveler's Depot 147

Views and Vistas
Alcazar Garden 94
Aqua Adventures 18
Balboa Park 92, 166, 181, 226
Black's Beach 155, 228, 232
Carlsbad Flower Fields 97
Christian Community Theater 207
Coronado Bay Bridge 226
Cowles Mountain 217
Crystal Pier Hotel 126
Embarcadero Marina Park North 121
Fiesta Island 70, 75, 161
French Gourmet at Elario's 114, 228
La Jolla Cove 166
Laurel Street Bridge 226
Mission Trails Regional Park 216
Montgomery Waller Community Park and
    Recreation Center 234
Mount Helix 176
Mount Soledad 229
Ocean Beach Pier 38
Oceanside Photo and Telescope
    Astronomical Society 107
Palm Canyon 219
Palomar Mountain 156
Palomar Observatory 157
Presidio Hill 212
Presidio Park 168
Quince Street Bridge 87
San Diego Harbor Excursions 19, 168, 231
Seaport Village 89, 168
Shelter Island 168
Silver Strand 72
Spruce Street Suspension Bridge 85
Tavern on the Green 124
Top of the Hyatt 228
Top of the Park 229
Tunaman's Memorial 134
University of San Diego 166

LOCATION INDEX

Balboa Park
Alcazar Garden 94
Balboa Park Puppet Guild 173
Bea Evenson Fountain 226
Botanical Building 181
Cactus Garden 94
Casa Del Prado 91
Ebony Pride 125
El Prado Way 22, 226
Flying A Squares 193
House of Charm 218
House of Pacific Relations International
    Cottages 66
Japanese Friendship Garden 94
Jarrett Meeker Foundation 18
Laurel Street Bridge 226
Marie Hitchcock Puppet Theater 173
Marston Point 226
Mingei International Museum 153
Miniature Train 157
Model Railroad Museum 88, 143
Museum of Man 54, 214
Museum of Photographic Arts 88, 141
Old Globe Theater 95, 181, 204
Palm Canyon 219
Philippine Cultural Arts Festival 84
Recital Hall 193
Reuben H. Fleet Science Center 88, 157, 181
Saint Francis Chapel 54
San Diego Aerospace Museum 134, 146, 147
San Diego Automotive Museum 23
San Diego Hall of Champions Sport
    Museum 193
San Diego Historical Society 20, 35, 58
San Diego Mycological Society 91
San Diego Natural History Museum 88,
    217, 218
San Diego Zoo 18, 57
Semi-Spontaneous Shakespeare Society 181
Spooky Sleepovers 18
Spreckles Organ Pavilion 88
Starlight Musical Theatre 207
Tavern on the Green 124
Timken Museum of Art 88
Veterans Memorial Center and Museum 134

War Memorial Building 193
Zoro Garden 181

Bankers Hill
Chatterbox Café 101
Hob Nob Hill 38
Liaison 90
New Creation Church of Christ 125
Quince Street Bridge 87
Royal Food Mart 101
Spruce Street Suspension Bridge 85

Bay Park
Andres' Patio Restaurant 69
Genghis Khan 112
Hauser Patio & Rattan 112
Light Bulb House 112
Light Bulbs Unlimited 112
Mex-Art Pottery & Home Accents 112
Morena Club 150
O'Connell's 150
St. Mary Magdalene's 33

Center City
San Diego Maritime Museum 187
Star of India 187

Chollas View
Villa Montezuma 107

Clairemont Mesa
Action Thrift 208
Game Empire 92

College Area
Blessed Sacrament 33

Downtown
4th and B 66
Asian Story Theater 21
Bandar 163
Bayou Dining & Jazz 152
Bitter End 131
Café 828 118
Children's Park 58

Comic-Con International 64
Computer Museum of America 142
Croce's Jazz Bar, Restaurant 113
Dime Store Retro 175
Dizzy's 113
El Cortez Hotel 64
Fall Back Festival 58
Faz 222
Field, The 44
Fumari 190
G.I. Joe Army Surplus Store 47
Gran Havana Cigar Factory 190
Horton Grand Hotel 106, 107, 200
Horton Plaza 199
Le Travel Store 147
Lyceum Theater 22, 205
Mariott Suites 222
Martini Ranch 130
Molly's 49
Momo 47
Nutter's 162
Ramada Inn and Suites 119
Red Circle 130
Rei do Gado 36
Royal Thai Cuisine 202
San Diego Children's Museum 58
San Diego Chinese Historical Society
    Museum 146
San Diego Convention Center 64, 153
San Diego Harbor Excursions 19, 168, 231
San Diego Public Library 16, 88
San Diego Repertory Theatre 204, 205
Single Gourmet 186
Sledgehammer Theatre 204
St. Cecilia's Playhouse 204
Thomas Cook Currency Service Inc. 71
Top of the Hyatt 228
U.S. Grant Hotel 199
USA Hostels San Diego 127
Walkabout International 218
Waterfront, The 102
Westgate Hotel 199
William Heath Davis House 107
Wine Bank, The 233

East Village
Soon Lee Chinese Laundry 60
Sushi Performance and Visual Art 205

Golden Hill
Big Kitchen 51

Harbor District
Cancer Survivors Park 194
Coronado Ferry 79
County Administration Building 73
Navy Aircraft Carrier Memorial 135

Hillcrest
5th Avenue Books 35
6th @ Penn Theatre 208
Abbey, The 13
Alibi, The 149
Anatomy Day Spa and Boutique 191
Babette Schwartz 176
Balboa Park Inn 126
Ballroom Boutique 28
Ben & Jerry's Ice Cream 124
Bingo and More 33
Blue Stocking Books 35
Bountiful Books 35
Brass Rail, The 124
Bread and Cie 26
Bronx Pizza 170
Buffalo Exchange 221
Caliph, The 165
Candy Depot 50
Celadon Royalty Thai 201
Champion Ballroom Academy 28
City Deli 118
Column One 110
Corvette Diner 103
Cottage, The 130
Crest Café 219
Crypt on Park 81
David's Coffee House 60
Dietrich Coffee 60
Flame, The 125, 193
Flashbacks Recycled Fashions 222
Hamburger Mary's 102
Hash House A Go Go 180
Heidi's Frozen Yogurt 124
Hillcrest Cinemas 50, 140
Hillcrest Farmer's Market 78
Holy Smoke 189
Ichiban 196
Inhale 189
Jimmy Carter's 37
John's 5th Avenue Luggage 148
Kickers 69
Lesbian, Gay, Bisexual, Transgender
    Community Center 123
Lips 74

Longevity Herbs 108
Lotus Thai Cuisine 109
Mint 183
NuNu's 149
On Comic Ground 65
Ono Sushi & Pacific Spice 196
Our Lady's Chapel 52
Park Manor Suites 229
Pet Pleasers Bakery 164
Puff N Stuff Smoke Shop 189
Rich's 124
San Diego Astrological Society 22
San Diego Design Center 84
San Diego LGBT Pride 123, 125
Scripps Mercy Hospital 52
Sensual Delights 172
Seven 131
Starbucks Coffee 124
Taste of Italy 170
Terra 76
Top of the Park 229
Trader Joe's 215
Tribute Garden at San Diego Hospice 95
Unlimited Adventures 187
Uptown District 61
Vermont Street Pedestrian Bridge 87
Xen Hookah Lounge and Coffee Shop 190
Village Hillcrest 50, 140

Kearny Mesa
94th Aero Squadron 47, 186
Cigarettes Cheaper 190
Convoy Street 77
Emerald Chinese Seafood 77
Four Points Sheraton Hotel Skies Lounge 186
Montgomery Field 48
Nijiya Market 78
Southern California Comics 65
Tofu House 224

Kensington
Ken Cinema 140
Kensington Coffee Company 63
Kensington Community Church Recreational
     Hall 193

La Jolla
Black's Beach 155, 228, 232
Children's Pool 29
Cottage Restaurant, The 230
Flour Power Custom Bakery 25

French Gourmet at Elario's 114, 228
Galoka Gallery and Restaurant Bar 224
Helga's Yarn Boutique 121
Hotel La Jolla 115
La Jolla Cove 166
La Jolla Playhouse 96, 204
La Jolla Shores 70
Marine Street Beach 70
Mount Soledad 229
Museum of Contemporary Art 20, 155
Scripps Institute of Oceanography 232
Scripps Park 166
Seal Rock Mammal Reserve 30
Stuart Collection 179
Sushi on the Rock 195
Torrey Pines Glider Port 228
University of California at San Diego 153, 179

Linda Vista
Founders Chapel 54
Immaculata 54
University of San Diego 166

Little Italy
Absolutely Dancesport 28
Caffe Italia 61
Filippi's 170
Firehouse Museum 146
Princess Pub and Grille 43

Loma Portal
Adult Depot 15
Black Angus 121
Chuck E. Cheese's 57
Comics-N-Stuff 64
Kite Country 121
Kobey's Swap Meet 119
Mardi Gras Café and Market 151
Sports Arena 15, 119
Ultrazone 57

Marina District
Café 222 229
Embarcadero Marina Park North 121
Kite Flite 121
Seaport Village 89, 168

Middletown
Club Montage 124
Cottage Café 172
El Indio Mexican Restaurant 215

Shakespeare's Corner Shop 43
Shakespeare's Pub & Grill 43
Six Degrees 125

Mira Mesa
Seafood City Supermarket 83

Miramar
Flying Leatherneck Museum 146
Independent Luggage Repair 148

Mission Bay
Aqua Adventures 18
Bahia Hotel 19
Budweiser Beer School 32
Dolphin Interaction Program 17
Fiesta Island 70, 75, 161
Hilton San Diego Resort 120, 166
Mission Bay 70, 120, 166
Over the Line Tournament 161
Pacific Islander Festival 89
Rocky Point Preserve 17
Santa Clara Point 70
Seaforth Boat Rentals 19
SeaWorld 17, 32, 57
Trainer for a Day 17

Mission Beach
Belmont Amusement Park 59, 197
Cheap Rentals 72
Giant Dipper Rollercoaster 59, 197
Liberty Carousel 59
Mission Beach Club 72
Plunge, The 197
South Mission Beach 70
The Mission 38
Thunder Boats 59

Mission Gorge
Iowa Meat Farms 132
San Diego Brewing Co. 42

Mission Hills
A La Francaise 26
Falafel King 183
Junipero Serra Museum 168, 212
Lamplighter, The 150
Mission Hills Café 150, 151
Phil's BBQ & Ice Cream 102
Pioneer Park 49

Presidio Hill 212
Presidio Park 168
Saffron Chicken 203
Saffron Noodles & Sate 97
Sausage King 133

Mission Valley
Albie's 165
Cookies by Design 27
El Torrito Mexican Cantina 202
Fashion Valley Mall 139, 160
Hazard Center 141
In Cahoots 67
Madstone Theaters 140
Mission Center 160
Mission San Diego de Alcala 55, 138
New York Pizza Department 170
Pacific College of Oriental Medicine 108
Qualcomm Stadium 177
TGI Friday's 202
Todai 47
Try Thai 202
Waffle Spot, The 230

Normal Heights
Novelty & Crafts 122
Ould Sod 44
Pet Me Please 164
Prince and the Pauper Collectible
    Children's Books 35
Rosie O'Grady's Irish Pub and Grille 45
Sew Fine 122

North Park
Auntie Helen's 209
Bienestar San Diego 125
Bud Kearns Memorial Pool 197
Cabernet Cellar 233
Chicken Pie Shop 56
Chito's Shoe Repair 148
Controversial Bookstore 34
Gen Min Acupuncture and Herb Center 108
Haar Ethiopian Restaurant 76
Herb Shoppe 110
Johnny's Family Restaurant 39
Jyoti Bihango 223, 224
Mission, The 38
North Park Library 134
Red Fox Room 165
Ringold Alley 82

Rudford's Restaurant 220
San Diego Velodrome 72
Sierra Club 217
St. Vincent's Specialty Shop 209
Starlight Dance Studio 28
Wolf's 124
Zone, The 124

Ocean Beach
Cecil's Café 38
Dog Beach 75
Galactic Comics 65
Hodads 102
Kaiserhof, The 178
Ocean Beach 70, 78
Ocean Beach Farmer's Market 78
Ocean Beach International Backpackers
   Hostel 129
Ocean Beach Park 75
Ocean Beach People's Organic Food
   Cooperative 108
Ocean Beach Pier 38

Old Town
Basic Brown Bear Factory 201
Bazaar del Mundo 206, 215
Casa de Pico 215
Chapel of the Immaculate Conception 55
Chuck Jones Studio Gallery 48
Creations and Confections 51
Immaculate Conception Church 55
Kelly's 149
Mrs. Burton's Tea Room 225
Old Mission Beach Athletic Club 161
Old Town Trolley Tours of San Diego 107
Theatre in Old Town 206
Victorian Heritage Park Bed & Breakfast
   Inn 129
Whaley House 104

Pacific Beach
Banana Bungalow Beach San Diego 127
Chateau Orleans 151
Crystal Pier Hotel 126
Da Kine's 120
International Professional School of Body
   Works 131
International Society for Krishna Con-
   sciousness Temple 88
Karinya Thai 202
Lotsa Pasta 214

Pacific Beach Town Council 56
Play It Again Sports 132
Rocky's Crown Pub 102
Rose Creek Cottage 55
Sinbad Café and Hookah Bar 190
Surfer Motor Lodge 120
Sushi Ota 195
Traveler's Depot 147
Vishions Smoke Shop 98

Point Loma
Feng Shui Warehouse 81
Umi Sushi 196

Rolando Park
Ray and Joan Kroc Corps Community
   Center 198

San Carlos
Cowles Mountain 217

Serra Mesa
A Walker's Luggage and Shoe Repair 148

Shelter Island
Humphrey's 115, 168
Japanese Friendship Bell 168
Tunaman's Memorial 134

Sorrento Mesa
WineSellar, The 234

Sorrento Valley
Karl Strauss Brewery 39

Tierrasanta
Mission Trails Regional Park 216

University City
Café Japengo 195
Thomas Cook Currency Service Inc. 71
University Towne Center Mall 71

University Heights
Bourbon Street 34, 152
Brian's American Eatery 220
Buddha's Light Bookstore 46
Café Caspian 163
Diversionary Theatre 207
Hsi Fang Buddhist Temple 46

Lesbian and Gay Historical Society of San Diego 21
Twiggs Coffeehouse 63
Vermont Street Pedestrian Bridge 87

Outside of City Limits

Alpine, California
Viejas Casino 33, 34
Viejas Outlet Center 161
Anza Borrego, California
Anza-Borrego Desert State Park 99, 107
Little Blair Valley 107
Campo, California
San Diego Railroad Museum 144
Cardiff, California
V.G. Donuts and Bakery 25
Carlsbad, California
Athletic Singles Association of Southern California 186
Bellefleur Winery and Restaurant 160
Bit O'Britain 44
Carlsbad Company Stores 160
Carlsbad Flower Fields 97
Carlsbad Inn Beach Resort 39
Children's Discovery Museum of North County 58
Chopra Center 74
Daily News Café 39
Guided Adventures in Nature 218
La Costa Resort and Spa 74
LEGOLAND California 57
Museum of Making Music 142
Ruby's Diner 160
Tiptop Meats 179
Village Fair Shopping Center 58
Chula Vista, California
ARCO/US Olympic Training Center 159
Filipino Family Day 83
Knott's Soak City USA 59, 83
Coronado, California
Bikes and Beyond 71
Coronado Brewing Co. 42
Coronado Farmer's Market 79
Coronado Playhouse 181
Gondola Company, The 100
Hotel Del Coronado 71, 100, 106, 147, 200
Museum of History and Art 147
Night & Day Café 220
Outdoor Summer Shakespeare Festival 181
Silver Strand 72

Del Mar, California
Del Mar Thoroughbred Club 89
Freeflight 19
Jimbo's Naturally 109
Milton's 117
El Cajon, California
East County Performing Arts Center 155
Kaelin's 133
Swallows Sun Island Club 156
Sycuan Casino 33
Thrift Korral 209
Tyler's Taste of Texas 221
Unarius Academy of Science 85
World War II Flying Museum 146
Encinitas, California
Melodia Brazilian Seafood and Vegetarian Kitchen 36
Moonlight Beach 30
Quail Botanical Gardens 95
Self-Realization Fellowship Retreat and Hermitage Grounds 96
Terra Brazil 36
Escondido, California
California Center for the Arts 98
Deer Park Winery and Auto Museum 23
Golden Door 191
Jimbo's Naturally 109
Kit Carson Park 153
Lawrence Welk Resort 122
Rancho Zosa 173
Walk on the Wild Side Tour 18
Wild Animal Park 18, 57
Fallbrook, California
Exotic Limes and Fruits 24
Rancho Fruit Market 24
Imperial Beach, California
Midnight Adult Book and Video Center 16
Open Sandcastle Competition 177
Julian, California
Eagle and High Peak Mine 99
La Mesa, California
All Things Bright and British 44
Aswan African Restaurant 75
Christian Community Theater 207
DZ Akins 115
La Mesa Women's Club 29
Mount Helix 176
Old Country Restaurant and Deli 178
Rotating Home 176
San Diego Swing Dance Club 29

Leucadia, California
  Beacon's Beach 30
  Leucadia State Beach 30
National City, California
  Conching's Café and Ice Cream Parlor 83
  Contract Tours 211
  Filipino Press 83
  Seafood City Supermarket 83
Oceanside, California
  Brother Benno's Thrift 210
  California Surf Museum 143
  Greystokes Bar & Grill 124
  Guajome County Park 175
  Mission San Luis Rey 139
  Oceanside Photo and Telescope Astronomical Society 107
  Rancho Guajome Adobe 175
Otay Mesa, California
  Montgomery Waller Community Park and Recreation Center 234
Pala, California
  Mission San Antonio de Pala 138
Palomar, California
  Palomar Observatory 157
Poway, California
  Hamburger Factory 103
  St. Bartholomew's Thrift Shop 209

San Ysidro, California
  San Diego Factory Outlet Mall 160
  World Duty Free Shop 190
Santa Ysabel, California
  Crossroads Gift Shop 26
  Dudley's 26
  Julian Pie Company 27
  Santa Ysabel Indian Mission 27
Santee, California
  Chua Van Hanh Vietnamese Buddhist Temple 45
Solana Beach, California
  Anthony's Shoe Repair 148
  Belly Up Tavern 111
  Cedros Gardens 111
  Icons 111
  Leaping Lotus 111
  Solana Beach Train Station 153
  South Cedros Avenue 111
Tijuana, Mexico
  Avenida Revolucion 211
  Mercado Hidalgo 211
Vista, California
  Cal-A-Vie 191
  La Paloma Restaurant 174
  Rancho Buena Vista Adobe 174

ALPHABETICAL INDEX

4th and B 66
5th Avenue Books 35
6th @ Penn Theatre 208
94th Aero Squadron 47, 186

A La Francaise 26
A Walker's Luggage and Shoe Repair 148
Abbey, The 13
Absolutely Dancesport 28
Action Thrift 208
Adult Depot 15
Albertson's 25
Albie's 165
Alcazar Garden 94
Alibi, The 149
All Things Bright and British 44
AMC Theaters 139
Anatomy Day Spa and Boutique 191
Andres' Patio Restaurant 69
Anthony's Shoe Repair 148
Anza-Borrego Desert State Park 99, 107
Aqua Adventures 18
ARCO/US Olympic Training Center 159
Asian Story Theater 21
Aswan African Restaurant 75
Athletic Singles Association of Southern
    California 186
Auntie Helen's 209
Avenida Revolucion 211

Babette Schwartz 176
Bachman Place 185
Bahia Hotel 19
Balboa Park 92, 166, 181, 226
Balboa Park Inn 126
Balboa Park Puppet Guild 173
Ballroom Boutique 28
Banana Bungalow Beach San Diego 127
Bandar 163
Basic Brown Bear Factory 201
Bayou Dining & Jazz 152
Bazaar del Mundo 206, 215
Bea Evenson Fountain 226
Beacon's Beach 30
Bellefleur Winery and Restaurant 160
Belly Up Tavern 111

Belmont Amusement Park 59, 197
Ben & Jerry's Ice Cream 124
Bienestar San Diego 125
Big Kitchen 51
Bikes and Beyond 71
Bingo and More 33
Bisexual Forum 125
Bit O'Britain 44
Bitter End 131
Black Angus 121
Black's Beach 155, 228, 232
Blessed Sacrament 33
Blue Stocking Books 35
Botanical Building 181
Bountiful Books 35
Bourbon Street 34, 152
Brass Rail, The 124
Bread and Cie 26
Brian's American Eatery 220
Bronx Pizza 170
Brother Benno's Thrift 210
Bud Kearns Memorial Pool 197
Buddha's Light Bookstore 46
Budweiser Beer School 32
Buffalo Exchange 221

Cabernet Cellar 233
Cactus Garden 94
Café 222 229
Café 828 118
Café Caspian 163
Café Japengo 195
Caffe Italia 61
Cal-A-Vie 191
California Center for the Arts 98
California Institute of Technology 156
California Surf Museum 143
Caliph, The 165
Cancer Survivors Park 194
Candy Depot 50
Carlsbad Company Stores 160
Carlsbad Flower Fields 97
Carlsbad Inn Beach Resort 39
Carltas Company 97
Casa de Pico 215
Casa Del Prado 91

Cecil's Café 38
Cedros Gardens 111
Celadon Royalty Thai 201
Champion Ballroom Academy 28
Chapel of the Immaculate Conception 55
Chateau Orleans 151
Chatterbox Café 101
Cheap Rentals 72
Chicken Pie Shop 56
Children's Discovery Museum of North
     County 58
Children's Park 58
Children's Pool 29
Chito's Shoe Repair 148
Chopra Center 74
Chopra, Deepak 73
Christian Community Theater 207
Chua Van Hanh Vietnamese Buddhist
     Temple 45
Chuck E. Cheese's 57
Chuck Jones Studio Gallery 48
Cigarettes Cheaper 190
City Deli 118
Club Montage 124
Coco's 37
Column One 110
Comic-Con International 64
Comics-N-Stuff 64
Computer Museum of America 142
Conching's Café and Ice Cream Parlor 83
Contract Tours 211
Controversial Bookstore 34
Convoy Street 77
Cookies by Design 27
Coronado Bay Bridge 226
Coronado Brewing Co. 42
Coronado Cays 100
Coronado Farmer's Market 79
Coronado Ferry 79
Coronado Island 70, 79
Coronado Playhouse 181
Corvette Diner 103
Cottage Café 172
Cottage, The 130
Cottage Restaurant, The 230
Country Craftsman of San Diego 225
County Administration Building 73
Cowles Mountain 217
Creations and Confections 51
Crest Café 219
Croce's Jazz Bar, Restaurant 113

Crossroads Gift Shop 26
Crypt on Park 81
Crystal Pier Hotel 126

Da Kine's 120
Daily News Café 39
Darlena's Turning Point 186
David's Coffee House 60
Deer Park Winery and Auto Museum 23
Del Mar Thoroughbred Club 89
Denny's 37
Designated Drivers Association 90
Dietrich Coffee 60
Dime Store Retro 175
Diversionary Theatre 207
Dizzy's 113
Dog Beach 75
Dolphin Interaction Program 17
Dudley's 26
DZ Akins 115

Eagle and High Peak Mine 99
East County Performing Arts Center 155
Eat Leather 82
Ebony Pride 125
El Cajon 79
El Cortez Hotel 64
El Indio Mexican Restaurant 215
El Prado Way 22, 226
El Torrito Mexican Cantina 202
Embarcadero Marina Park North 121
Emerald Chinese Seafood 77
Exotic Limes and Fruits 24

F Street Adult Video and Gifts 16
Falafel King 183
Fall Back Festival 58
Fashion Valley Mall 139, 160
Faz 222
Feng Shui Warehouse 81
Field, The 44
Fiesta Island 70, 75, 161
Filipino Family Day 83
Filipino Press 83
Filippi's 170
Firehouse Museum 146
Flame, The 125, 193
Flashbacks Recycled Fashions 222
Florida Canyon 226
Flour Power Custom Bakery 25
Flying A Squares 193

Flying Leatherneck Museum 146
Founders Chapel 54
Four Points Sheraton Hotel Skies Lounge 186
Freeflight 19
French Gourmet at Elario's 114, 228
Fritz Theater 206
Fumari 190

G.I. Joe Army Surplus Store 47
Galactic Comics 65
Galoka Gallery and Restaurant Bar 224
Game Empire 92
Gen Min Acupuncture and Herb Center 108
Genghis Khan 112
Giant Dipper Rollercoaster 59, 197
Golden Door 191
Gondola Company, The 100
Gran Havana Cigar Factory 190
Greystokes Bar & Grill 124
Guajome County Park 175
Guided Adventures in Nature 218

Haar Ethiopian Restaurant 76
Hamburger Factory 103
Hamburger Mary's 102
Harbor Drive 184
Hash House A Go Go 180
Hauser Patio & Rattan 112
Hazard Center 141
Heidi's Frozen Yogurt 124
Helga's Yarn Boutique 121
Herb Shoppe 110
Hillcrest Cinemas 50, 140
Hillcrest Farmer's Market 78
Hilton San Diego Resort 120, 166
Hob Nob Hill 38
Hodads 102
Holy Smoke 189
Horton Grand Hotel 106, 107, 200
Horton Plaza 199
Hotel Del Coronado 71, 100, 106, 147, 200
Hotel La Jolla 115
House of Charm 218
House of Pacific Relations International
    Cottages 66
Hsi Fang Buddhist Temple 46
Humphrey's 115, 168

Ichiban 196
Icons 111
Immaculata 54

Immaculate Conception Church 55
In Cahoots 67
Independent Luggage Repair 148
India Street 61
Inhale 189
In-N-Out Burger 103
International Professional School of Body
    Works 131
International Society for Krishna Consciousness
    Temple 88
Iowa Meat Farms 132

Japanese Friendship Bell 168
Japanese Friendship Garden 94
Jarrett Meeker Foundation 18
Jimbo's Naturally 109
Jimmy Carter's 37
John's 5th Avenue Luggage 148
Johnny's Family Restaurant 39
Julian 26
Julian Pie Company 27
June gloom 231
Junipero Serra Museum 168, 212
Jyoti Bihango 223, 224

Kaelin's 133
Kaiserhof, The 178
Karinya Thai 202
Karl Strauss Brewery 39
Kelly's 149
Ken Cinema 140
Kensington Coffee Company 63
Kensington Community Church Recreational
    Hall 193
Kickers 69
Kit Carson Park 153
Kite Country 121
Kite Flite 121
Knott's Soak City USA 59, 83
Kobey's Swap Meet 119

La Costa Resort and Spa 74
La Jolla 79
La Jolla Cove 166
La Jolla Playhouse 96, 204
La Jolla Shores 70
La Mesa Village 44
La Mesa Women's Club 29
La Paloma Restaurant 174
Lamplighter, The 150
Landmark Theaters 140

Laurel Street Bridge 226
Lawrence Welk Resort 122
Le Travel Store 147
Leaping Lotus 111
LEGOLAND California 57
Lesbian and Gay Historical Society of San
    Diego 21
Lesbian, Gay, Bisexual, Transgender
    Community Center 123
Leucadia State Beach 30
Liaison 90
Liberty Carousel 59
Light Bulb House 112
Light Bulbs Unlimited 112
Lips 74
Little Blair Valley 107
Little Italy 43, 61
Longevity Herbs 108
Lotsa Pasta 214
Lotus Thai Cuisine 109
Lyceum Theater 22, 205

Madstone Theaters 140
Mann Theaters 140
Mardi Gras Café and Market 151
Marie Hitchcock Puppet Theater 173
Marine Street Beach 70
Mariott Suites 222
Marston Point 226
Martini Ranch 130
May gray 231
Melodia Brazilian Seafood and Vegetarian
    Kitchen 36
Mercado Hidalgo 211
Mex-Art Pottery & Home Accents 112
Mexico 210
Midnight Adult Book and Video Centers 16
Midnight Madness 73
Milquatay Valley 144
Milton's 117
Mingei International Museum 153
Mini Cab Company 136
Miniature Train 157
Mint 183
Mission, The 38
Mission Bay 70, 120, 166
Mission Beach Club 72
Mission Center 160
Mission Hills Café 150, 151
Mission San Antonio de Pala 138

Mission San Diego de Alcala 55, 138
Mission San Luis Rey 139
Mission Trails Regional Park 216
Model Railroad Museum 88, 143
Molly's 49
Momo 47
Montgomery Field 48
Montgomery Waller Community Park and
    Recreation Center 234
Moonlight Beach 30
Morena Boulevard 112
Morena Club 150
Mount Helix 176
Mount Soledad 229
Mrs. Burton's Tea Room 225
Museum of Contemporary Art 20, 155
Museum of History and Art 147
Museum of Making Music 142
Museum of Man 54, 214
Museum of Photographic Arts 88, 141

Navy Aircraft Carrier Memorial 135
New Creation Church of Christ 125
New York Pizza Department 170
Night & Day Café 220
Nijiya Market 78
North Park Library 134
Novelty & Crafts 122
NuNu's 149
Nutter's 162

O'Connell's 150
Ocean Beach 70, 78
Ocean Beach Farmer's Market 78
Ocean Beach International Backpackers
    Hostel 129
Ocean Beach Park 75
Ocean Beach People's Organic Food
    Cooperative 108
Ocean Beach Pier 38
Oceanside Photo and Telescope Astronomical
    Society 107
Old Country Restaurant and Deli 178
Old Globe Theater 95, 181, 204
Old Mission Beach Athletic Club 161
Old Town Trolley Tours of San Diego 107
On Comic Ground 65
Ono Sushi & Pacific Spice 196
Open Sandcastle Competition 177
Ould Sod 44

Our Lady's Chapel 52
Outdoor Summer Shakespeare Festival 181
Over the Line Tournament 161

Pacific Beach Town Council 56
Pacific College of Oriental Medicine 108
Pacific Islander Festival 89
Pacific Theaters 140
Palm Canyon 219
Palomar Mountain 156
Palomar Observatory 157
Park Manor Suites 229
Pet Me Please 164
Pet Pleasers Bakery 164
Phil's BBQ & Ice Cream 102
Philippine Cultural Arts Festival 84
Pimp Daddy Limos 169
Pioneer Park 49
Play It Again Sports 132
Plunge, The 197
Presidio Hill 212
Presidio Park 168
Prince and the Pauper Collectible Children's
    Books 35
Princess Pub and Grille 43
Puff N Stuff Smoke Shop 189

Quail Botanical Gardens 95
Qualcomm Stadium 177
Quince Street Bridge 87

Ralph's 25
Ramada Inn and Suites 119
Rancho Buena Vista Adobe 174
Rancho Fruit Market 24
Rancho Guajome Adobe 175
Rancho Zosa 173
Ray and Joan Kroc Corps Community
    Center 198
Recital Hall 193
Red Circle 130
Red Fox Room 165
Rei do Gado 36
Reuben H. Fleet Science Center 88, 157, 181
Rich's 124
Ringold Alley 82
Rocky Point Preserve 17
Rocky's Crown Pub 102
Rose Creek Cottage 55
Rosie O'Grady's Irish Pub and Grille 45
Rotating Home 176

Royal Food Mart 101
Royal Thai Cuisine 202
Ruby's Diner 160
Rudford's Restaurant 220

Saffron Chicken 203
Saffron Noodles & Sate 97
Saint Francis Chapel 54
Samahan Dance Company 84
San Diego Aerospace Museum 134, 146, 147
San Diego Astrological Society 22
San Diego Automotive Museum 23
San Diego Brewing Co. 42
San Diego Children's Museum 58
San Diego Chinese Historical Society
    Museum 146
San Diego Circulators 193
San Diego Convention Center 64, 153
San Diego County Farm Bureau 78
San Diego Design Center 84
San Diego Factory Outlet Mall 160
San Diego Hall of Champions Sport
    Museum 193
San Diego Harbor Excursions 19, 168, 231
San Diego Historical Society 20, 35, 58
San Diego LGBT Pride 123, 125
San Diego Maritime Museum 187
San Diego Massage Professionals 132
San Diego Mycological Society 91
San Diego Natural History Museum 88,
    217, 218
San Diego Public Library 16, 88
San Diego Railroad Museum 144
San Diego Repertory Theatre 204, 205
San Diego Swing Dance Club 29
San Diego Tall Club 186
San Diego Trolley 210
San Diego Trust & Savings 223
San Diego Velodrome 72
San Diego Velodrome Association 72
San Diego Zoo 18, 57
San Diego's Finest City Squares 193
Santa Ana 231
Santa Clara Point 70
Santa Ysabel Indian Mission 27
Sausage King 133
Scripps Institute of Oceanography 232
Scripps Mercy Hospital 52
Scripps Park 166
Seafood City Supermarket 83
Seaforth Boat Rentals 19

Seal Rock Mammal Reserve 30
Seaport Village 89, 168
SeaWorld 17, 32, 57
Self-Realization Fellowship Retreat and
    Hermitage Grounds 96
Semi-Spontaneous Shakespeare Society 181
Sensual Delights 172
Sessions, Kate 94
Seven 131
Sew Fine 122
Shakespeare's Corner Shop 43
Shakespeare's Pub & Grill 43
Shelter Island 168
Sierra Club 217
Silver Strand 72
Sinbad Café and Hookah Bar 190
Single Gourmet 186
Six Degrees 125
Sledgehammer Theatre 204
Solana Beach Train Station 153
Soon Lee Chinese Laundry 60
South Cedros Avenue 111
South Mission Beach 70
Southern California Comics 65
Spooky Sleepovers 18
Sports Arena 15, 119
Spreckles Organ Pavilion 88
Spruce Street Suspension Bridge 85
St. Bartholomew's Thrift Shop 209
St. Cecilia's Playhouse 204
St. Mary Magdalene's 33
St. Vincent's Specialty Shop 209
Star of India 187
Starbucks Coffee 124
Starlight Dance Studio 28
Starlight Musical Theatre 207
Stuart Collection 179
Surfer Motor Lodge 120
Sushi on the Rock 195
Sushi Ota 195
Sushi Performance and Visual Art 205
Swallows Sun Island Club 156
Swim hotline 198
Sycuan Casino 33

Taste of Italy 170
Tavern on the Green 124
Terra 76
Terra Brazil 36
TGI Friday's 202
Theatre in Old Town 206

Thomas Cook Currency Service Inc. 71
Thrift Korral 209
Thunder Boats 59
Tijuana 79
Timken Museum of Art 88
Tiptop Meats 179
Todai 47
Tofu House 224
Top of the Hyatt 228
Top of the Park 229
Torrey Pines Glider Port 228
Trader Joe's 215
Trainer for a Day 17
Traveler's Depot 147
Tribute Garden at San Diego Hospice 95
Try Thai 202
Tunaman's Memorial 134
Twiggs Coffeehouse 63
Tyler's Taste of Texas 221

U.S. Grant Hotel 199
Ultrazone 57
Umi Sushi 196
Unarius Academy of Science 85
University of California at San Diego 153,
    179
University of San Diego 166
University Towne Center Mall 71
Unlimited Adventures 187
Uptown District 61
USA Hostels San Diego 127

V.G. Donuts and Bakery 25
Vermont Street Pedestrian Bridge 87
Veterans Memorial Center and Museum 134
Victorian Heritage Park Bed & Breakfast Inn
    129
Viejas Casino 33, 34
Viejas Outlet Center 161
Villa Montezuma 107
Village Fair Shopping Center 58
Village Hillcrest 50, 140
Vishions Smoke Shop 98
Von's 25

Waffle Spot, The 230
Walk on the Wild Side Tour 18
Walkabout International 218
War Memorial Building 193
Waterfront, The 102
Westgate Hotel 199

Whaley House 104
Wienerschnitzel 178
Wild Animal Park 18, 57
William Heath Davis House 107
Wine Bank, The 233
WineSellar, The 234
Wolf's 124

World Duty Free Shop 190
World War II Flying Museum 146

Xen Hookah Lounge and Coffee Shop 190

Zone, The 124
Zoro Garden 181